PSYCHOANALYTIC PERSPECTIVES ON WOMEN AND THEIR EXPERIENCE OF DESIRE, AMBITION AND LEADERSHIP

Psychoanalytic Perspectives on Women and Their Experience of Desire, Ambition and Leadership considers how these factors can be understood, nurtured, or thwarted and the subsequent impact on women's identity, authority and satisfaction.

Psychoanalysis has long struggled with its ideas about women, about who they are, how to work with them, and how to respect and encourage what women want. This book argues that psychoanalytic theory and practice must evolve to maintain its relevance in a volatile landscape. Each section of the book begins with a chapter that reviews contemporary ideas regarding women, as well as psychoanalytic history, gender bias, and societal norms and deficits. Three composite clinical stories allow our distinguished contributors to discuss the contexts within which individual experience can be affected, and the role that clinical work may have to mobilize and advance passion and vitality. In their discussions, the interplay of clinical psychoanalysis, sociopolitical context, and understanding of gender, combine to offer a unique perspective, built on decades of scholarship, personal experience, and clinical expertise.

Psychoanalytic Perspectives on Women and Their Experience of Desire, Ambition and Leadership will serve as a reference for all psychoanalysts and psychoanalytic psychotherapists as well as gender studies scholars interested in the progress of psychoanalytic theory regarding women in the 21st century.

Stephanie R. Brody, Psy.D., is a Supervising and Training Analyst at Boston Psychoanalytic Society and Institute, and Lecturer in Psychology, Department of Psychiatry (part time), Harvard Medical School and a Clinical Associate in Psychology and Attending Psychologist, McLean Hospital. She is the author of *Entering Night Country: Psychoanalytic Reflections on Loss and Resilience* (Routledge, 2016). Dr. Brody maintains a private practice in Lexington, MA, USA.

Frances Arnold, Ph.D. is on the Faculty of the Boston Psychoanalytic Society and Institute and is a Lecturer in Psychology, Department of Psychiatry (part time), Harvard Medical School and a Clinical Associate in Psychology and Attending Psychologist, McLean Hospital. Dr. Arnold maintains a private practice in Cambridge, MA, USA.

PSYCHOANALYTIC PERSPECTIVES ON WOMEN AND THEIR EXPERIENCE OF DESIRE, AMBITION AND LEADERSHIP

Edited by Stephanie R. Brody and Frances Arnold

Routledge
Taylor & Francis Group

LONDON AND NEW YORK

First published 2019
by Routledge
2 Park Square, Milton Park, Abingdon, Oxon OX14 4RN

and by Routledge
52 Vanderbilt Avenue, New York, NY 10017

Routledge is an imprint of the Taylor & Francis Group, an informa business

British Library Cataloguing in Publication Data
A catalogue record for this book is available from the British Library

Library of Congress Cataloging-in-Publication Data
A catalog record for this book has been requested

ISBN: 978-1-138-84266-3 (hbk)
ISBN: 978-1-138-84268-7 (pbk)
ISBN: 978-1-315-73129-2 (ebk)

Typeset in Bembo
by Taylor & Francis Books

Printed and bound in Great Britain by
TJ International Ltd, Padstow, Cornwall

CONTENTS

ACKNOWLEDGEMENTS

This book project reflects the arc of our careers, as well as our engagement with colleagues, friends, and family members who have deeply touched our work and our lives. Our story begins with our experience as young psychologists who were fortunate to be in a department at McLean Hospital, led by trail blazers, including Irene Stiver and Judy Jordan, who were co-founders of the Stone Center at Wellesley College and prolific writers of "a new psychology of women." Their work, and that of their colleagues, demystified female experience and helped transform psychoanalytic thinking. They served as not only our intellectual leaders, but also our professional guides, providing opportunities and support, and shaping our early careers.

I am also grateful for my more recent McLean "home" at the Personality Disorder Program. My involvement there, with its remarkable group of clinicians and scholars, has been central to my clinical work and the development of my ideas about desire, ambition, and leadership and their role in personal development. Finally, this book would never have happened had I not become a psychoanalyst, and without my intellectual and collegial community at Boston Psychoanalytic Society and Institute (BPSI). I am grateful to many BPSI colleagues, including James Frosch, Susan Pasternak, Catherine Kimble, Alexandra Harrison, Andrea Celenza, Holly Housman, Trude Kleinschmidt, Jack Foehl, Cary Friedman, Richard Gomberg, Joe Schwartz, Walker Shields, and many others.

At the heart of this book is the engaging friendship and intellectual partnership Stephanie and I have enjoyed and relied on for over 30 years. We have shared intellectual interests, passionate ambitions, professional and personal highs, and of course, inevitable lows. We have partnered in our clinical work, our academic teaching, and our institutional communities. We have shared countless projects while raising families, and we have been able to collaborate with, and challenge each other, over decades. I could not have done this project alone and I am deeply grateful for Stephanie's friendship, honesty, creativity and superb writing ability.

The other heart of this book is our patients, from whom I have learned so much. They have taught me what I know about desire, ambition, and leadership, including what inhibits desire, ambition, and leadership, what frees them, and what sets them on fire. I thank all of them for their enormous generosity.

I cannot say enough about our contributors. We are so lucky to have their voices for this project. The book is a mosaic that has been created by many minds and diverse experiences. It has been a pleasure to watch the project unfold in ways that have been remarkably spontaneous. I want to give special thanks to my friend and colleague, Katy Aisenberg, whose thoughtful suggestions and careful, editorial eye proved invaluable.

Love and gratitude goes to my family who have been both inspirational and extraordinarily patient. My husband, Bob Stern, offered numerous ideas while devotedly reading, and re-reading, so many chapters. Always a steadfast support, he is both my biggest fan and the one who most challenges me. Our daughters, Diana, Laura, and Jennifer, are an inspiration and the book is a tribute to them; we have watched them mature into vibrant, active women who are full of life, each exploring her desires and ambitions in her own way. My force field mother would have thought our topic rocked; my father, who inspired me to become a psychoanalyst, would feel I was fulfilling his wish that I spend more time writing about what is most important to me.

Frances Arnold

August 30, 2018

ACKNOWLEDGEMENTS

We are grateful to all of the contributors to this book, some who received invitations to participate in this project over four years ago, when it appeared that the concept of women and leadership would be a reality in America, rather than an idea. Over the course of these years, not only have they generously partnered with us, they have waited patiently for the publication of this project. They have offered support and understanding as we have addressed the events of life that often interrupt, disrupt or delight us. Marriages, deaths, births, health issues, and political upheavals have conspired to slow us down, even to discourage us from our path to completion. But we have persisted, and we are thankful to our colleagues for their commitment.

I am equally grateful to my partner in this endeavor – Frances Arnold. Over many years, our clinical work and our interest in women's desire and ambition has been a focus of our attention: the numerous ways in which context – family, society, and hierarchy – influence the leadership potential that has been part of our consulting rooms and our lives. We have collaborated over the years on many projects, and our lives have become intertwined now in so many ways – I remain admiring of her clinical expertise, her personal vitality, and enormous warmth, without which this project would not have been possible.

To our patients: this project would not have existed without your stories and first-person perspectives. You have been the reporters on the ground, who have offered insights, challenges, and strategies for navigating the changing landscape for women (and men) in 2018. We appreciate your transparency, and your willingness to invite us into your lives, to help, and to understand.

To our readers: It is our sincere hope that this book cracks open the psycho-analytic door, offering an invitation to those in our field who want to expand opportunities for women by changing our own embedded ideas. We also hope this book offers a hand to those outside of psychoanalysis, who might discover that psychoanalytic ideas about women have changed, and are changing still.

To my mother: The image on the cover of this book was drawn by my mother, Ruth Brody – an exceptional artist, art director, wife, mother, and grandmother who died at 93 in September 2017. Her fortitude and energy has been, and will always be, an inspiration to my family. She was a leader before it was acknowledged, a creative force field, a powerhouse in any setting. Her drawing of the strong, dominating woman seemed exactly the right image to adorn our cover. I only wish she could be here to see my love and appreciation of her.

To my family – Rick, and Josiah, who have encouraged me towards the completion of this project by supporting me and giving me the space to work, and have fed and entertained me with music and poetry: my love for them is deep and enduring. But I especially want to express my appreciation for my daughter, Rebecca. I cannot overstate my gratitude for her grace, strength, and intelligence. When I thought it would be too hard to complete this project, she inspired me to push on, to make my voice heard. It is my hope that when she expresses *her* desire, ambition, and leadership, she will do so with the authority that comes from freedom, and the knowledge that she is loved beyond measure.

Stephanie Brody
August 27, 2018

CONTRIBUTORS

Frances Arnold, Ph.D., is a Clinical Associate in Psychology and Attending Psychologist at McLean Hospital, and a Lecturer in Psychology in the Department of Psychiatry (part time) at Harvard Medical School. She is also a psychoanalyst and faculty member at Boston Psychoanalytic Society and Institute (BPSI), where she is currently Vice-Chair of Curriculum. Her academic and teaching interests include theories of therapeutic action and psychoanalytic technique, personality disorders, trauma, and infant parent mental health. She has written and presented on topics including Borderline Personality Disorder, trauma, attachment disorders, female development, psychoanalytic technique, and women and psychoanalysis. She serves on the Planning Committee of the American Psychoanalytic Association (APsaA) and for many years, has co-led (with Stephanie Brody) an APsaA discussion group on Women's Experience of Competence, Ambition, and Leadership. She is in full time private practice in Cambridge, MA, where she sees children, adults, and families

Rosemary H. Balsam, F.R.C.Psych., (London), M.R.C.P. (Edinburgh), is Associate Clinical Professor of Psychiatry in the Yale Medical School; Staff Psychiatrist, Yale Student Mental Health and Counseling; Training and Supervising analyst at the Western New England Institute for Psychoanalysis. Teaching, and in private practice of psychoanalysis and psychotherapy for many years, her special interest is in the role of the body, female development, and the analyses of young adults. She lectures nationally and internationally and has been the National Psychoanalytic Woman Scholar for APsaA. Her book *Women's Bodies in Psychoanalysis* (Routledge, 2012) describes how the body is theorized in psychoanalysis. She has written widely on the topics of gender, mothers and daughters, and the neglected theory of pregnancy and childbirth. She is on the editorial boards of *Psychoanalytic Quarterly*, and *American Imago*, with her husband Paul Schwaber, is an editor of the Book Review section of *The Journal of the American Psychoanalytic Association*.

Brenda Bauer, Psy.D., is a clinical psychologist and psychoanalyst in New York on the faculty of the Institute for Psychoanalytic Education (affiliated with the New York University School of Medicine Department of Psychiatry). She has a particular interest in issues pertaining to women and girls, impediments to achievement, and parenting.

Stephanie Brody, Psy.D., is a Training and Supervising Analyst and Faculty member at Boston Psychoanalytic Society and Institute where she is Editor of the *BPSI Bulletin*. She is a Clinical Associate in Psychology and Attending Psychologist at McLean Hospital, and a Lecturer in Psychology in the Department of Psychiatry (part time) at Harvard Medical School. During the last several years, Dr. Brody has led two discussion groups at the American Psychoanalytic Association meetings – Facing the Facts: Self Disclosure and the Analytic Relationship, and Women's Experience of Competence, Ambition and Leadership (co-led with Frances Arnold). Dr. Brody is the author of *Entering Night Country: Psychoanalytic Reflections on Loss and Resilience* (Routledge, 2016). She in private practice in Lexington, MA.

Andrea Celenza, Ph.D., is a Training and Supervising Analyst at the Boston Psychoanalytic Society and Institute, Assistant Clinical Professor at Harvard Medical School. Dr. Celenza is the recipient of several awards and offers two on-line courses: Sexual Boundary Violations: How Do They Happen? and What, Where is Psychoanalysis: Classic Concepts, New Meanings. She has authored two books. *Sexual Boundary Violations: Therapeutic, Supervisory and Academic Contexts* was published by Jason Aronson in 2007. Her new book, *Erotic Revelations: Clinical Applications and Perverse Scenarios* is published by Routledge. She is in private practice in Lexington, MA.

Dianne Elise, Ph.D., is a Personal and Supervising Analyst and Faculty member of the Psychoanalytic Institute of Northern California, a Training Analyst member of the International Psychoanalytic Association, and she has served on the Editorial Boards of the *Journal of the American Psychoanalytic Association* and *Studies in Gender and Sexuality*. Dr. Elise has written a series of papers over two decades examining gendered aspects of early developmental experiences, sexuality, and erotic transference. Nationally recognized for her innovative contributions to the psychoanalytic literature on gender and sexuality, she has consistently challenged conventional accounts of development. Her writing includes publications in the *Psychoanalytic Study of the Child*, *The Psychoanalytic Quarterly*, *JAPA*, *Psychoanalytic Dialogues*, *Studies in Gender & Sexuality*, *Psychoanalytic Inquiry*, as well as several book chapters. She is currently working on a book of her papers for Routledge, titled *Creativity and the Erotic Dimensions of the Analytic Field*. She practices in Oakland, California.

Adrienne Harris, Ph.D., is Faculty and Supervisor at the NYU Postdoctoral Program in Psychoanalysis and Psychotherapy. She is also on the faculty of the Psychoanalytic Institute of Northern California. She is the author of *Gender as Soft Assembly* and essays on gender, clinical process, speech and semiotics, self care and the work of Sandor Ferenczi. In 2012, she, Lewis Aron and the late Jeremy Safran founded the Sandor Ferenczi Center at the New School. She is an Editor of the Relational Perspectives in Psychoanalysis Book Series, which has published close to 100 volumes.

Dorothy Evans Holmes, Ph.D., ABPP, FABP, is a Teaching, Training, and Supervising Analyst in the Psychoanalytic Center of the Carolinas. She is Professor Emeritus at the George Washington University where she was Program Director and Director of Clinical Training of the Professional PsyD Program. She is also Teaching, Training and Supervising Analyst Emeritus at the Washington Baltimore Center for Psychoanalysis. Dr. Holmes has written extensively on intra-psychic influences of race and gender and their impact on psychoanalytic treatment process. She has served on boards, committees, and editorial boards of numerous national organizations, including currently serving as Chair of the Committee on Race and Ethnicity in APsaA's Department of Psychoanalytic Education and on the American Council of Psychoanalytic Education, Inc. Dr. Holmes' honors for her career-long scholarly focus on cultural factors and cultural trauma include having been an APsaA Plenary Speaker in 2016 and for the American Association for Psychoanalysis in Clinical Social Work in 2017. This year, she will be the Freud lecturer at the Institute for Psychoanalytic Education, NYU School of Medicine, and the Ritvo lecturer at the Yale University Child Study Center.

Nancy Kulish, Ph.D., is a Professor, Department of Psychiatry, Wayne State Medical School and Adjunct Professor of Psychology, University of Detroit/Mercy. She is a Training and Supervising Analyst at the Michigan Psychoanalytic Institute, where she is past president. She was chosen as the National Woman Psychoanalytic Scholar of the American Psychoanalytic Association for 2005. Currently she is on the Editorial Boards of the *Psychoanalytic Quarterly* and the *International Journal of Psychoanalysis*. She has published and presented on topics ranging from female sexuality, gender, transference/countertransference, and adolescence to termination. She was on the plenary panel on sexuality at the International Psychoanalytic Congress in Mexico City, in August, 2011. With Deanna Holtzman, she is the co-author of *A Story of Her Own: The Female Oedipus Complex Reexamined and Renamed*, published in 2008 and *The Clinical Problem of Masochism* published in 2012. She is in private practice in Birmingham, Michigan.

Vivian B. Pender, M.D., is a Clinical Professor of Psychiatry at the Weill Cornell Medical College and a Training and Supervising Psychoanalyst at Columbia University, Center for Psychoanalytic Training and Research. She is a Trustee of the American Psychiatric Association. She has won honors and awards for her excellence in teaching medical students. At the United Nations she represents the International Psychoanalytical Association and the American Psychiatric Association. Until 2011, she chaired the NGO Committee on the Status of Women and now chairs the NGO Committee on Mental Health. During that time, she assisted in the establishment of UN Women. She recently co-hosted a UN conference on Youth and Gun Violence. She is a volunteer Asylum Evaluator for Physicians for Human Rights. In 2015, she founded Healthcare Against Trafficking, Inc., a non-profit organization dedicated to promoting education and advocacy in the healthcare sector. She is a co-investigator on a Weill Cornell Department of Internal Medicine innovative grant to study "Experiences of Sex Trafficking Victims in Healthcare Settings." Published in 2017 is a book chapter on violence against women and to be published in 2018, a chapter on psychoanalysis and the law. She produced four documentaries of conferences at the United Nations on mental health, human rights, human trafficking, hatred, and violence. She is the Editor of *The Status of Women: Violence, Identity and Activism*, Karnac, 2016.

Dionne R. Powell, M.D., is Training and Supervising Psychoanalyst, Columbia University Center for Psychoanalytic Training and Research, Clinical Assistant Professor of Psychiatry, New York-Presbyterian Hospital, Weill Cornell Medical College, and Adjunct Assistant Clinical Professor of Psychiatry, the New York Presbyterian Hospital, Columbia University College of Physicians and Surgeons. Dr. Powell's immersion in psychoanalytic and psychiatric education spans three decades. She has served as Columbia Psychoanalytic Center's faculty representative to the Executive Committee, Chair of the Training and Supervising Analyst Committee, and co-chair of the Columbia Looks Ahead (COLA) discussion groups. At the national level, Dr. Powell has been member of APsaA's Executive Committee, Task Force on Governance and Structure, and served as Secretary of the Board on Professional Standards. She is vice-president of the American Association for Psychoanalytic Education. Dr. Powell has presented and published widely on topics including affect tolerance, "stuck" analyses, psychoanalytic governance, race and the African American experience in psychoanalysis and has appeared on *In Treatment: Private and Confidential*, an HBO documentary based on the series, first aired in Spring of 2019. She is in full time private practice in New York City.

Arlene Kramer Richards, M.D., is currently on the Faculty of the Contemporary Freudian Society, American Institute for Psychoanalysis, and Institute for Psychoanalytic Research and Training, and Tongjin University Medical School, Wuhan, China. Dr. Richards is the author of *Myths of Mighty Women* (Karnac, 2015) and is editor of *Psychoanalysis: Listening to Understand – selected papers of Arlene Kramer Richards* (International Psychoanalytic Books, 2012), and of Richards, Spria and Synch (Eds), *Encounters with Loneliness: Only the Lonely* (2015). Dr. Richards is in private practice in New York City.

INTRODUCTION

Stephanie Brody

The idea for this book emerged almost three years ago when the United States Presidential election of 2016 was only just beginning to enter the national consciousness. As we considered our topic, how modern psychoanalysts view women's experience of desire, ambition, and leadership, we felt sure that the prospects of a first female president would shape our discussion. Indeed, we hoped that the results of the election might well serve as evidence that many of the embedded layers of gender bias would be of minimal impact, that qualifications of the candidates that would prove to be most important to the political debate would be measured by competency, grasp of fundamental human values, and especially a respect for democracy and the American Constitution. As we finalized this book, now 18 months after the inauguration of the new President, one who lost the popular election by over 3,000,000 votes, but won the presidency nevertheless, we are bound to reflect on the nature of gender and wonder, to what extent might we integrate our topic into current events. Indeed, it is next to impossible to address this topic without reflecting on how America responded to the rise of a national leader who is also a woman and wonder to what degree gender issues played a part in the politics and the result.

The affective landscape of our country is purposefully diverse and heterogeneous, and our history has been built on the shoulders of women and men from many countries, backgrounds, and ethnicities. Yet we are now shaken by the politics of divisiveness, especially in the way that efforts to resist and rise above the restrictions of unconscious bias, sexism, racism, and "shock politics" have been dismissed as irrelevant and ineffective. We are told that those who dispute or argue for the values of democracy, dissent, a free press, and the rule of law, have no hope against the power of the executive office and the officials who support denial, dismissal, and indifference in a way that undermines empathy, inclusion, and compassion. We cannot look at our topic without wondering about our own privilege: how the composite case examples that we have included in our book describe women who, despite being impacted by the internal and external ingredients of family, history, temperament, genetics, socioeconomic environment, and education, have nevertheless, been able to achieve measures of success that are beyond the purview of many other women and men in the America of 2018. Still, we have included these stories because we believe they represent the reality for many, even those who have been able to defy the odds of our modern society, have achieved "success," and yet have encountered interference and confounding limitations. How might we under-stand the restrictions that continue to dominate, and then find a way to explain why so many are forced to alter their contributions, censor their imaginations, and contain their futures? Do they rightly expect that they live in a world that has no interest in or may even thwart the uniqueness of their potential and forever constrain them? We believe that our desire, our ambition and our capacity to lead is connected deeply to the world in which we live, in the social soil in which it has room to grow. The America of 2018 calls out to us as a landscape that also needs to be understood as we enter this discussion, and while we may wonder, as psychoanalysts, about the individual psychic geo-graphy of our patients, we believe that we must consider the landscape of exclusion that has the power to control or nurture freedom in each of us, to reflect on the humanity of our democratic values and ask how psychoanalysts may shape the discussion and stem the insidious growth of bias and exclusion.

The discussants that we have invited to contribute to our book are all leaders in the world of psychoanalysis. The topics that have been of interest to them throughout their professional lives have distinguished them as writers, master clinicians, and pioneers who have shaped and continue to impact the world of psychoanalysis. We are honored that they have agreed to contribute to our discussion and each reflects a perspective born out of years of personal reflec-tion and clinical experience. Though they may have encountered impediments along the way, they have also found and cultivated the environment that allows the expression of what the author Paulette Jiles describes in her book. *Enemy Women* as the "internal fire" of the soul, where "every breath" is a "letter to the world" (Jiles, 2007). We welcome the force of their spirit and intellects in the space of our pages.

August 27, 2018

Reference

Jiles, P. (2007) *Enemy Women*, New York: Harper Perennial

PART I
Desire

1

DESIRE

What women want

Stephanie Brody

There is a statue in Rome that refuses to be ignored. Though I have seen it before, I am drawn over and over to the clean white marble, and the two dynamic forms, alive in the stone. Daphne and Apollo stand frozen, inviting attention. A moment in time, entwined in desire, conflict, and terror. Apollo has abducted Daphne, and drawn by her beauty, he seeks possession. She cries out in fear – this is no requited love. She calls to her father, to her mother, for help, for she has no wish for capture. The parental response is full of irony. She is not given a weapon to slay her captor, nor strength to overcome his muscular control; she is not offered authority to persuade him of his insolence, or cunning to outwit or ensnare him. She is granted no power for escape. Rather, she is transformed where she stands, into a laurel tree. Though Bernini's artful capacity to render marble as supple flesh is mesmerizing, it is the delicacy of transformation that transfixes. Her mouth open, her body bound to the earth, her fingers changing to leaves before our eyes, her toes rooted to the ground, we imagine that Apollo now has no use for her since her body may no longer be overtaken and entered. But a price has been paid to avoid possession. Her agency is now limited to the stretch of her boughs and the depths of her roots. There is no freedom. How do we understand the meaning of this painful solution? There has been no choice for Daphne, just the exchange of one prison for another. Apollo eternally wears a laurel wreath around his head, a memento of his lost, briefly held possession. But Daphne is powerless, deepening her rooted life in a habitat for other living creatures, but removed from her human life – the future of possibility in her own desire, thwarted.

Now, in a darkened opera house, I listen to the story of Iolanta, the young princess who grows up unaware that she is blind. Her father, fearful that this knowledge will lead to frustration and despair, secludes Iolanta, and demands that the few attendants who provide her with companionship comply with his wish for secrecy. They agree to the deception, but it is laced with disdain. Iolanta cannot see how they mock her innocence, or capitalize on her naiveté. Surrounded by pretense and deception, Iolanta senses that something is wrong, though she cannot identify the source, or its meaning. As the opera unfolds, a local doctor informs her protective father that a cure is possible, but only if Iolanta is made aware of her blindness, and then, only if she seeks to be cured.

Enter the stranger, defying the ominous threat of death to all that cross the threshold of Iolanta's home. Overcome by her beauty, he is instantly in love. It is only when he speaks of color and realizes that Iolanta does not understand the meaning of the word, does he finally comprehend that she is blind. "What does it mean to see?" she asks. As he describes the gift of light, she explains to him that she is able to joyfully experience the world in numerous ways, through sensations that are fully available to her. He is enthralled by her sense of appreciation for what she has and his love for her deepens. She too feels love for him, but remains confused by the idea that she lives in deprivation. When the lovers are discovered, the doctor suggests that Iolanta, now aware of what she is missing, might be driven to seek a cure.

But Iolanta does not react with longing for what others say she lacks – she does not miss what others take for granted, and has no motivation to change. For her frustrated father, the promise of cure quickly fades and he is perplexed that she has no desire for a human asset others so value. Confounded, her father feigns rage toward her lover and threatens to kill him if Iolanta remains indifferent, if she squanders this opportunity. Holding no true wish for sight, she fears the death of her new love; motivated through this unlikely link, she finds the desire that brings her cure and the security of the relationship that matters most. The opera ends with Iolanta reunited in love, but confused by the world of light and color that has been thrust upon her.

Fast forward.

1942. *Woman of the Year*, a film starring Katherine Hepburn and Spencer Tracy in their first cinema collaboration, depicts Tess Harding, a brilliant career woman who falls in love with a sportswriter, Sam Craig. Though awed by her beauty and sophistication, her academic and worldly knowledge, Sam is frustrated by their differences in class and interest. The social worlds that she navigates smoothly make him feel uncomfortable, clumsy, and inept, while his environment of baseball and boxing rings puzzles or appalls her. Their romance is combustible, sexual, and in mid-twentieth century United States, unique and somewhat subversive. Impulsively, they marry, and quickly the disparate lifestyles and his gendered expectations conflict. Neither is willing to give up the deeply satisfying benefits of their careers, and the character of Sam, though respectful of her massive intellect, still expects her to put her career in second place to her responsibilities as a traditional wife. Her refusal to give up her achievements and the possibility of ongoing contributions to the world stage leads to a dramatic separation. He cannot live with who she is. Pressed to make the inevitable binary choice between career and relationship, Tess decides that she is not only unwilling give up her marriage, but she can achieve as much success in the traditional domestic realm as she has in the global. In a desperate attempt to win him back, she tries to prove her capability – in the kitchen – and makes a mess of it. In fur coat and career dress, she proves only that she has never before made a cup of coffee for anyone, including herself. Tess is the competent career woman, revealed to be the pathetic, perhaps unworthy, wife. Pleading with Sam to restore the relationship, she points out that she is now willing to make a sacrifice: "Don't you see?" she says, "I'm going to quit my job." He responds in frustration: "And do what? Run for President?" The story ends as Sam allows Tess back into his life, but only after he throws her young male assistant off a pier, and makes Tess take his name. She is now Tess (Harding) Craig. Kiss and fade out.

It is 1980. Another brilliant young woman is scrambling. Her ambitious political husband has been delivered a humbling loss and is now unemployed. This early setback hurls the family into unanticipated financial risk. They are too young to have accrued any personal wealth. Though she has worked to bridge connections within a community that regards her as a foreigner, her husband's rejection seems to intensify her sense of difference in her, now even more unfriendly, hometown. They have a young infant, and crumbled by humiliation, this recently successful man seems paralyzed and depressed. Until this point, she has been holding back, sensitive to her environment, aware that she must shape her desires to fit the expectations typically associated with a political spouse. She has carefully maintained the role that is required in her conservative community: supportive wife. Ever attentive to the potentially negative reactions that others might have to her personal achievements, she hides her enormous light under a bushel. Only those closest see her potential more fully. But now, taking stock of the landscape, she picks up the phone and leverages her own network and broad expanse of personal connections. She makes sure to remind others of her skill, her ability to work harder and smarter than anyone else in the room. There is no choice now but to reenter the field. The challenge, though formidable, does not crush her. Indeed, this sort of humbling is familiar, perhaps even the recipe for advancement. Her aspirations remain in the distance. She is practical, and though there is anxiety and uncertainty, something long limited has been released. This is a challenge that engages, and may even be relished in its long delayed expression of self, aspiration, and agency. Here is someone we have all come to know, visible on the world stage. Is this the story of the first woman to become President of the United States?

We could say that these four stories tell us something about desire, how we think of it, how it is reflected in myth, fiction, culture, and politics. It is also about women and desire, though the narratives that are described occur not at the beginning of each life, but at a choice point, somewhat *after* the personal characteristics have been shaped by internal process, external realities, relationship values and dynamics, and social and cultural expectancies. Is this a story of desire, of how desire is born, or of how desire may be gathered, personal and particular to the self, in its own special time? Ideas about desire have changed over the course of psychoanalytic history, reflecting profound shifts in the understanding of instinct, conflict, relationships, and gender. The theory is not a women's story, but the story has had an impact.

The psychoanalytic story of women: desire as envy

Psychoanalytic theory regarding women, and the development of the female psyche, has a regrettable history. The male father of psychoanalysis is at the beginning of the story, creating a myth about men, explained and elaborated, followed by another myth about women. Women's psychic development was based on the absence of a penis, and therefore, the absence of the all-important part of the first myth: the Oedipus and castration anxiety. Freud's theory, a reflection and response to social and political changes, his personal experience (Stolorow and Atwood, 1979, p. 53) an effort to explain and maintain a status quo.

For Freud, women were a perplexing challenge – the psychological development of women did not immediately comply with the neat formulations regarding male identity that had been Freud's first focus. Constructing a theory about the male psyche, Freud held that, for men, psychological health depended on conflict resolution and identification, especially around the Oedipal.[1] "Rivalry, desire, anxiety and guilt are central themes, and the consolidation of the male psyche and identity is triggered by the dread of fantasied castration" (Brody, 2016, p. 62). For Freud, the son's unconscious maternal desire must be thwarted in order to avoid castration punishment, a path to parental approval and eventual rewards of society. According to Freud, little boys (and men) regarded girls as castrated boys – forever wounded. For Freud, this anatomical difference was a deprivation with lifelong implications. Psychoanalysis would argue that without the fearful dread of castration (for women, it had already occurred), women were unmotivated to earn the approval healthy men sought and attained. Unable to achieve the full developmental advantages that the resolution of the Oedipal conflict offered to their male counterparts – a higher level of morality, the access to a lawful society, heterosexual object choice, and the rewards of identification with the powerful father – women remained less than, flawed, inferior.

Since the fantasied dread of castration played no direct role in women's psychic world, an alternative was introduced. Freud's perspective on women's desire was to frame it within the phallocentric dimension: It was the wish for what men had that motivated women. The longed for physical "advantage" shaped the psychological motivation, but only within specific stereotypical (for the time) norms. Thereafter, a woman who sought actual benefits of male advantage, rather than the substitute satisfaction from pseudo-ownership via genital penetration, and the addition of a baby – "a glorified poor man's penis" (Balsam, 2000, p. 1338) – was to be regarded (within psychoanalytic constructions) as neurotically fixated. Penis envy was the cause of the neurotic derailment (Freud, 1924, 1925, 1933). Any woman that sought power, authority, and autonomy, or the wish for influence, status, or personal benefit, should be understood according to this unilateral developmental theory. "Behind this envy for the penis, there comes to light the woman's hostile bitterness against the man, which never completely disappears in the relations between the sexes, and which is clearly indicated in the strivings … of 'emancipated' women" (Freud, 1918, p. 205).

Inevitably, such women could be targets of disapproval. A woman who wanted the privileges of men could be vulnerable to criticism, easily defined as flawed for not conforming to the trajectory of the newly institutionalized theoretical explanation. Women were regarded as more susceptible than their male counterparts to envy and jealousy, always wanting "something more" because they had "something less" (Kofman, 1985, p. 177). Appearance, personal demeanor, or the absence of stereotypical "feminine" physical attributes, were decoded as misplaced needs. Any woman who sought or held power, engaged in assertive, competitive or aggressive behavior could be tagged as a deviant female, out of line with male defined perspective.

Though psychoanalysts have not been alone in elevating male status, Freud's specific theory seemed to added authority to the belief that women might really be "inferior." This formulation has had far-reaching implications for psychoanalysis and its role in understanding women whose significance in the family, society, and political realms, was described in a limited and phallic oriented perspective. To speak out in the public arena requires a courage that resonates with risk, triggering historical links to our analytic history and the skepticism that is accorded to women's stories. Egregiously, Freud's abandonment of the seduction theory confirmed the dismissal of women whose narratives were interpreted as fantasy stories, and became grist for Freud's theories regarding hysteria, sexuality, and the unconscious. Lear (2005) notes that though Freud often had a "need to trace the 'symptom' back to a real life event" (p. 250), in many other clinical matters, his wholesale rejection of women's stories of trauma remain a betrayal, another piece of theoretical authority that undermines women's public voice and credibility. Trauma, violation, harassment are treated with skepticism or dismissal. Until recently, when women sought to challenge these role restrictions, in the consulting room, in the global sphere, or the workplace, they were often pathologized, and diagnosed. Much like Tess Harding, women are reproached for their achievements, aspirations, and honesty, a form of denigration to which no man would be subjected. "Whether consciously or unconsciously, directly or in sublimated fashion, penis envy thus always persists, exercising its more or less harmful effects: in any case its importance is unquestionable" (Kofman, 1985, p. 176). Not unlike the story of Iolanta, who was surprised to discover that the world saw her as lacking, it is not always easy to see whose blindness is more damaging.

Private and public

There are many instances where desire's destiny has already been determined by limitations others set in stone, evidence of the pervasive intersection between the theories of women and the expression of such theory in daily life. Because women's bodies express a presence in ways that seem to challenge rules and standards of control – full of power, desire, and sexual meaning – women become the objects of disavowal and mistrust. The tears, the blood, the milk, the mess, residues of sex and reproductive assets, are experienced as a kind of "body pollution"

(Douglas, 1966, p. 145) to be controlled, cleaned up, or avoided. The symbolic implications are far-reaching. The bodies that give women the power of nature have been regarded as a threat (Ortner, 1974, p. 76) to be "subordinated" and tamed (ibid., p. 73). When women's power, physical presence, intellectual authority or change of status elicits uncontrollable attractions, aggressions and desires, it is the fault of the unruly, feral female.

The woman who is free to experience her own desire, unencumbered by the restrictions and forced choices imposed by others, may be regarded as subversive. It is not safe for women to forcefully desire self-valuing goals, money, status, or authority. Men, but also women, criticize and demonize women. Those women who forge unapologetic pathways to success, desire to reach higher, or to change social or economic position or policy, can be labeled as disobedient, or unfeminine. When women spill out of the predictable prescriptions of patriarchy, they are regarded as domineering, dangerous, and suspicious. Cast as a dangerous enchantress, "dirty goddess" or a "carnal scapegoat" (Dinnerstein, 1999, p. 124), women who refuse to be seduced, stalked, possessed, and controlled, become targeted, labeled, and indicted. It is a not so subtle form of devaluation, chronically present where such actions are common, normalized, and unchallenged. Possession of personal desire requires that women walk a tightrope, carefully negotiating the thin line between what is expected, what is feared, and what matters most. As a scholar of Henry James says, regarding the character of Isabella Archer in *The Portrait of a Lady* – "her field of action … has never been free" (Gorra, 2012, p. xviii) and "the decisions of others have always impinged on her own" (ibid., pp. xviii–xix) "like some wild, caught creature" (James, 1996, p. 137), no less trapped than a bird in a cage. Though autonomy and exceptionalism hold particular value in America (Gorra, 2012, p. 114), many stories of women reveal the external forces that limit freedom. Like Isabella, the great American dream of individual autonomy may not be available to women, where the "real offence … (is) of having a mind at all" (James, 1996, p. 552).

This familiar scenario has been a part of mainstream popular culture, family and politics, where it has the power to take hold insidiously, unselfconsciously, and with little challenge. Psychoanalytic perspectives, dominant in the post-World War II culture, held sway in popular culture. A *Life* magazine (*Life*, 1956) devoted to the "Role of Women" offered a worried view of marriage, divorce rates and women who are not "feminine enough" (Coughlan, 1956, p. 109). After interviewing several well-known psychiatrists of the era, the male journalist concluded that, as traditional roles begin to blur, "the highest temporal necessity of human existence" is at risk: *the survival of the species* (my italics) (ibid., p. 109). "The career woman … may find many satisfactions at her job, but the chances are that she, her husband and her children will suffer psychological damage, and that she will be basically an unhappy woman" (ibid., p. 116). "If they are feminine women, with truly feminine attitudes, they will – without self-conscious exhortations about the delights of domesticity – accept their wifely functions with good humor and pleasure" (ibid., p. 116). The baby boom of the 1950s is evidence that women are comprehending "the penalties of feminism" (ibid., p. 118) as the article optimistically concludes "the social prestige of motherhood has penetrated," perhaps reversing the ominous trend of identity ambiguity. In this popular issue, women who desired a role in medicine, politics or academia were considered legitimate, but only if willing to maintain a traditional domestic role as well. The desire to make a difference on global scale could be accepted only if remuneration was absent, if there were a Mrs. at the front of her very successful husband's name. It was, and still is, sexism – a justification for patriarchy that is determined and controlled by men.

As feminists would argue for decades, Freud and his followers have done women no favors. There has been backlash, a wholesale rejection of Freud's theories – deemed so sexist as to threaten the theoretical validity and clinical utility of psychoanalysis itself. The risk that our field may become extinct is clear to anyone who works in academic settings, clinical training programs, or high school psychology classrooms. It is painful to reflect on this aspect of psychoanalytic history, to acknowledge the manner in which desire was attributed to women in this specific way, and how this view shaped and validated bias – clinical, theoretical, and cultural. To reflect on this now, means a deconstruction of desire, a rethinking of the famous Freudian frustration – how to understand what women want, not through Freud's eyes, but through others'.

Desire through the eyes of women

The psychoanalytic attempt to understand femininity seemed doomed to failure, though the introduction of women's voices at various points over the last century worked to make progress, often in the context of intense political and organizational efforts to oust the purveyors of these alternatives. Of female desire, Horney (1926) identified the inherent distortions in a theory bound by "phallic monism." Horney strongly questioned the validity of a psychology of women that was derived entirely from the point of view of men thus: "how far has the evolution of women, as depicted by men … been measured by masculine standards," perceptions that confirm a male oriented understanding of female psychology and development (ibid., p. 327). The overarching phallocentrism argues for the inferiority of women. "[T]his is the reason why in most varying fields inadequate achievements are contemptuously called 'feminine', while distinguished achievements on the part of women are called 'masculine' as an expression of praise" (Ibid., p. 326). Though there are instances in which penis envy may be relevant, Horney radically introduced women as agents of their own desire: object seekers with healthy sexuality, desirous of an equal sexual partner. Assertively, she noted that women seek pleasure from men. Perceived by women as an attractive and appealing sexual object, the penis is erotic and desired (ibid., p. 337). Adding to that was her assertion that the role of motherhood was a unique anatomical *privilege*. To Horney, pregnancy was pleasurable and affirming – an enviable, though overlooked, female asset. Women were hardly lacking. Rather, they were different, and this difference was to be respected as unique rather than inferior.

Joan Riviere (1929) spoke of the sexual life of women, perhaps as a response to her own analyst, Ernest Jones, who introduced his ideas in "The Early Development of Female Sexuality" (Jones, 1927). Describing a specific type of women who "wish for masculinity" (Riviere, 1929, p. 303), Riviere seemed to tweak the earlier theory about the resolution of penis envy through childbearing by considering an alternative. Though initially describing "the overtly masculine type of woman" (ibid., p. 303), Riviere goes on to observe the woman who must wear "womanliness ... as a mask, both to hide the possession of masculinity and to avert the reprisals expected if she was found to possess it" (ibid., p. 306). Women who display intellectual gifts, talent, and power also realize that such qualities may activate the anxiety of men in their social groups. As a result, women make efforts to enhance their traditional "womanly" attributes and social interpersonal style, to soothe their male counterparts. Though hardly revolutionary, Riviere's discussion of jealousy in the case of a female patient, suggests the possibility that "the desire for a *preferential position* over some other person" (Riviere, 1932, p. 418) went beyond the theoretical dogma of its day to consider a woman whose wish for importance and power went beyond the acquisition of anatomy.

Lampl-De Groot (1933) grappled with the reframing of the psychology of women, arguing that girls and boys had equal intensities of desire:

> the female is not from the beginning a passive, yielding being who permits herself to be loved, but ... reveals active as well as passive tendencies often not to be differentiated from those of the boy, even quantitatively. The little girl, like the boy, courts with actively directed love, as long as the mother is still the love object. It is necessary, then, to explain how it happens that the little girl, in the course of normal development, renounces her activity.
>
> *(Lampl-De Groot, 1933, p. 495)*

Though Lampl-De Groot returns to the familiar certainty regarding the young girl's wish for a penis, and sense of deprivation without it, she includes boys (as does Horney). In the calculation, the boy's envy of pregnancy is regarded as less intense than the girl's penis envy, as its frustration is located in the far future. More significant is her effort to challenge the acquisition of passivity as "normal" for ideal female development. Having described the developmental process, for boys *and* girls, Lampl-De Groot challenges the certainty of the path. She notes: "this course of events seldom occurs in real life" (ibid., p. 518) and "subordination of active libido to passive never completely succeeds. Even where complete femininity in love-life is achieved, more or less vigorous active tendencies are demonstrable" (ibid., p. 517). In this way, she seems to crack open a door to the possibility that many women are capable of harnessing active tendencies for the purpose of pleasurable and fulfilling activities, but only by "utilizing a bit of her masculinity in the service of nourishing and caring for her child and later in educating it" (ibid., p. 513). But she disappoints in the final paragraph: only by harnessing maleness, may women, briefly, achieve. "It is no wonder," she says, "that the super-ego of the woman enables her to achieve less significant social and cultural contributions than the man" (ibid., p. 518).

Over forty years later, Chasseguet-Smirgel (1976) attempted to revisit the meaning of Freud's ideas about female development. Though the issues of desire are somewhat obscured in the more significant argument regarding Freud's phallic monism and the "blind spots" associated with his perspective, she articulates with greater clarity a fundamental question:

> if a subject as fundamental as female sexuality causes such disagreement among analysts after almost 80 years of clinical practice, it must be because it stirs up certain internal factors in a particularly intense way which somehow interferes with our progress towards knowledge. Our differences of opinion about female sexuality are such that in the melee we lose sight of the truth.
>
> (Chasseguet-Smirgel, 1976, p. 275)

Theoretical battles, she boldly states, must include the possibility that the enduring understanding of "female sexuality as a series of lacks" (ibid., p. 281) conceals underlying helplessness that has been unconsciously *split off* by the anxious male/psychoanalyst, who would otherwise be overwhelmed by the power of the female; she argues that the early experience of dependency on the mother, the unequivocal need for her in order to survive, casts the mother as an omnipotent other and reveals a narcissistic vulnerability in men, that is unbearable to acknowledge consciously. The psychoanalyst/male whose origin is the same as any other boy, must perpetuate the denigration of women in order to manage the intensification of need and inadequacy that is activated in early male sexual development, and this leaves traces in adulthood.[2] It is a bold assertion that attempts to explain why, even now, Freud's theory of women has endured, a normalization of the denigration of women, despite clinical contradiction and vigorous debate. Stating that:

> Freud attributed to man a "natural scorn" for women. This scorn originated in the fact of their lack of a penis. My experience has shown me that underlying this scorn one always finds a powerful maternal imago, envied and terrifying. A passing devaluation of the mother is "normal" and allows the boy to narcissistically cathect his own sexual identity, but it should not be prolonged into adulthood except in the guise of protective feelings towards the woman.
>
> (Ibid., p. 283)

Her article ends with a barely veiled chastisement that could be seen as a communication to her psychoanalyst colleagues who perpetuated this perspective and failed to regard the impact on women as either destructive or in need of alteration: "Scorn in the adult is never 'normal' and reveals personal uncertainty about one's own self-worth" (ibid., p. 283). Negative responses to powerful and important women reflect the feelings of inadequacy in the person who scorns, is fearful, and is unable to manage a view of women that does not conform to phallocentric perspectives.

Contemporary Perspectives: prime numbers, mothers and identity

Is it possible to locate desire in its purity – a "prime number" sense of desire – before it is infiltrated by the layers of life that will shape the arc of its development; the nascent experience of a desiring self, before the introduction of limit, judgment or outcome? If we begin with the premise that desire is an inherent aspect of human psychological experience, then we can begin to deconstruct the intervening factors that shape desire for each individual and what differences affect the unfolding.

At first, desire is a kind of hunger, held in the body, as physical need, and drawn to the focus of the object source as provider. Here, all that is known is desire *as survival*. Desire as *must have*. Hunger desire is shaped by the inevitable obstacles or favorable contexts that sculpt and shape the need: human responsiveness, attunement or misalignment – satisfaction, gratification, and frustration. Hunger desire serves to regulate the body's capacity to engage, to create a response, to build contacts that are reliable. It also establishes memories as forms of comfort, dismissal or rejection that are layered into traces of body contact, interaction, and fulfillment.

Central to Dimen's long consideration of the topic of desire is the essential distinction between want and need. Dimen, quoting at length from her own perspective on the topic states that:

> want and need appear culturally as unequal strangers. Wanting, associated with adulthood, active will, masculinity, is better than need, linked to infancy, passive dependency, and femininity. Adults therefore try to distance their dependency needs by regarding their longings for love, tenderness, and care as weak, childish, "womanish"
>
> *(Dimen, 1989, pp. 41–42, Dimen, 1991, p. 348)*

Hence, two aspects of what we think of when we explore desire, are themselves gendered, burdened by the embedded expectations and judgments associated with long standing bias. "I want" is an assertion, laced with power and dominant expressions of expectation and clarity. It can be bombastic and loud, often entitled, demanding, and concrete. Need, however, is associated with hunger, deficit, and depletion. It is about survival, common to men and women, but quickly seems to change meaning as it becomes gendered over time. The whining and whimpering, a negative often associated with dependency, is a highly gendered image, and the satisfactions that meet a woman's need are evidence of autonomous failure.

To Benjamin (2004, p. 47), desire occupies a continuum of experience:

> We consider the gradations of the desire to reach the other, the frustrated desperation to get in accompanied by the urgent need to discharge, the different inflections of the wish to enter or be entered, that is, from the wish to be held safely to the urge to break in forcibly, from the wish to be known to the wish to be cracked open.

With her focus on the experience of female sexuality, arousal, and body-to-body contact, Benjamin's use of the word desire is fluid and energetic, reflecting the interplay of intimacy and responsiveness in the context of sexual activity:

> A subject who owns passivity, with its pleasure and vulnerability, need not *passivize the other*. Such a subject can have desire for another subject without reducing him or her to a will-less or overwhelming object who, in turn, renders him helpless before his own impulses.
>
> *(Benjamin, 2004, p. 53)*

But Benjamin's description of this dynamic interaction could resonate in many ways, reflecting the ideal potential for engagement in numerous human endeavors, as long as there is equality, mutuality, and vitality. "Owning desire" (ibid., p. 53) is a concept that can be created singly, and in collaborative or negotiated complementarity. This is the messy but sometimes liberating possibility in any dyad, though commitment and the risk of loss must also be included in any calculation of outcome.

Just as gender is "an extremely complicated nonlinear system of meanings that an individual constructs and co-constructs with his or her environment" (Balsam and Harris, 2012, p. 42), so too is desire. Much like chaos theory would suggest, desire, is *or can be,* "emergent, patterned, organized, but unpredictable" (Balsam and Harris, 2012, p. 39). "Subtle moves, subtle shifts in experience, produce very wide variation and experience" (ibid., p. 40), and "very small shifts in just one or two matters can produce massive changes and organizations" (ibid., p. 39).

Mothers and daughters

Who figures prominently in the pathway of development? How does each person respond to moments of synchrony, gratification, or frustration? Is the social and cultural field populated by inspiring, nurturing, stimulating figures, or will there be impediments, biases, or restrictions? The interlocking layers of history, action, and affective meaning become part of the complexity of each life, sometimes making it more and more difficult to remember or believe there was ever a pure desire, unencumbered by the strands of disappointment, obstacle or restriction – when prime number desire was thrown off course by expectations, limits or obligations. There can be no flourishing of pure desire in an environment dominated by others, where the essential cry for personal autonomy is not respected. If we are not careful, desire can look like Daphne's transformation to the laurel tree, exquisite but frozen in place and possibility.

Desire intersects with the multilayered acquisition of identity. The possibilities associated with its plasticity, and the actual dynamics of identity, defy Freud's representations of women. "Identity emerges as multiple, not uniform or unitary, as emergent not stable, differentiated not seamless, always contested" (Dimen, 2003 p. 78). Idealization can shape desire, emerging as a wish for loving attention, similarity, or inclusion. Attachment and idealization are linked, as are aspects of desire in the context of relationships. For women, identification must be understood within a context of social complexity, gender bias or favorability, and the interplay with the idealized (and equally influenced) other. Aspirations connect with loving attachment, fear of loss, or necessity, shaping the evolution of both desire and identity. As Dimen suggests, it is vital to understand identity as a complexity of multiplicities (Dimen, 1991), that include a combination of gender and the construction of identity from many different locations. Female desire in contemporary psychoanalytic literature is centered on the mother–daughter relationship.

In the first issue of the psychoanalytic journal, *Studies in Gender and Sexuality*, Dianne Elise asks: "Why is it not clear what women want?" (Elise, 2000, p. 126). Why, she asks, "does some element of mystery … prevail; women's desire is veiled, has a hidden, shrouded quality" (ibid., p. 126). Elise asserts that the origin of female desire is clear: it is "to re-experience the early sensual atmosphere with the mother" (ibid., p. 132) who "the girl originally desires, relates to intensely, and then loses as a romantic/erotic object." Women, Elise proposes, must foreclose their desire for mothers, a consequence of the heterosexual mother's rejection. The chronically disappointed woman is forced, ultimately, into a "second best" alternative – the husband/father. Her premise is that: "full recognition and expression of women's desire, given the cultural expectations, would threaten this highly valued love relationship for women; thus, women are likely to back-pedal on one form of desire (sexual) to achieve another (relational)" (ibid., p. 141). Under these circumstances, desire dies.

Butler (1995) locates the meaning of desire within the context of identification, loss, and repudiation, emphasizing the underlying basis for the heterosexual position and the renunciation of homosexual longing. The question of loving attachments and the irreconcilable mourning for unlived possibilities (ibid, p. 176) resonate with Elise's version of women's desire. The foreclosure of the mother leaves the individual in a state of chronic desire and melancholy, often unacknowledged and disavowed. This ongoing state of despair for repudiated love in the service of social convention results in identity that has attained its coherence through the act of prohibition and exclusion.

Chodorow's (1974, 1976) groundbreaking perspective regarded the profound value of the mother-daughter relationship and challenged the oft stated expectation: women and men need to renounce love for the mother in order to progress into healthy psychological maturity. In an early paper, Chodorow (1974) notes that:

> Feminine identification is based not on fantasied or externally defined characteristics and negative identification, but on the gradual learning of a way of being familiar in everyday life, and exemplified by the person (or kind of people – women) with whom she has been most involved.
>
> *(Ibid., p. 51)*

Here, Chodorow embraces the notion that female identity is powerfully nurtured in the affective container of the significant relationship between mother and daughter. How mother–daughter or parental relationships facilitate or nurture desire is a complicated mix of internal experiences that are intergenerational, internal, and intersubjective. In a follow-up reflection, decades later, Chodorow notes the importance of challenging the "tyranny of biological explanations of gender" (Chodorow, 2012, p. 57) that derive female psychology almost entirely from differences in anatomy (ibid., p. 58). She also admits that her description of the centrality of the mother–daughter relationship was "written from a daughter's point of view," a lens that could not draw on the "transformative claims that motherhood makes on identities and a sense of self" (ibid., p. 61). This awareness, made personal when she became a mother herself, clarified for her the "vast variety of individual patterns of interpreting, creating, and changing reality" (ibid., p. 61).

Kulish and Holtzman use the myth of Persephone to highlight the powerful relationship between mother and daughter, one that includes identification (Kulish and Holtzman, 2008, p. 16), the awakening of sexual desire, and the possibility of independence (ibid., p. 47). As daughters mature, the onset of menstruation heralds a change in status, a signal of reproductive possibility, of sexual desire, and greater equality with mother. In a healthy relationship, mothers convey the vitality that may be felt in the female body. This primary, deeply affirmative sense of femaleness, is in significant contrast to the idea of the body as impure (ibid., pp. 146–148).

Enigmatic and Pragmatic knowing occupy Atlas' (2016) exploration of desire. Her work focuses on the creation of the dyadic relationship, parental and analytic. Her perspective explores the intersection between parent (mother) and child, and the development of desire through the expression of body, sensuality, sexuality, and erotic knowledge, a process that can be Pragmatic: "sensible, logical, operational, definable, practical, hardheaded, and sober" and Enigmatic: "opaque to observation, puzzling, riddled, polysemous" (Atlas, 2016, p. 2). She utilizes these templates to argue for a desire that is expressed in sexual awakening, longing, and interpersonal tension. Though relationships define the context within which desire is amplified, much can remain mysterious, "like poetry … never fully exposed, and every attempt to describe it will distort its essence" (ibid., p. 3). Grappling with "forbidden" desire, the way desire "awakens the hidden parts of ourselves" and "the deepest experiences of our own body" (ibid., p. 116), Atlas attempts to place desire in the liminal space of what is known and unknown. She regards desire that is, at turns, resonant with expected norms and markers, while alternately obscured by elusive unprocessed experience. Like Douglas (1966), and Kulish and Holtzman (2008), Atlas recognizes the familiar representation of women's bodies as containers with objectionable leakages of body fluids related to sexual acts, procreational capacity, and childbirth. When desire leads to body expression, Atlas argues that, rather than accept the patriarchal view of women as offensive and requiring exile and purification, women can transition towards an opposite self-representation, one that views desire, procreation, and body mastery as a developmental asset with enormous impact: "women share a secret, the secret of femininity, and in that sense are superior, exceptional" (ibid., p. 126). Body representation in desire heralds the acquisition of power only possible for the female of the species.

Desire derailed

Not all desire is received with pride and accurate attunement. There are too many situations, "climates in which … desires are eradicated or deadened, blocking the pathway to felicitous adult sexuality" (Wrye and Welles, 1998, p. xvii), an interference with ideal developmental progress and necessary "transformation" (ibid., p. xvii). Wrye and Welles note the presence of a special "horrible, dry, hollow" (ibid., pp. 138–139) that derails desire. This is especially visible in attachment disturbances, where the experience of separateness and individuality have become compromised. Like a Winnicottian "primitive agony" (Winnicott, 1974, p. 104), the sense of aloneness is so desperate that all desire becomes focused on regulating contact to avoid annihilation.

When desire is received with humiliation, the consequences are likely to register as a limiting force, attached to conflict, risk, and shame. Layton states that:

> Humiliation and the wish to be loved play a primary role in the splitting of attributes not considered gender-appropriate. Some of those attributes have been attained through complex identifications; many of them, however, are gender neutral, inborn capacities for agency and attachment that develop in relationships that are culturally gendered, with men and women who are culturally gendered.
>
> *(Layton, 2000, p. 57)*

The decision of "*not me*" may register just as powerfully as the desire to be "*just like.*" Desire may be activated toward the process of dis-identification, an assertive pivot from aspects of the self or other that are regarded as damaging or aversive. Most significant relationships can hold many features of both. The obstructive, influential, or facilitating presence of external reality exerts an impact. Relationship value affects the acquisition of identity and the processing of desire – on both sides of the relationship. No individual is immune to the influences that allow for, shape, or limit the full expressive force of identification.

> Identifications (that) arise through different process: mimesis, introjection, incorporations, and internalization each yield up distinct form of identification. Identifications may be global or partial … Powerful unconscious aspects of identification may lie right at the surface of the body or deep in our psychic core.
>
> *(Harris, 2009, pp. 126–127)*

Imagination and the arc of desire

When reviewing the psychoanalytic literature for this book, perspectives on women and desire are organized around several specific threads of meaning: the erotic body that ignites desire; reverberations between the desired and the aroused; implications of sensuality, satisfaction or frustrations of sexual need; the maternal icon as a life sustaining necessity or controlling and dangerous threat. Powerful and important understandings of identification are entwined with the language of pro-creation, situated specifically within the mode of family relationships, decisions to be a mother – or not; to be a caretaker – or not. Women as maternal, reproduc-tive, and nurturing are engaged in the work of supply and satisfaction. Though not without meaningful rewards, it is a wonder that other aspects of creative activity, invention, and impact are missing in the theoretical understanding of women's psychology and women's lives.

Though hardly dismissive of the profound value of the female body, whose reproductive power is awe inspiring and worthy of envy, or the importance of maternal relationship, there is an absence of focus on the unique intellectual impact of women: "that the body you come into the world with exists as a housing for expressing your mind" (Balsam and Harris, 2012, p. 43) and that this singular perspective offers special value.

When women desire to be part of the public arena, there are still individual, inter-personal, societal, political and psychological tensions. Though perhaps less pervasive in other progressive countries, in the United States of 2018, it is still a challenge. That this remains a question is noteworthy. Why wouldn't a woman desire to be part of the social, political, and cultural fabric of the world; to have an impact, to desire to make the world more inhabitable, safe, and innovative? Introducing her book, *Gender as Soft Assembly* (Harris, 2009), Harris again references the question that seemed to baffle Freud and many in our psychoanalytic community: "what do women want?" and then asks, "how do women want?" (ibid., p.18). Freud's mystification and his theories continue to have decisive impact. There is much to be said for requiring the classical analysts to stand back and give room to what Layton (2004) describes as the ongoing resistance to acknowledging the multidimensional factors that shape contexts within which women and their desire are conceptualized:

> When cultural context is considered, it often appears as an add-on to such traditional psychodynamic constructs as dependence-independence, enmesh-ment-separateness, or the capacity for love. I would like to see American psychoanalysis recognize that gender, race, class, and sexual orientation are not add-ons to psychodynamics; they constitute psychodynamics. They entail and put limits on the very way we Americans define our sense of agency, our feelings of dependency, our way of loving.
>
> *(Layton, 2004, p. 248)*

And, our wish to enlist desire in order to have an impact on, and change the world that we inhabit.

The incubator of fantasy and imagination

Though fantasy often occupies the realm of the symbolic and the metaphorical – a path to the meaning of self and representations of others, the expressed and resolved wish, or impossible scenario, there is more to fantasy that must be considered as we address the topic of desire. Occupying a crucial role in the understanding of the unconscious, fantasy remains an iconic focus of psychoanalytic theory and clinical exploration. Fantasy is what Jonathan Lear calls a "living form ... of imaginative capacity ... that contains many remnants of the past" (Lear, 2005, p. 112). Fantasy resides in the liminal space between inner and outer, real and unreal, wish and frustration, present and past. As an emergent potential, fantasy always:

> seems to be located exclusively within the domain of opposition between subjective and objective, between an inner world, where satisfaction is obtained through illusion, and an external world, which gradually, through the medium of perception, asserts the supremacy of the reality principle.
>
> *(Laplanche and Pontalis, 1968, p. 2).*

When Freud described the value of "building castles in the air" (Freud, 1908, p. 145), he conceived an imaginal vision, a day dream, that might offer pleasurable satisfactions not always possible in the here and now of life. In the "closed psychical system," castles are elusive, a form of wishful thinking and "pleasure play" (ibid., p. 144). Fantasy dwells at the intersection between psychic reality, "a reality at least as valid as the material world" (Laplanche and Pontalis, 1968, p. 2), and the hard facts of existence. But inevitably, there will be an intersection, clash, or collision between unconscious fantasy and external reality. At that very point of contact,

> at the very moment when fantasy ... is discovered, it is in danger of seeing its true nature obscured by the emphasis on an endogenous reality ... which is itself supposed to be in conflict with a normative, prohibitory external reality, which imposes on it various disguises.
>
> *(Ibid., p. 7)*

Though we may agree that individual psychic reality remains hardy over time, the idea that psychic reality, fantasy, and imagination are immune to incursions and influences from external and internal experience no longer fits what we know. From the first breath, existence is layered with multifaceted interactions that shape how we think, feel, and relate, how we establish identity and our engagement in the world. That is, over time, the lived life grounds fantasy into a life where desire is attached to the future, and fantasy bakes in imaginal possibilities and purpose.

The mind that makes fantasy is no less than a creative incubator. Fantasy is where imagination is born and where the possibilities of a future self are formulated and eventually intersect with the forces of the external experience: family, values, societal norms and expectations, stereotypes, and limitations. "What really matters," says Lear, "is acquiring a practical understanding of how this vibrant imagination is woven into conscious life" (Lear, 2005, pp. 112–113).

Though psychoanalysis has often materially failed to offer understanding and support for women's psychic power, entitlement, and imagination, fantasy provides *the medium* for desire, utilized as "something more" than the evidence of an unconscious life. Fantasy can be seen to nurture desire, building the architecture of aspiration into visions of the future. Hence, rather than thinking of desire as sealed off, a contained unconscious process located in the world of fantasy, it is worth considering the identification of desire as a developmental skill that begins in the world of fantasy and *moves* into the world of creativity and imagination – a necessary ingredient for a passionate life.

Desire evolves and becomes rooted in a variety of contexts throughout our lifetimes, existing in the complexity of unconscious process, individuality, and intersubjective and relational space. As with the acquisition of any essential human competence, there are moments that reveal detours, interruptions and emotional surges; specific events, conflicts, or relational patterns that, when explored deeply, uncover how desire was transformed, thwarted, or even squelched entirely. The maturation of desire supports the unique exigencies of the individual, allowing for expression, complexity, and opportunity. As a platform for the integration of the personal, familial, cultural, and sociopolitical landscape, fantasy can be utilized to clarify the desires that are marinating in the unconscious and that seek expression in the real world. To identify internal desires and then, to create the conditions where those desires may develop and flourish, would be the goal of any facilitating environment, including the psychoanalytic consulting room.

Clinical meaning and process

In the context of our discussion of women, we must consider the social constructs that limit development. That each individual is "grounded" within a larger social context (Layton, 2004, p. 233) means that desire will be limited by, facilitated, and deeply affected by the particular world into which each of us is born. Internal experience will inevitably be shaped by the individual's response to the world, who shares the space, and the interactional patterns that layer on, influence, and in turn, impact the experience. Culture, racism, social class, gender bias, and misogyny bring incursive layers of impact, an encumbrance that burdens healthy development. Can we ever know when our desires have not been altered by influence, when our "choices" have *not* been pre-determined? Are the skills that women seem to be "good" at, such as empathy, relationship building, and emotional sensitivity, really inherent, or are they dismissed leftovers, often regarded as "soft": a transparent reference to second sex status. Perhaps, even more potential is being lost by women and men as a consequence of predetermined and rigid barriers to change – embedded bias and intrusions on desire that are resistant to modification.

By the time we psychoanalysts see our patients, desire has been shaped by an inevitable intersection between fantasies of desire, fantasies of expectation, and the real experience of the individual in the world. We must find the threads of meaning, often obscured in elements of family dynamics and patterns of thwarted interests and identifications. As with any valued developmental skill, when growth is restricted, all aspects of an individual, personality, identity, relationships, and self-esteem, are affected deeply. Fortitude, courage, intellect or artistry – ideal ingredients for development – may run into roadblocks.

If it is possible to free desire from the ropes of external restrictions, the desire that is buried by the need for self-protection, or obscured by the fear of disapproval, or loss of love, may be liberated, and find a developmental pathway that is unencumbered, even celebrated.

The corrosive and damaging impact of obstructed developmental aims must be a focus that looks around the patient, and within the patient. Our clinical explorations must be free to include the role of social, cultural, and familial impact, and if those contacts afford moments of respect, indifference, or contempt. The clinical consulting room may bring its own version of interference, as psychoanalysts are themselves vulnerable to embedded biases, unconscious beliefs, desires (Celenza, 2010), and expectations that have become gendered and skewed by our own theoretical history and personal experience.

A more contemporary approach to clinical work might explore the ideal conditions in which inchoate wishes and imaginal capacity become organized into an understanding and respect for a desire that translates into essential personal knowledge – a developmental pathway whose ultimate achievement is the acquisition of the confident and robust ability to actualize aspirational goals and the movement from internal desire to action.

This is an urgent need, not only because we are entering an historic time of female influence and leadership, but because, despite this shift, we see a resurgence of external forces that would seek to interfere with the full representation of women's desire, the intensification of gender bias in the face of real women with real power in our consulting rooms, and on the global stage.

Absent from the discussion, is the consideration of women's bonds with each other, the desire for mentors, collaborators, and friends and the value that such engagement can afford. These relationship paradigms often reveal intense intimacy and mission in private and public spaces. The impact of women's power in numbers, as opposed to single efforts, is an example of such meaning. The recognition that intense desire can be asserted more easily when it can claim space with others cannot be underestimated in the context of public space. The capacity to voice desire as a human right is revealed in the context of gender injustice, workplace values, and equity. Individual privileges voiced singly have less impact than those communicated as a chorus. When desire is shared within a group, the force of its potential is liberated.

In the ideal, autonomous desire would arise, much like a developmental achievement, from a convergence of parental scaffolding, cultural flexibility, intellectual stimulation, creative imaginal capacity, and social and relational support as well as the individual strengths and inherent genetic capacities. Within that context, women, and men, are free to develop their own unique agenda for desire, and their ambitions are defined and shaped by agentic competence, a rich affective awareness, and the assurance of intimate connection – whatever the action. Desire becomes part of identity. If we are to give desire its due, we will recognize desire as an indispensible human asset and that no matter what world we inhabit, or how desire is restrained: "nothing once desired or brought into a relation of attachment and longing is ever fully relinquished" (Harris, 2000, p. 246).

I think, therefore I desire

Desire, I assert, is not in the body alone, but in the mind, and in the way the mind enters the world. Desire is expressed in the global arena, in the wish to have impact, to improve the world, to achieve justice for others, to facilitate empowerment for the disenfranchised. Desire mobilizes one's place in the world, the search for a mission that defines identity, and shapes the future. Desire uses the mind *and* body, and represents a hunger for the animated experience, expressed in the service of satisfying challenging goals – to be open to the fullness of affect, risk, and any uncertain possibility that life supplies. Desire, often expressed in imagery of an empty, fillable container (womb) is not just about wanting and wishing, but about *aiming*. It is about a wish that materializes, from the engaged whole person, embodied – yes, but also imagining the outcome, a movement towards an enlivened existence, and a belief that such an existence is possible.

Each body that enters this world is affected by the other bodies that connect with the history of their own desire, also shaped by hunger, loss, deprivation, prejudice, or privilege. The complexity of many entwined elements may seem too difficult to unravel, but this is exactly the challenge of desire – to locate its most important origins – the spark in imagination, passion, and meaning – and cultivate and nurture its growth. To lift the long tendrils that obscure or choke the movement of desire into action is a difficult endeavor. Too often, desire suffers in the wasteland of dismissal, despair or denial. Deprived of a suitable and sustainable growing environment, even the most powerful of desires can founder, or dry out. It is not always easy to confront the forces of resistance, and to remain loyal to one's own ardent path. "To find the full heart of desire and stake one's claim to it in this world is a formidable, perhaps heroic task" (Brody, 2016, p. 6).

So it is that desire does not develop in a vacuum, but depends on multiple factors to flourish. Some, like our random arrival in a particular family, society or world, can make all the difference, as can DNA or temperament, or even luck. We are not alone on our path through desire. It matters who joins us, partnering, encouraging or disparaging the tiny seeds that need the right soil to take root.

"So many of the developmental stories in gender theory use the language of psychic sculpting. Elements of the self are foreclosed, repudiated, disidentified in a kind of psychic Bauhaus aesthetic, [of] 'less is more'" (Harris, 2000, p. 246). Though Bernini could make marble appear supple, sculpting the illusion that Daphne might move and breathe, hard rock has no give. Daphne was trapped – unable to possess her life, her desire stolen from her. Though we each face the possibility that desire may be similarly embedded in stone, shaped by others who would limit our potential and forfeit our dreams, we must remember that, when desire is animated, its form cannot be frozen, not by restraint, not by humiliation, not by denial. Desire is a force that will refuse to be ignored, and when free, will find its wings.

And then, take flight.

Notes

1 A description of Freud's understanding of male development is not included here, as the psychoanalytic history of male development is not the focus of this book. Interested readers have many options but should regard Freud's 1924 paper on the dissolution of the Oedipus complex as a primary resource.
2 Chasseguet-Smirgel's assertion sounds remarkably like a similar argument made by D.W. Winnicott in an obscure 1969 paper, "Some Thoughts on the Meaning of the Word Democracy" (Winnicott, 1969, p. 416) in which women are experienced as an ongoing threat due to the earliest experience of dependency that evolves into an "universal fear of domination" (ibid., p. 417). Further discussion of this paper can be found in Chapter 11.

References

Atlas, G. (2016) *The Enigma of Desire*. New York: Routledge.

Balsam, R. (2000) Integrating Male and Female Elements in Women's Gender Identity, *JAPA* 49: 1335–1360.

Balsam, R. and Harris, A. (2012) Maternal Embodiment: A conversation between Rosemary Balsam and Adrienne Harris. *Studies in Gender and Sexuality* 13(1): 33–52.

Benjamin, J. (2004) Deconstructing Femininity. *Annual of Psychoanalysis*, 32: 45–57.

Brody, S. (2016) *Entering Night Country: Psychoanalytic Reflections on Loss and Resilience*. New York: Routledge.

Butler, J. (1995) Melancholy Gender. *Psychoanalytic Dialogues*, 5: 165–180.

Celenza, A. (2010) The Analyst's Need and Desire. *Psychoanalytic Dialogues*, 20(1): 60–69.

Chasseguet-Smirgel, J. (1976) Freud and Female Sexuality – A Consideration of Some Blind Spots in the Exploration of the "Dark Continent". *IJP* 57: 275–286.

Chodorow, N. (1974) Family Structure and Feminine Personality. In M. Rosaldo and L. Lamphere (eds) *Woman, Culture and Society*. Stanford, CA: Stanford University Press.

Chodorow, N. (1976) *The Reproduction of Mothering*. Berkeley: University of California Press.

Chodorow, N. (2012) The Reproduction of Mothering: Reconsiderations. In *Individualizing Gender and Sexuality*, New York: Routledge.

Coughlan, R. (1956) Changing Roles in Modern Marriage in *Life (Special Issue) The American Woman: Her Achievements and Troubles*, 41(26): 108–118.

Dimen, M. (1989) Power, Sexuality, Intimacy. In A. Jaggar and S. Bordo (eds) *Gender/Body/Knowledge*. New Brunswick, NJ: Rutgers University Press.

Dimen, M. (1991) Deconstructing Difference: Gender, Splitting, and Transitional Space. *Psychoanalytic Dialogues*, 1: 335–352.

Dimen, M. (2003) *Sexuality, Intimacy, Power*. Hillsdale, NJ: Analytic Press.

Dinnerstein, D. (1999) *The Mermaid and the Minotaur*. New York: Other Press, (originally published, 1976New York: Harper and Row).

Douglas, M. (1970) *Purity and Danger: An Analysis of Concepts of Pollution and Taboo* (originally published, 1966). Harmondsworth: Penguin.

Elise, D. (2000) Women and Desire: Why Women May Not Want to Want. *Studies in Gender and Sexuality* 1: 125–145.

Freud, S. (1908) Creative Writers and Day Dreaming. In *SE, Volume IX, (1906–1908) Jensen's 'Gradiva' and Other Works*, 141–154. London: Hogarth.

Freud, S. (1918) The Taboo of Virginity (Contributions to the Psychology of Love III). In *SE, Volume XI; Five lectures on Psycho-Analysis, Leonardo daVinci and Other works*, 191–208. London: Hogarth.

Freud, S. (1924) The Dissolution of the Oedipus Complex. In *SE, Volume XIX (1923–1925): The Ego and the Id and other works*, 171–180. London: Hogarth.

Freud, S. (1925) Some Psychical Consequences of the Anatomical Distinction between the Sexes. In *SE, Volume XIX (1923–1925): The Ego and the Id and other works*, 242–258. London: Hogarth.

Freud, S. (1933) Femininity, (Lecture XXXIII). In *SE, Volume XXII New Introductory Lectures on Psychoanalysis and Other Works*, 112–135. London: Hogarth.

Gorra, M. (2012) *Portrait of a Novel: Henry James and the Making of an American Masterpiece*. New York: Liveright Publishing Corporation.

Harris, A. (2000) Gender as Soft Assembly: Tomboys' Stories. *Studies in Gender and Sexuality* 1: 223–250.

Harris, A. (2009) *Gender as Soft Assembly*. New York: Routledge.

Horney, K. (1926) The Flight from Womanhood: The Masculinity Complex in Woman, as Viewed by Men and by Women. *IJP* 7: 324–339.

James, H. (1996) *The Portrait of a Lady*. Ann Arbor: State Street Press.

Jones, E. (1927) The Early Development of Female Sexuality. *IJP* 8: 459–472.

Kofman, S. (1985) *The Enigma of Woman* (translated from the French by Catherine Porter). Ithaca: Cornell University Press.

Kulish, N. and Holtzman, D. (2008) *A Story of Her Own*. New York: Jason Aronson.

Lampl-DeGroot, J. (1933) Problems of Femininity. *Psychoanalytic Quarterly* 2: 489–519.

Laplanche, J. and Pontalis, J.B. (1968) Fantasy and the Origins of Sexuality. *IJP* 49: 1–18.

Layton, L. (2000) The Psychopolitics of Bisexuality. *Studies in Gender and Sexuality* 1(1): 41–60.

Layton, L. (2004) Dreams of America/American Dreams. *Psychoanalytic Dialogues* 14: 233–254.

Lear, J. (2005) *Freud*. New York: Routledge.

Ortner, S. (1974) Is Female to Male as Nature is to Culture? In M. Rosaldo and L. Lamphere (eds), *Woman, Culture and Society*. Stanford, CA: Stanford University Press.

Riviere, J. (1929) Womanliness as Masquerade. *IJP* 10: 303–313.

Riviere, J. (1932) Jealousy as a Mechanism of Defence. *IJP* 13: 414–424.

Stolorow, R. and Atwood, G. (1979) *Faces in a Cloud*. New York: Jason Aronson.

Winnicott, D.W. (1969) Some Thoughts on the Meaning of the Word Democracy. Reprinted 2017, in *Collected Papers of D. W. Winnicott*, Vol. 3, pp. 407–422. Oxford: Oxford University Press.

Winnicott, D. W. (1974) Fear of Breakdown. *International Review of Psychoanalysis* 1: 103–107.

Wrye, H.K. and Welles, J.K. (1998) *The Narration of Desire*. Hillsdale, NJ: Analytic Press.

2

MARIE

A story of desire

Stephanie Brody

Introduction

In the first clinical case description, you will read the story of a woman who experiences some of the challenges we often have encountered in our consulting room space. The responses to her story, by our three contributors – Rosemary Balsam, Andrea Celenza, and Dianne Elise – offer unique perspectives on some factors that might have contributed to the narrative under discussion. Rather than drawing conclusions, each psychoanalyst uses her personal lens to capture aspects of the story that could play a role in the unfolding of this story. Rosemary Balsam considers first, how Freud might have understood Marie, and then provides a contemporary perspective that considers the erotic, the assertive, and the creative aspects of desire that are inherent in the story. Balsam underscores the juxtaposition between body awareness, sex, and gender, and how these factors shape Marie's relationship to the world and her internal conflicts. Andrea Celenza considers the complexity of Marie's parental identifications and the degree to which her desire is deadened, and then revived in the context of relationship conflict. Dianne Elise focuses on the interruption of healthy adolescent development, an incubator for erotic desire, and how libidinal life is ignited within the parental matrix.

It is likely that you, the reader, have heard a story like Marie's. This is a woman who has struggled at midlife and looks toward the psychoanalytic process to help her navigate the rough waters of internal turbulence and the ever challenging external obstructions that are too familiar and always painful. She has survived, she has achieved, but her desire has been sabotaged. Can modern psychoanalysis offer an alternative perspective to help us untangle the threads of desire? This is the story of "Marie."

Marie

The first time Marie called me, she was frazzled and ambivalent about starting therapy. The only reason she even had time to schedule an appointment was because she had been out of work for the past few days, trying to deal with a stubborn respiratory infection that prevented her from attending an annual business meeting. She was so congested that her doctor had forbidden her from getting on a plane. When she arrived for her appointment, she was dressed for a work meeting that she felt must attend, but coughed regularly and spasmodically as she shared her story. She looked worn and thin, disheveled, though she was dressed in stylish business attire. She became tearful almost immediately. The gist of it was that she was burned out.

Marie is a 50-year-old married mother of three. Raised in an upper middle class family, she is the third child of five siblings. Her childhood, and early family life look fairly conventional. She grew up in the Midwest suburbs of a large city. Both parents were college educated. Her mother, a teacher, gave up her profession when she became pregnant with her first child. Her father attended business school and eventually took over a successful family business. When Marie was 12, her father became disabled following a serious car accident. Though he was cognitively intact, chronic pain and fatigue made it impossible for him to run his business as before. Fearing that his disability would impact the public perception of the business, the family made a modest financial settlement to him and he was forced to retire. The disability became a humiliation that burdened him and threatened the family's financial security for the remainder of his life. The family maintained a façade of financial stability. Mom returned to teaching in the local public school, and took care of everything else, managing finances frugally.

Within this atmosphere, Marie developed a sense of self-sufficiency and focus. She followed the rules set for her by her parents and caused no trouble. A member of the Future Entrepreneurs of America and the field hockey team at her high school, Marie was a good student with an impressive academic and sports record. She worked herself through college with a combination of loans, scholarships, and part-time work as a waitress. At college, she met Scott, the man who eventually became her husband. Marie had little self-confidence with men, and found the attention from someone whom she described as "the life of the party" a welcome surprise. Though she was uncertain of his ambitions or their intellectual compatibility, her ambivalence could not override the worry that she would end up single. Scott was a persistent suitor, and so she agreed to marry him when they graduated.

With a degree in liberal arts, Marie entered the work force with no idea of what she might do. She fell into a banking job that offered on site training, and did well because she was a diligent and responsible employee who learned quickly and excelled at her tasks. She was promoted rapidly, with increasing management responsibilities. Her husband, on the other hand, seemed to have trouble at work. Though charming in social situations, his temper flared in a highly structured environment. A sales position with more flexibility and less oversight did not prove to be a success for him. As Marie became increasingly aware of Scott's work challenges, she leveraged a tuition benefits plan at her workplace and entered an evening program at a local graduate school, working towards an MBA. Holding down her job and taking on an academic program was challenging. When she became pregnant in her final year of coursework, pregnancy-related nausea was so intense that she briefly was hospitalized. Reluctantly, she decided to take a leave of absence from her academic work, planning completion in the year after her first child was born. She worked until she went into labor and then took four weeks of maternity leave. Fearful that she would be seen as expendable during her absence, she called into work daily to offer guidance on a significant project that she had initiated early in her pregnancy. Convincing Marie that their finances could weather the risk, Scott proposed to start his own home-based business with the savings they had planned for a down payment on a home. This, he said, would allow him the flexibility to stay home with their new baby when she returned to work, and would give him the autonomy that he needed to launch his own successful career. But soon it became clear that Scott was unable to consolidate his business plan smoothly. Marie agreed to help with the administrative and organizational tasks that he found tedious.

Less than a year later, Marie became pregnant again. Now, she and Scott agreed that it was probably better for him to be a fulltime dad and he sold his business. This change gave Marie more time – now she was able to focus on her own work without the distractions of Scott's business, or even the parenting responsibilities that had affected her daily schedule. But she noticed that her relationship with Scott had shifted. She felt unimportant compared to the children. Guilty, she noticed that she felt competitive with her children for her husband's attention, sulking when he chose to spend time with them, instead of her, on weekends. She wondered if Scott cared about her at all. When the third child arrived, it became clear that the only way to remain financially stable was for her to continue to work fulltime. Marie was never able to complete her business degree.

Now, with three children under the age of five, Marie's increased responsibilities at work assured her of her job security and increasing advancement up the corporate ladder. Business travel was inevitable. Marie recalls the wrenching feeling when she left home, sneaking away while her children were asleep so as to avoid goodbye. Marital conflict increased around the control of finances and parenting decisions. Now, in charge of a large corporation, Marie felt distant from her family, especially her husband. Depleted after the successful completion of a work project, Marie was out of town having a drink in the hotel bar when one of her colleagues suggested that they initiate a sexual relationship. The culture of her corporation was rife with extramarital affairs, but this was new for her, and different. Marie was exhilarated and confused by her unbidden arousal, and excitement. She had forgotten what it was like to be the object of another person's interest. Until that moment, she had been certain that her disinterest in sex with Scott was a result of chronic fatigue, and she was stunned that the proposal activated such a strong reaction in her. Impulsively, she agreed to the invitation, responding to a flood of desire that she had not known existed. Changing her travel plans, she could not turn off the intensity of her awareness and allowed an evening of sexual intimacy. It was as though a part of her that she had not known had suddenly emerged, filling her with a sense of aliveness that had been out of reach. The next day, she felt embarrassed and exposed. She fled for her home, and swore to put the incident out of her mind, maintaining a strict and uncomfortable boundary with her colleague.

Increasingly detached from her husband, she would arrive after a trip in need of replenishment and rejuvenation. Her efforts to contribute to the family culture, attending church, planning family vacations, participating in her children's school activities and later, their college application process, were dominated by her husband's need for control. She felt like an outsider in her own home. Pressured at work to maintain high levels of productivity, Marie regularly worked 12–16 hours a day, contacting teams of employees in different time zones and rarely getting more than four hours of sleep a night. Her health began to suffer. She lost weight and always seemed to have a cold. After a bout with pneumonia, she could not contain herself. Abandoning her mask of self-sufficiency, she went to her primary care doctor and confided that her marriage, her job, and her life overwhelmed her. Her doctor referred her for psychotherapy.

At our first meeting, Marie told me that her doctor advised her that she needed to take a medical leave. Always proud of her stamina, she was deeply ashamed that her body had failed her. She had thought a week or two off would be enough. She could not even remember her last vacation. Marie carefully spelled out her dilemma: though she enjoyed the status and financial security her job gave her, she didn't feel passionate about her work, or that her success would have a positive and lasting impact on people. Her marriage seemed irreparably damaged by her husband's need to control her. She resented his domineering attitude, but rarely argued with him. As their children became more independent, she felt her family life unraveling. Distant from her children, now young adults, she felt that she had missed much of their lives and didn't know if it was possible to improve these relationships. Increasingly the lavish life style of the family seemed to chain her to her job. Though she had no alternative ideas, the dream of changing her job, or scaling back her hours seemed impossible. She and Scott had little in common now and she resented that he rarely acknowledged her for how hard she worked.

First in psychotherapy and then psychoanalysis, we began to see the far-reaching impact of her family dynamics and her work history. As her career was on the ascent, she believed it was important to "sterilize" her femaleness in order to maintain expectations regarding successful business practices. Though she knew that this success was defined from a male perspective, it was a reality that dominated her workplace. Sent to an executive coach when frustration at work brought her to tears, she was taught how to control her emotional expressiveness. Coaching, she told me, was considered a "work perk": an endorsement of her competence and an effort to bring her to her highest potential. She became adept at shutting her feelings down. A powerhouse of authority at work, she was so apprehensive about talking to her husband that she gave in to all of his decisions, even when she disagreed. So numb and detached from her feelings, she functioned like a robot, not only taking orders from her husband, but aware of an internal dictator who was critical and harsh, expecting high performance at work even under circumstances of emotional and physical deprivation.

Over time, she described another aspect of her hidden life. Though she had fled from the first brief affair, she now felt increasingly drawn to seek out sexual contacts with men whom she met during her business travel. Often strangers at restaurants or bars, she described her experiences as "experimental liaisons," efforts to re-engage her body sexually, to reassure herself that she was capable of sexual sensation, but without the risk of emotional attachment. She described these encounters as "relief holidays." Though she convinced herself that she was able to assess her physical safety in these situations, there was a worrisome absence of awareness regarding the possible danger inherent in her casual sexual hook ups.

Though she craved the focused attention that she received in the analytic dyad, she was conflicted about her immersion in the experience, and feared dependency. Even though she appreciated the comfort she felt in our relationship, and noticed an expanding capacity for self-expression, she was wary of me and at times dismissive of the therapeutic process, looking for quick results and "outcomes" that could be measured. Slowly she realized how powerfully she avoided conscious desire. Exploring ideas about what she wanted led her to feel anxious and confused. Paradoxically, when the external routine and rules in which she had to conduct her work life, marriage and emotional state were relaxed, she felt lost. We learned that the driven climb to success had distracted her from a feeling of emptiness. Marie reflected that, when she took the time to look, she found nothing was inside of her.

Aware that she could no longer endure the long hours, Marie gave up her management role and took a position in the company that reduced her responsibilities, offering significant flexibility, but less income and authority. Marie described a meeting with colleagues to review contracts and bidding guidelines. Reflecting on her position in the room as the only person over 50, and the only woman, she was struck by the ambitiousness that she saw in her younger, mostly male, counterparts. The discussion was boring to her and she felt trapped. She dreaded the 360-review that would occur – to be coordinated by a recently hired male colleague, much younger and much less experienced. But he had been an academic hot shot, had excelled in business school. Her colleagues saw him as a "catch" when they recruited him successfully away from a competitor. Her meetings with him always infuriated her – he showed no respect for her previous experience. But she had to admit that her ambivalence about her job was so high that she was not very motivated. Money seemed less important to her, and she continued to wonder what value her job brought to others.

As she described the meeting to me, she included many observations and details, but little affect that would reveal what she had experienced in the moment. Noting that a large power point display rolled out the figures and territories, Marie recalled that the chart revealed with certainty that she would not reach her "numbers" for the quarter. It dawned on her that discussion was circling around the ramifications for an "underperforming" employee – perhaps like her. As the meeting continued, she described an increasing awareness of her post-menopausal self and the subliminal shifts that communicated to her that her age, her body, her sexuality and indeed her gender were out of place in this room, full of hungry young colleagues. But none of this awareness helped her to stem the growing anxiety that soon erupted into a full-blown panic attack. She excused herself from the room, feeling overheated, dizzy and nauseous. Packing up her belongings, she went home, wondering if she could ever go back to work.

As we reconstructed the event, Marie became aware of the unbearable anxiety that rolled over her when she deviated from the path set by others. Surfacing as well was the resentment and fury: unappreciated for her accomplishments she felt angry and devalued, powerless and lost. Life felt suddenly fragile, and risk felt like a seduction that was especially intense in the absence of clarity about what would happen next. We wondered together what purpose she envisioned for her life, why she had been able to manage with so little and with so few relationships that felt intimate and satisfying. What had happened that might explain the emptiness and how might we better understand the distance between herself and her elusive desire?

3

A CLINICAL CASE OF DESIRE

Rosemary Balsam

"Desire," "ambition," and "leadership" are profoundly entwined elements in the psychic lives of both women and men. *Women's* desire is the sub-topic of this chapter. My focus here is on female sexed and gendered aspects of Eros and its libidinal drives. It will necessarily involve Marie's ambition and her attitudes to leadership as well as her subjective sense of erotic and assertive, creative desire. Her story is a clinical instance of how we might use these lenses to think about some specific psychic dilemmas of a female life.

Orienting comments

From the beginning of his vision in the "Project" approximately 1886 and on, Freud created a theory of mind that always kept central the material body. The early work that he did on women was perhaps his most worthwhile concerning the actual female body, because he approached the body more as a whole and not just as separate genitals or part objects (Freud 1886–1899). There was a rich introductory period of genuine exploration regarding *both* women and men, e.g., "The Interpretation of Dreams" (Freud 1900–1901), or in Dora, whom he analyzed in 1900 (Freud 1905a), and in "The Three Essays" (Freud 1905b; even though he misunderstood female masturbatory involvement of the clitoris as "masculine"). But his views changed. Freud's ultimate *one-sex male* theory of female development was annunciated suddenly in 1908 in "On the Sexual Theories of Children" (Freud 1908) added to the 1915 edition of the "Three Essays," further fixed in 1925 in "Some Psychical Consequences of the Anatomical Distinction between the Sexes" (Freud 1925) and ultimately, set in stone in 1933 in "Femininity" (Freud 1933; see for discussion of this, Balsam 2017). Unlike shifts that he effected in other aspects of his general theory over the years, (for example, the changing versions of anxiety theory), after 1908 Freud never budged on his "male" concept of young females.[1] Two differing bodies just did not exist for him, even though his palette of gendered so-called "femininity" was suggestively ranging, and included the concept of bisexuality. His "one-sex" male theory (*necessarily* convoluted if trying to force a female creature into it) was more compatible with an ideal unified patriarchal heterosexual Oedipus Complex for all, where Father ruled all. It was not until Stoller's work in the 1970s (e.g. Stoller 1976), and the work of academic feminists that a helpful separation was brought about in sexuality theory between sex (biology) and gender (psychological reactivities). Freud's original all-purpose meshed term, "sexuality," could then be spoken of as "sex and gender" for *either* a male or a female. Two bodies could exist. New variants of gender portraits that were not specifically tied to sexual object choice or gender role identity were now more easily able to be noticed, and there was room for gays and lesbians to inhabit their respective bodies and be recognized as having developmental paths to maturity.

A woman like Marie – in the old version of Freud's sexuality – would automatically have been considered simply as an obvious bad case of penis envy, and as a woman trying to be a *man* and live like a "rightful" man. This judgment would have been reached because of her breaking social patriarchal convention by donning the *external* trappings of favoring work outside the house over a domestic role; by her lack of devotion in supporting her "man" in his "rightful" role in doing outside work and being the main provider of the family; by her snatching this role away from him, for herself. In the newer versions of sex and gender, there is much more room to allow Marie to be the *woman* she is, while asking broader questions such as: what *kind* of woman is Marie internally, in her expressions toward work ambition and domesticity? Where are her important familial object identifications? How did she develop up to this point? And how does she seem to factor in her natal female body? Where are her passions and erotic desires? The latter is another broad question that can *assume* her possession of them as a female equal to a male, rather than the old-fashioned reading of desire as emergent only from "masculine" libido. Disturbances in her female body's eroticism would then be seen as worthy of exploration, to find out what had happened to it during development.

Despite Freud's stubborn and culturally biased misinformation about female sexuality, he and his immediate followers did keep a laudable faith in and recognition of the *physicality* of the body, much more so than neo-Freudians or in later variant off-shoot schools of analysis. Some analysts of current differing schools believe that any *true* theory of intrapsychic process should ignore biology – as if the biological housing of humans were a contaminant of "concreteness" that degraded a pure and superior abstraction (see as an example, the often admired "Three Commentaries on Gender…" of the ego psychologists, Grossman and Kaplan, 1988).[2] A strong case can be made for this attitude merely being a denial of the body, and in particular the female body. I believe it important that those with female anatomy be recognized as natal *females*, while simultaneously every variant of gender fantasy that exists can surely be granted its own psychic and, if chosen, conscious legitimacy, including actions that may accompany these variants like transgender states. The subject will inhabit her own body morphology with varieties of ease, or with varying degrees of denial or rejection. Modern gender portraits possible for natal females thus include cis-gendered hetero- and homosexuals, and all 50 variant categories available on Facebook.[3] Modern analysts can own the biologically obvious, if you will: that a girl is born female, and that she senses and reacts in complicated ways to her *own* body during her development, and that she may have many "female genital anxieties," that include *birthing* anxieties that involve her version of reproduction – just as does a boy experience his own "castration anxiety" and others in tune with a male body. Karen Horney's 1926 correction of Freud's girl's changeling fantasy is what we now return to as Freud's missed opportunity (Balsam 2015).

All of that said though, interestingly, the *female* sexed body continually seems to get lost over and over again in psychoanalysis, in developmental interests and in clinical materials. It is often obviated as a vital and shaping stimulus to that woman's mental life, behavior, and actions (Balsam 2012, 2013). Once one becomes alerted to this phenomenon of female body neglect, one realizes how very odd and unexplained this is (except for explanations that involve profound archaic anxieties[4] aroused in both patients and analysts of both sexes).

So far, in this analysis of Marie, in relation to my focus on the sexed body and gender, I think we observe a minimized *sexed* body (which I offer not as a criticism, but to draw attention to the less spoken voice of her womanhood). There are current references to her body as debilitated and in pain in the account, and, it is implied, in need of "care." These elements are very real and they are conscious and so express her wish for tender care in the here-and-now. But they *may* also indicate an unconsciously regressive and submissive position that she is expressing right then, in tune with her "burn-out."

Marie's embodied sexuality, or her "sex and gender," does seem to me to play a major role in the script. The analysis as a whole is progressing beautifully and deepening. Essential issues of trust are deepening. Marie is increasingly comfortable in allowing her analyst (henceforth "Dr. Jane Doe") to hear her intimate life. To date the analysis seems to proceed along more pre-oedipal or "agendered" lines. The analyst mentions at one point that Marie "craves" attention in the dyad with her, but also resists it. This seems indeed a description of a wish for an intense pre-oedipal dyadic relation. This state is not really described further, nor is any other transference. But for the sake of discussion, I am going to risk some suggestive speculations on the basis of elements in the narrative, so that I beg the indulgence of the analyst who is actually in the room with Marie, and also the reader.

In "pre-oedipal" analytic spaces I often find that sex and gender seem to take a back seat in an analyst's thoughts, probably because we are used to thinking that we need higher levels of integration and a more developed Oedipal arena in an analysis to be able to think of or expect associations to the body, sex, and gender. I plan here to use some of the materials available in this rich narrative of Marie's life that the analyst has shared, to try to show a possible relevance of an underlying body/sex/gender story to Marie's ultimate collapse into this "feeling of emptiness" and "avoidance of conscious desire."

Marie's presentation

In the opening panic attack that is the last straw that pushes Marie into treatment and that introduces her case, the 50-year-old patient eventually in the treatment opens up some psychic content surrounding the panics. (I am unsure of the time frame from the first meeting with Dr. Doe to the last misery reported, that seems to me to be psychologically linked.) Marie describes ultimately being surrounded in her work by hungry ambitious young *males*, and that she essentially feels her side-lined status as a *past-prime female*. Perhaps we might consider her panics as a "midlife gender identity crisis" – and that the "nothing" that she ultimately complains of as "emptiness," is not so much a brand new recognition of a whole *lifetime* of a lack of desire (as an analyst might worry about), but an acute confrontation with a profound lack of direction that contrasts vividly with her previous strong identity and well-known to her (if guilty) desires. She is said to be "lost." In this last big business meeting, confronted with her fall from the glory of Executive power to the lowly (humiliated)[5] position of risking a pink slip for not making her figures for that quarter, to my ear, internally, she suddenly feels herself to be at the mercy of fantasies of being both a "failed man" *and* a "failed woman" – being a "no-thing," a no-body … literally a *no body*. She does not want to go "home" to a repudiated domestic life. She is devastated, empty, panicked, and without direction. The opening panic and "burnout" with body breakdown and regression may have been a foretaste and a paler echo of the last panic that is described more fully. (Other more minor panics when she was younger along her career path, perhaps evoked from similar shapes, may have been taken care of temporarily by the mentioned coach, who would surely help lighten her superego reaction to elements of full-on competition and aggression within her Corporate world.)

Marie's development

The following is an approximate map of female developmental territory relevant to Marie. The reason it becomes hard to separate "desire" from "ambition," in Freudian theory is that – also following Loewald (1989) – the libidinal drive fuels the person's internalized object relational attachments and models that transform into growth, and fantasy and trial action towards, say, a person's visualization of a lived future. A child envisions (him- or) herself growing "big," and into an adult (or "a leader" – from that growing child's perspective). A female will play and think of herself as growing from a girl into a mature (big, powerful, sexual) same-bodied woman in the future roles, say, of any of the adults who surround her – a homo- or heterosexual partner, a parent, likely a "mother" with a baby, and thus possibly a "leader" in her family with often some social occupation – a teacher, a doctor, a nurse, a scientist, an astronaut, a business woman. In her fantasy life of alternatives, she may live out a girl-boy identity, growing hesitantly into a nubile asexual and intellectually dominated adult; or she might flee altogether from her female body developmentally (Horney 1926), and fantasize herself as a boy or *boy*-girl growing towards an ideal of manhood. In any variant, she will, at some points in her life, sooner or later have to own up to acknowledging or rejecting her natal female body qua female. This can be a gradual process or a series of unwelcome confrontations through menstruation and puberty; and/or in pregnancy and childbirth; and/or in menopause. Whether or not she chooses to *employ* her body's female capabilities, and her caretaking modes for what aims during her life, is a different matter.

Marie, by high school, saw herself as independent, a "good girl" and one of the "Future Entrepreneurs of America." Being educated, as were her parents, she would likely call on these images for internalized identifications. Marie's father was an important businessman before she was 12. Then presumably around her puberty when her gender identity would be burgeoning and in flux, her body maturing, and her affects in full force, a tragic car accident led her likely admired father into a downward spiral. It was said he would have "humiliated"[6] his family by his public representation of them in that business. That is a tragic plunge from the peak of his male powers. He was for Marie a major family psychic resource for her work ambitions, as we see in her adolescent membership of the Young Entrepreneurs. Marie's father was first a leader, and then forced by circumstance to be more of a follower. Marie's career path seems to follow her Father's arc – from climbing the corporate ladder to a major leadership position in early middle age, possibly guiltily outdoing both this once-heroic but later wounded father. She outstripped her mother also in work ambitions, possibly forming an additional source of guilt. Mother *retired* from work when she had her first child. This would have given her girl child Marie the message that this is the gold standard, and the "true" thing to do in one's life as a female. The idealizable parental models confronting Marie, then, form a conventional split between a "phallic" man at the height of his powers in business, and a "womb-centered" female at the height of her powers, bearing her first child and being solely domestic. Only when Father breaks down and fails in his phallic earning status, mother is then unwillingly, one imagines, pushed out into a work world that she had relinquished in better days. One has a sense of the parents' mutual discomfiture in these arrangements. Marie reactively grew to depend more on herself, we are told. She likely reversed parent-child dependency roles, trying to help her stressed parents out, due to each of them being unhappy and self-preoccupied.[7]

I think that Marie's early panic in college about being "single" probably encodes her first overt gender-identity crisis. It signals the war inside her mind about her parental gendered allegiances. In approaching the terror of early adult life after graduation, she is suddenly more aware of her lack of gender integration and immaturity, the limitations of her "good school-*boy*/girl" role, and is confused about the stark binary internal division that she imagines for the future. In anxiety she focuses on a forced *female* future of babies like Mother. (This aspect of her desire and fantasy becomes focused on being "like Mother" and having what Mother had, as represented by a husband and babies, for which she'd need a man.) Might she have been out of touch with her female body, either as "asexual" or operating more in *boy*/girl mode as a "Young Entrepreneur" mode, more

identified with her father, or being his best "son"? It is possible that her "femaleness" and the possession of her female body was never well integrated in adolescence with her "maleness," as the exaggerated femaleness seems to emerge in
sudden fits and starts, either as idealized or repudiated, when her more favored
male identifications fail her. (I would suspect that in a simple way she also likes her
father better than her mother.) The husband Scott, with whom she has three
children (the births described in amazingly passive language as "happening to" her
almost,[8] one imagines, half against her will), morphs into a stay-at-home nurturer
of their three children. It is unclear in the narrative if she ever felt erotic love for
him, but I do believe this is evidence of a desire to compete with her mother as
female, and have as many children as she could countenance – three, as she was the
third child herself (and beyond that, the other two siblings may have been jealously
despised babies). I cannot imagine that Scott's take-over in the upbringing of the
children could be done without extensive collusion on her part. She may have
wanted an identity of "Mother-with-kids," to solve her post-college early adult
gender crisis. But simultaneously she may have been repelled by a fuller identification with "Mother-as-caretaker." One wonders if she got enough "female"
action to calm her gender crisis by achieving the gendered role of "wife," *plus* the
empowering female body expertise in birthing, but she was repelled by maternal
caretaking (a sign to me of problems with her own mother). Conveniently, and
collusively, her husband does this job readily. This aspect of their marital match is
quite good, in fact. (It would be interesting to hear her talk of her marriage contrasted with that of her parents.)

It strikes me that this gender "solution" with her husband Scott relieves her once
again, as in high-school, to return to her more comfortably passionate competitive
position of aspiring to be the "best," or to please the "adults," or even to become a
better version of her Father as well as her working-Mother. Who knows if Marie's
Fatherly role may also encode in fantasy an erotic pursuit of her mother?[9] Suffice
to say that Marie successfully morphed more and more into her ideal "Young
Entrepreneur of America." It is likely to me that in work she happily inhabited this
gender identity and role, and was full of desire – but in a split-off though *uncon-
flicted* fashion – even if she may have been *sometimes* guilty off and on, that she had
little desire to be a domestic female with her babies, modeled on Mom.

Marie may have had tremendous guilt about sailing so close in her father's field
and far and away surpassing him. Is her crisis in mid-life like Icarus, who flew too
close to the sun, and whose wings melted?

Marie's mother and her mothering

Marie's life as a mother is given curiously short shrift in this narrative. I interpret
this absence as a function of the split portrait of Marie that we are working with.
The three births are described in chillingly passive language. Her children are not
given sexes, nor are they even named. Marie behaves in this story as if she were
very uncomfortable in the mothering aspect of her female skin. I always find it of

negative significance if such a patient talks consistently of "the kids" without names or gender. I feel it as part of a wish to annihilate their identities and perhaps their existence.

Let us assume then that this reflects an extremely one-sided life, and a one-sided internal Father-engendered existence, where mostly all of her energies and interests were focused inside her corporate family. (One might learn in her analysis that this style may in some fashion *also* reflect her own mother in a Mother imago that is acceptable to her.) Marie's sexual excitements, whenever her female erotic aspects emerged forcefully, were also professionally based as brief encounters at professional meetings. She was seemingly using her female body as enjoyably female in these moments, with a real ability to express sexual excitement. We can note that this *sexual* female aspect of Marie may be akin to her real-life female body abilities in giving birth three times. But these talents are quite split-off from her maternal female caretaking sensibilities. Mother gave up work with her first child. Marie, in contrast, seems to have resisted the idea of even taking any time off in her first pregnancy. If anything, she escalated her work over the span of her three births. This suggests to me her possible desire to be the *opposite* of Mother. Is that also some form of competition with Mother? Can Marie be an exciting erotic woman, but not a "dull domestic" one like Mother? She can try for a version of her young mother who attracted her successful businessman father, but not the older woman who ended up disappointed in her lot. This is all a further iteration of her ongoing interior sexed gender wars. Jennifer Stuart (2011) in her research on motherhood and work, based on her Yale Alumna cohort from 1984, concluded that women who smoothly became mothers *and* comfortably worked outside the home, were the daughters of women – not necessarily who themselves had worked – but who had *joyfully* inhabited the roles of motherhood. I somehow doubt that Marie's mother was that fortunate, and Marie bears the scars.

Marie's elusive desire

Dr. Doe poses the question to us about her patient's absent or "elusive desire." She writes, puzzling:

> why [Marie] had been able to manage with so little and with so few relation-ships that felt intimate and satisfying. What had happened that might explain the emptiness and how might we better understand the distance between herself and her elusive desire?

Having a "distance between herself and her desire" shows its "elusive" character as overly cautious – a defense, possibly against her guilt or rage. At the end she helpfully does get to her fury for not being appreciated for her accomplishments.

Marie does not seem to me like a person who is fundamentally lacking in pas-sions or incapable of making relationships, even if, at the end of the write-up, she is in a depressive self-castigating mode as if mourning a totally "wasted life." With the collapse of her work world, Marie has lost an enormous amount. Hers had to be a challenging, but for her a highly rewarding interpersonal world, even if full of competition or thorniness. She negotiated her ascension with skill to a very senior executive position in a significant company.[10] Thus she was ambitious, talented, and energetically applied herself and had to have related to others to accomplish this feat. It appears that Marie's "elusive desire" is/was deeply involved in these work achievements with possibly gleeful and enjoyable aggression at times. Marie may have been *guilty* about her possible previous joy or veiled joy, and filled with guilty satisfactions in revenge over the acquisition of power. I wonder therefore about fear of and a reaction against these powerful and successful aggressive drives that brought her ambitiously to a peak of internal triumph over her Father (and Mother as worker). Perhaps this triumph could not be borne, possibly because of masochistic guilt in relation to how damaged Father became, just when she was entering into puberty and launching into her adolescent prowess. In the melting decline that seems to have happened to her whole professional self and identity all during the therapy and analysis with Dr. Doe, could she be grieving her past glory? Here are my speculations about her transference at the end of the write-up: Could her work decline be an unconscious attempt to try to "preserve" and create a softer and less competitive "dangerous" relation with her "Father"/analyst in particular, by making a masochistic atonement to "him/Dr. Doe" for having been so ambitious in the past and being, say, "too" competitive and "destructive" towards him (as in the Icarus myth)? Marie is overly caught up in stereotypic binary opposites about what it would be to be a wife and a mother to children *versus* what it is like to be a successful business executive. While in positive work identity, that I suspect she associates with "maleness," she was "a powerhouse" (joyfully?), but perhaps also in a split-off way, a guilty "bad girl" for not living out a more "good girlie" existence, like Mother, with her babies? Is she now trying to limit herself and her successful ambitiousness to prove to herself and to Dr. Doe that she is not as "destructive" as she is convinced she has been in killing off Father, as it were? Is she joining Father in his decline to atone for her desire to succeed and outshine him and her Mother?

It is as if Marie cannot conceive of sufficient internal gender integration to be a wife, a mother and also a business executive. I have suggested that Marie is an example of a woman who likely has experienced and is experiencing a sexed and gendered war inside herself. The million dollar question for me is how Marie developed the way she did, with such an apparently vast split between her male/father identification and her female/mother embodiment and identification. The line of speculation that I have been pursuing, far from either an absence of important relationships or an *absence* of desire, is a picture of unconscious or preconscious *thwarted* desires that constituted her young boy-girl identity of giving "no trouble" – rageful desires, bitter conflicted desires, and guilty fear of owning positive desires; a life of lauding and disappointment in Father combined with turmoil with Mother, and who knows what with her siblings (also not mentioned, as if non-existent). Marie is just beginning a long journey of analytic work to analyze her mid-life disintegration, her troubled internal relationship with her parents, probable enactments with Dr. Doe no doubt, in an effort to try to rehabilitate herself with Dr. Doe's help, in a more integrated gender fashion suited for her next phase of life.

I would like to thank the editors for generously sharing these materials, and for the opportunity to contribute to this discussion.

Notes

1 A very late in life recognition occurred in 1940 about girls' wishes for babies that predated penis envy (but, according to him, still driven by their long pre-oedipal period and "male" sex drive towards their mothers – *never* by their female identifications with their same-bodied mothers!).

2 With Stewart, Grossman had previously offered helpful ideas about the role of fantasies of social power and thus metaphors that constituted "penis envy" (Grossman and Stewart 1976).

3 Facebook, in 2015, added a tab for "custom" alongside "male" and "female," with some 50 options, including "agender," "androgyne," "pangender" and "trans person" (as well as an option for controlling who can see the customized version).

4 Before the recent election in the USA, I thought that we were beginning to "know better" nowadays than to attribute a woman's strength of intelligence, abilities to sustain power and ambition to her "penis envy," her "masculinity," and her "pretense" at being a male, because of course it may well represent femaleness in abundance. Sadly, however, as part of the political defeat of the only female *ever* to have had the courage and outstanding abilities to run for President here, Hillary Clinton, the outpouring of public vituperation and hatred (no doubt fuelled by just these very archaic fears), against her so-perceived "manly" qualities, has been staggering, because of say, crushing her male opponent in debate. Her male opponent's name-calling of these qualities to damn her successfully to an overly eager populace has been both breathtaking and profoundly depressing to experience. I must ask myself then – who are "we" who "know better"? Certainly not our fellow Americans who swept Trump to victory – although "we," whoever we are, can comfort ourselves that Hillary *did* win this election by the tally of the popular vote. But can *any* American woman manage to break through this sadly continuing cultural and archaic oppression? But we therapists still do have the power to help one Marie at a time with the common internalization of this hatred of femaleness exhibited in the culture.

5 Like Father in his decline.

6 As in Marie's final fall in her Company.

7 This analysis is giving her an opportunity now to luxuriate in more dependency and expansiveness with the reliable Dr. Doe, so that she hopefully can begin to tackle her rage at such affective foreclosures, and possibly shed light too on her intolerance of her own children's early maternal dependencies. In this regard it would be interesting to keep open the possibility that she might be quite nurturant to young work colleagues, because she clearly is *not* their mother. So her problem may not be a global inability to nurture, but one tied to her problem with thinking of herself as "mother."

8 She "became pregnant" … and "became pregnant again" … and "the third child arrived" till she had three children under the age of five. Her "wrenching feeling" as she was sneaking away to work and avoiding goodbyes may well be guilt about the anticipated pleasure in escaping her dreaded identification with Mother as the caretaking drudge.

9 This could only be detected within the intimacy of analytic work, and through her dreams or other less controlled associative materials.

10 Work with faculty at the Yale School for Organization and Management has alerted me to the strength and bonding of such competitive relationships. This seemed more the locus of Marie's "family passions" if you will, than the care of the little children whom she had given birth to.

Bibliography

Balsam, R. (2012) *Women's Bodies in Psychoanalysis*. London; New York: Routledge.

Balsam, R. (2013) (Re)membering the Female Body in Psychoanalysis: Childbirth. *Journal of the American Psychoanalytic Association* 61(3): 446–470.

Balsam, R. (2015) Oedipus Rex: Where Are We Going, Especially with Females? *Psychoanalytic Quarterly* 84: 555–588.

Balsam, R. (2017) Freud, the Birthing Body and Modern Life. *Journal of the American Psychoanalytic Association* 65(1): 61–90.

Freud, S. (1886–1899) Pre-Psycho-Analytic Publications and Unpublished Drafts, *S.E.* 1: 1–411. London: Hogarth.

Freud, S. (1900–1901) The Interpretation of Dreams (Second Part), *S.E.* 5: 339–723. London: Hogarth.

Freud, S. (1905a) Fragment of an Analysis of a Case of Hysteria, *S.E.* 7: 1–122. London: Hogarth.

Freud, S. (1905b). Three Essays on the Theory of Sexuality, *S.E.* 7: 125–245. London: Hogarth.

Freud, S. (1908) On the Sexual Theories of Children. *S.E.* 9: 205–226. London: Hogarth.

Freud, S. (1925) Some Psychical Consequences of the Anatomical Distinction between the Sexes. *S.E.* 19: 243–258. London: Hogarth.

Freud, S. (1933). Lecture 33: Femininity in New Introductory Lectures on Psycho-Analysis and Other Works. *S.E.* 22: 1–267. London: Hogarth.

Grossman, W.I., and Stewart, W.A. (1976). Penis Envy: From Childhood Wish to Developmental Metaphor. *Journal of the American Psychoanalytic Association* 24S: 193–212.

Grossman, W.I., and Kaplan, D. (1988) Three Commentaries on Gender in Freud's Thought: A Prologue on the Psychoanalytic Theory of Sexuality in *Fantasy, Myth and Reality. Essays in Honor of Jacob A. Arlow*, edited by H.P. Blum, Y. Kramer, A.K. Richards and A.D. Richards. Madison, CT: International Universities Press. p. 538.

Horney, K. (1926) The Flight from Womanhood: The Masculinity-complex in Women, as Viewed by Men and by Women. *The International Journal of Psychoanalysis*, 7: 324–339.

Loewald, H. (1989) *Papers on Psychoanalysis*. New Haven; London: Yale University Press.

Stoller, R.J. (1976). Primary Femininity. *Journal of the American Psychoanalytic Association* 24S: 59–78.

Stuart, J. (2011) Procreation, Creative Work, and Motherhood. *Psychoanalytic Inquiry* 31 (4): 417–429.

And so we have a number of dialectics held as complementary developmental imperatives: autonomy and intimacy, relationality and solitude, fortitude and receptivity, to name a few. These too can be gendered, but again, this is a facility of our own making and not to be viewed as inherent.[2] Fortitude/receptivity can be viewed through the traditional gender stereotype of a phallic/receptive dialectic, summoning the now well-worn and politically tainted masculine/feminine iconography.

Gender is one of many difference markers (Goldner, 2002) that poses a binary facilitating the organization of an early self, as the pre-oedipal child awakens to gender differences. In Goldner's (2002) words, "Gender [is] a transcendent social category whose truth, though false, remains central to thought" (p. 70). Other binaries may serve the same purpose (see, for example, Stoller, 1968, and Chodorow, 1978 for a discussion of the way gender may be used as an organizer of separation, Chodorow, 2004, 2011, for a discussion of the little girl/mother polarity, Chasse-guet-Smirgel, 1984, for a discussion of generational difference, and Laplanche, 1997, for a discussion of the child's negotiation of the primal scene). These gendered splits often form the basis of segregated or dissociated aspects of the self that need to be recuperated and reconnected, as in the post-oedipal recuperation of earlier bi-sexual self-other identifications (Bassin, 1996; Benjamin, 1998; Elise, 2002; see Celenza, 2012 for a discussion of how gendered splits can collude in the organization of cross-gendered identifications). These gendered dualities can sequester nonconscious, body-based aspects of self that may be unconsciously communicated in the "inter-mediacy" (Civitarese, 2016) of the clinical setting.

My stance is to engage this polarity (receptivity and potency), stereotypically definitional of femininity and masculinity, in order to expose this polarity as a false dichotomy, the poles of which are not actually opposite (thereby are not mutually exclusive) in any register of meaning. These reckonings and the particular individual's negotiation of each may define the ways in which gender is instantiated, experienced and expressed from within the embodied subject. They may also vary *intra*-individually as relational patterns shift and self-experience multiplies and expands. *Most importantly, I view these poles as liberated from any hierarchic power relation, in that neither pole is privileged,* though in any particular individual one may be.[3] Even in its disavowal, each pole of this duality will be relevant, along with multiple gendered and nongendered dualities revolving around this "force field" (Dimen, 1991). In this way, we could say, *the binary is not dead; it is not even binary.*

Disclaimed receptivity, dis-identifications and dysregulation

Where is Marie on this false binary of receptivity and potency? She has situated herself in the traditionally masculine role where "doing" is privileged over and against "being" and "feeling," where potency is valued over receptivity. Nowhere is it better demonstrated that a simple reversal only substitutes one set of disclaimers for another. In Marie, we see how a reversal of the traditional gender binary fails to facilitate transcendence, but instead begs several questions: Why choose among these vital capacities? What will happen to the inhibited, disclaimed urges? What are the psychical mechanisms by which Marie ends up on this path?

Marie finds comfort in achievement over embodied feeling. She describes several phenomena that indicate derivatives of early self-other identifications and defensive adaptations: an "internal dictator," self-sufficiency masking fears of dependency and an intense desire to achieve. These most certainly have their roots in Marie's nuclear familial experience. At the very least, we see in her husband, Scott, the re-incarnation of her father's disabilities and probably a guilt-laden attempt at cure. In her own commitment to support the family, we see an actualization of her identification with her mother, a kind of anti-oedipal commitment, I suspect, furiously maintained.

Early loss (and in Marie's case, the losses must include her father's difficulties at work, the humiliation of the loss of the family's business as well as his profound disability when Marie was only 12) often sets in motion a bargain struck in the unconscious: If I do X, then Y will never happen again. Or, another version: If I do X, then I will undo or make up for Y. We can speculate that Marie has struck some such unconscious bargain, promising achievement in order to undo, make up for or prevent another of her father's calamities, humiliating disappointments or even his death.

One symptom that is conspicuous to me is the report that Marie had "low self-confidence with men" when she met her husband Scott. Why might this be? In the absence of more detailed reminiscences about her relationship with her father, I will speculate about his temperament and the extent to which Marie's relationships with men may have become dominated by the patterns established early on. Perhaps her father was too fragile to bear the weight of Marie's anger toward him for his disabilities and emotional sensitivities. Perhaps her lack of self-confidence is a diffidence that masks constrained hostility, one which she sought to re-engage in her marriage to Scott. Perhaps Scott's persistence was the reassurance she needed that he could survive her aggression as her father (in her mind) had not. (After all, he had been injured.)

Then there's the mystery of Marie's mother, about whom we have little information and about whom I will speculate as well. Mothers bearing multiple children (I'd say four or more) tend to disappear in the family constellation as separate and independent force fields, becoming a responder to the needs of others and losing track of themselves as forthright beings. Marie had the misfortune of being the middle child, not just between two others, but among five – sandwiched with two on either end. Her unconscious bargain for this internally-felt "punishment," no doubt, entailed a promise never to complain or ask for anything for herself. We can only imagine what she missed in her early childhood development, but the absence of attunement and mirroring for her nascent developing self is a good bet.

It is wise to remember that there is nothing more supportive and soothing than a metabolizing other – one reason I question the distinction between psychoanalysis and psychotherapy. As Winnicott (1974) presciently stated, "[T]hink not of trauma but of *nothing happening* when something might profitably have happened" (p. 105, italics added). Here, paraphrasing from the same paper (Winnicott, 1974), it is easier for patients to remember trauma than to remember *something not happening*, an absence of soothing, especially when the needed regulating mother is physically present but her metabolizing function is absent. Green's (1997) writing of the dead mother is an exploration resultant from an absent other – the dead body that results from the absence of maternal regulating function. In Marie's case, there is the absence of two parents – the present absence of her mother (either tending to siblings or working) and the absent presence of her father (physically present but emotionally withdrawn).

Winnicott goes on to say, "[T]he patient fears the awfulness of emptiness, and in defence will organize a controlled emptiness by not eating or not learning, *or else will ruthlessly fill up by a greediness which is compulsive and which feels mad*" (Winnicott, 1974, pp. 106–7, italics added). Both of these statements have bearing on Marie's experience and resultant personality organization. Perhaps her reaction to the young, up-and-coming executive whose promotion threw her into a panic is a recrudescence of the calamitous birth of her younger sibling(s). In any event, Marie's anxieties and depression reflect a woman whose capacities to self-regulate and self-soothe are severely lacking, who searches for herself reflected in the eyes of others rather than in an embodied, felt-experience. These put one in mind of early mother–infant neglect or faulty and dysregulated bodily rhythms (see Beebe, Stern and Jaffe, 1979; Atlas, 2012; Benjamin, 2014).

An absent (or dead) mother can lead to a precocious dissociation between the body and the psyche, as between sensuality and tenderness, and a blocking of love (Green, 1997). Isolated enjoyment of the body is substituted for loving tenderness and intimate engagement between two persons. A preference for the more secure, concrete, tangible other can develop, a preference for the physical and sexual body over and against communion with *the being* of the other. As if to say, "If you can't know me, then touch me" or "I can't feel you, so touch me." Sometimes brute force or aggression-tinged physicality become necessary to more palpably conjure the other's presence. The body's sensate capacity substitutes for emotional regulation missed early in life. Here too, there can be an overinvestment in autonomous performance, thinking, and imagination as fantasy-based activities supplant dyadic, threatening emotionally-based relations.

Marie laments that "there is nothing inside." We can understand this in at least two ways, as a veridical statement reflecting a psychic deficit or as the phenomenal experience resultant from a complex defensive process. Green (1997) speaks of a *hole* left in the aftermath that may be revived in contexts of love, a sense of emptiness as a metaphor for the absence of self-soothing and self-regulating identifications. Perhaps, on the other hand, she is furious at the trauma she has endured through her mother's enslavement to her father and siblings and at her father's decline, a fury she is afraid to face and does not know exists. These disclaimed self-states can leave a hole as well.

Semrad (1980) is remembered for having noted that *there is no such thing as emptiness, there is only trauma that can't be talked about*. After all, Marie also admits to an internal dictator – she is not empty, she is overfull of something akin to dictatorial rage. Still, it is absence that likely was Marie's trauma and this is an occurrence that invokes the negative – absence, neglect and/or nonresponse over and against the more visible and palpable contours of abuse. By definition, there is a lack of figurability and shape – it is nonrepresentable. The dead or absent other is an unrepresentable figure, an unintrojectable other who, despite this, is continually sought.

In gendered terms, Marie's nuclear family presented her with patterns that represent a reversal of the traditional gender binary. (Conventionally, maternal identifications capture the receptivity to feeling while paternal identifications govern potency and achievement.) But reversal or no, we see reflected an absence of healthy concordant identifications derived from her relationships with her mother and an absence of healthy complementary identifications derived from her relationship with her father. She has introjected (taken in wholesale) her mother's ways of being (i.e. the do-er, worker, achiever – again, contrary to the traditional gender binary). Marie excludes anything she might unconsciously associate with a degraded femininity, her sexuality largely dormant, her *receptivity to feeling* numbed. Layered atop these patterns of being is a dis-identification with her father as the passive, humiliated, depressed figure of her childhood (again contrary to the traditional gender binary). All of these feed the internal dictator; all lead her to become the over-achieving persona by which she has become enslaved.

The child lives out the unlived life of the parent, another way of saying dis-identifications reflect the inevitable unconscious imprints of early attachments. Marie's devotion to work and achievement, well before her burnout, is an attempt to compensate for the soothing self-regulating functions she missed in early childhood. But these achievements, while addressing some measure of self-esteem and internal pride, rest on an unstable foundation. Her narcissistic investment in work is contained by a structure that rests on a fault-line waiting to erupt. These fractures threaten to destabilize the fundamental building blocks of her being and desire, now numbed to the emotional presence of the other. She finds herself unable to be aroused in her unconscious refusal to be receptive to internally generated and resonant affective states.

Marie's alternative pathway is to turn away from the receptive potential of her body and to define herself instead by the less threatening desire of the other – a sexualized feminine object. Scott persists, so she marries him. There's a ladder, so she climbs it. Others approach her, so she responds. It is as if Marie is in a trance for much of her early and mid-adulthood. Luckily, her body is beginning to break down and speak through its unconscious protest.

Postscript

This is a time in our cultural history when we can use our power to influence and create change. We can seize this moment as an opportunity, as exploitations come under scrutiny. We, as psychoanalysts and psychoanalytic practitioners, have the tools to understand this crisis more deeply and take leadership in accord with these understandings.

In this effort, it is important that we not lose our ability to think. We should avoid the temptation to let politics determine our differentiations. We should remain steadfast in the commitment to make fine discriminations freed from prejudice and preconception.

Notes

1 I realize articulating this binary can be misunderstood as promoting one pole over the other, in line with the ways in which Western culture traditionally organizes sexual and gendered splits. I am not supporting the traditional delegation of a host of (gendered and nongendered) relations associated with each pole to either female or male (e.g. femininity with passivity, to name the most prevalent). Risking this misunderstanding, I am proposing the articulation of this binary because it is helpful in describing clinical problems, ways in which individuals are trapped in gender polarities and splits, with the clinical aim of transcending these (see Dimen, 1991, and Benjamin, 1998, for further discussion of splitting and its interface with gender polarity).
2 Compare, for example, Schiller's (2012) labial framework of sexuality as a specifically female form of desire.
3 Compare Schiller's (2012) framework of female sexuality that she conceives as "existing alongside" the traditional phallocentric framework.

References

Atlas, G. (2012). Touch me know me: Erotic countertransferences: From boundary violations to therapeutic action. Paper presented at the Division 39 Spring Meeting, Santa Fe, NM.

Bassin, D. (1996). Beyond the he and the she: Toward the reconciliation of masculinity and femininity in the postoedipal female mind. *Journal of the American Psychoanalytic Association*, 44S, 157–190.

Beebe, B., Stern, D., and Jaffe, J. (1979). The kinesic rhythm of mother-infant interactions. In A.W. Siegman and S. Felstein (Eds.), *Of Speech and Time: Temporal Patterns in Interpersonal Contexts*. Hillsdale, NJ: Lawrence Erlbaum.

Benjamin, J. (1998). *Shadow of the Other: Intersubjectivity and Gender in Psychoanalysis*. New York, NY: Routledge.

Benjamin, J. (2014). Beyond doer and done to: An intersubjective view of thirdness. In L. Aron and A. Harris (Eds.), *Relational Psychoanalysis Volume 4: The Expansion of Theory* (Relational Perspectives Book Series) (pp. 91–130). New York: Routledge.

Celenza, A. (2012). From binarial constraints to gender multiplicity: Steve Mitchell's contributions to gender and beyond. Paper presented at the International Association for Psychoanalysis and Psychotherapy, New York.

Celenza, A. (2014). *Erotic Revelations: Clinical Applications and Perverse Scenarios*. London: Routledge.

Chasseguet-Smirgel, J. (1984). *Creativity and Perversion*. New York, NY: Norton.

Chodorow, N.J. (1978). *The Reproduction of Mothering*. Berkeley, CA: University of California Press.

Chodorow, N.J. (2004). Beyond sexual difference: Clinical individuality and same-sex cross-generation relations in the creation of feminine and masculine. In I. Matthis (Ed.), *Dialogues on Sexuality, Gender, and Psychoanalysis* (pp. 181–203). London, England: Karnac.

Chodorow, N.J. (2011). *Individualizing Gender and Sexuality: Theory and Practice*. New York, NY: Routledge.

Civitarese, G. (2016). *Truth and the Unconscious in Psychoanalysis*. London: Routledge.

Dimen, Muriel. (1991). Deconstructing difference: Gender, splitting, and transitional space. *Psychoanalytic Dialogues*, 1, 335–352.

Elise, D. (2002). The primary maternal oedipal situation and female homoerotic desire. *Psychoanalytic Inquiry*, 22, 209–228.

Goldner, V. (2002). Toward a critical relational theory of gender. In M. Dimen & V. Goldner (Eds.), *Gender in Psychoanalytic Space* (pp. 64–96). New York, NY: Other Press.

Green, A. (1997). The dead mother. In A. Green (Ed.), *On Private Madness* (pp. 142–172). London: Karnac.

Laplanche, J. (1997). The theory of seduction and the problem of the other. *International Journal of Psychoanalysis*, 78, 653–666.

Schiller, B.M. (2012). Representing female desire within a labial framework of sexuality. *Journal of the American Psychoanalytic Association*, 60, 1161–1197.

Semrad, E. (1980). *The Heart of the Therapist*. New York: Jason Aronson.

Stoller, R. (1968). *Sex and Gender*. New York, NY: Science House.

Winnicott, D.W. (1974). Fear of breakdown. *International Review of Psycho-Analysis*, 1, 103–107.

5

FRAZZLED DESIRE

Out of time

Dianne Elise

Marie's case report concludes with a question: "What had happened that might explain the [patient's] emptiness and how might we better understand the distance between herself and her elusive desire?" Immediately preceding, another question was posed: why had Marie "been able to manage with so little and with so few relationships that felt intimate and satisfying"? I surmise that the second question contains the answer to the first: Marie *had* been able, was forced to be able, to manage with relationships that were *not* intimate, those in her family of origin, most especially with her parents. As a result, an internal object world was constructed where people relate in terms of achievement, duty, and responsibility, where conflict and dissatisfaction are suppressed, and where desire goes dormant.

The sentence in the report that most catches my attention shows Marie as having little self-confidence with men, finding "the attention from someone whom she described as 'the life of the party,' a welcome surprise." We are told that Marie had worried that she would end up single. *Why?* Why does a young woman just out of her teens feel so surprised that anyone would be interested in her, especially sexually? Marie does not expect *to be desired*; that one fact alone tells us much about her relationship with her parents, and, I believe, most centrally about her early developmental experience with her mother. Parental care forms the erotic template for adult life.

Certainly we think of adolescence as a recreation and extension into adult sexuality of oedipal themes; is Marie's seemingly barren landscape of dating predated by a sense of being of little interest to her father? Quite likely. How did her father relate to Marie as a young child, as an adolescent? There appears to be no affirmation of her as a desired and desiring person specifically in relation to men. She ambivalently agrees to marry Scott, not on the basis of choosing him, but as a hedge against herself remaining the one not chosen. Her marriage derives from a position of default, not desire.

We would wonder also about the intimate life of the parental couple in Marie's family of origin: were her parents libidinally in contact with one another and each with his or her individual self? Or are we dealing with a deadened relationship in the parent's marriage? Marie may be replicating in her own quite unromantic life what she witnessed in her parents' relation to one another. Of profound significance, the impact on Marie of both oedipal life and of her view of her parents as a couple would layer upon prior developmental experience, that occurring within the pre-oedipal phase. Her experience within this early maternal matrix will be my central focus in this discussion.

Starting from earliest infancy, a child is held in the embrace of the primary caretaker, in Marie's case and most typically, her mother. A "seduction" of the infant takes place that is necessary for the development of an embodied sense of self (Freud, 1905; Laplanche, 1997), a feeling of aliveness and vitality (Winnicott, 1971) and for the emergence of desiring subjectivity. Marie appears to be almost completely devoid of these qualities, leaving us to imagine that they were lacking in the primary bond, and quite possibly in her mother as a woman. I emphasize that a mother's capacity for desire is crucial to the development of desire in her child; this connection may especially hold when that child is another female.

The encounter with the mother as erotic being brings into being a child's erotic self, both in the specifically sexual and in the most general sense: vitality in living, a curious and creative engagement with life – Eros, rather than functional adaptation. A mother relies on her eroticism in mothering her child; a child relies on the mother's eroticism in developing a vibrant sense of self (Kristeva, 2014). The mother/infant dyad relies on circulating eroticism within their pairing – a force of life, a pulsing that brings them together and sends them apart. The adult sexual couple must also be kept in view; maternal eroticism is not solely in relation to the child, for the child, but an aspect of the woman as a sexual being in fullness.

We as a species rely on our inheritance of maternal eroticism as crucial to our humanity – a generational transmission of tantalizing tenderness and fierce passions in an embodied relationship with mother, with self, and with the world (Elise, 2000, 2015a). In these developmental beginnings, the relation with the mother provides a sensuous matrix, a birthplace of meanings. Her sensual care maps each child's sexual body, giving life to erotic delights and desires. Ideally, these early erotic components then gather "steam" in the more complex, triangular oedipal configuration where various erotic strands intricately intertwine, extending into oedipal desire for the mother and for the father.

I have suggested that we think of maternal eroticism as stimulating, a stimulus – providing for both mother and child a flexible foundation, a springboard with movement, motility, momentum (Elise, 2000, 2015a). Imagine a diving board: there is give and take. It is flexible and firm, something to bounce off as well as into. We can envision an expansive exuberance – the ongoing creation of a sensually based atmosphere in which we imaginatively experience our bodily and psychic selves, our minds. This lusty experience of being in the world extends beyond the maternal orbit and beyond the purely sexual to a more general joie de vivre, a passion for life in its ups *and downs*. This encounter with maternal eroticism will reverberate throughout one's life (Kristeva, 2014). It will seed the capacity to keep desire alive in the face of obstacles and disappointments – the complex that we each struggle with as our oedipal destiny (Elise, 2015b).

In healthy development, maternal eroticism infuses a mother's relation to her child; it is within this matrix that a child experiences a sensually based relation with another where desire stirs within the rhythms of this primal interchange. Libidinal life is ignited. I emphasize that this dynamic pairing would ideally form the foundation for an experience of a couple relation that breathes – connecting in, releasing out, oscillating, but sustaining over time (Elise, 2015a). Maternal or paternal capacity in this regard forwards unique trajectories of self in multiple directions. Both adult development and that of a child rest on a parent's lively, passionate, creative investments, be those with a partner, with artistic pursuits, or in meaningful work and other projects.

This is of course an ideal picture of what we might hope is the case and often is not. Then we see patients such as Marie presenting with familiar problems of depression, meaninglessness, "burn-out" – a loss of joy, vitality, eagerness, and responsiveness. The "diving board" is now just a flat object with no spring; it can't be made use of; it seems useless to try, indicative of a deadened versus creative relation to the self and to one's objects.

Marie appears to have been profoundly disappointed – "dropped" – at an early stage. If something more alive in the maternal bond was present in infancy, it seems to have gone far underground. Marie's unique unfolding has been compromised, desire's potential collapsed. Marie is described as "frazzled," worn and thin, numb and robotic. She is completely detached from her husband and children. Her pressured work life expresses no passion. Even her affairs, "relief holidays" as respites from her pressured pace, are emotionally empty. We see a deep freeze of desire, (ice-) boxed in a life of superficial convention and driven responsibilities.

As I have been discussing, this pattern of conventional façade is most likely a repetition of her experience in her family of origin. What were any of her family members actually feeling, especially in relation to one another? Marie's parents appear to have blunted their own expression of desire. Her father seems to have been interested solely in work; her mother first gave up her profession, then later when the father was forced to retire due to a castrating disability, she returned to teaching and "took care of everything else." This history appears rife with stifled resentment and emotional withdrawal. In addition to emptiness within and between her parents, this lack of vitality likely infused the way they related to Marie, and then the way she came to relate to herself, forming the image of self that comes to be *her*.

Marie learns to mask her inner life with pseudo self-sufficiency. She strives, but she does not thrive in any deeper emotional sense (Elise, 2012). Her dependency needs go unmet, desires for nurturance denied. Her adult life paints a picture of her internal world. The picture is grim, one with very little color in a sea of gray hues. Marie's relationship to mothering her children, and to family life more generally, is drastically severed. She feels unimportant, uncared for, and "competitive with her children for her husband's attention." Here she voices what she most likely felt as a child, but is not yet able to consciously acknowledge. Marie is missing a parental presence, both in its maternal and paternal manifestations; this absence has been long-standing. Any stirring of desire is kept trapped below her surface. Buried as well is a profound resentment and fury.

After so much derailment of desire – ambition without passion, a libidinally flat expression of endless latency – when "a flood of desire she had not known existed" bursts forth in her first affair, Marie is stunned by this contact with a "sense of aliveness that had been out of reach." She flees. Significantly, desire only belatedly shows up in Marie's life in a forbidden, clandestine, "cheating" of family relation-ships – an aggressive attack on her barren existence. She immediately cordons off this experience, maintaining a strict boundary, using more pressured productivity to force out of her mind this troubling registering of self. She becomes even more depleted and requires a doctor's parental function to tell her to stop. Desperate, she finally seeks the help of a therapist.

Attacked by panic, *Marie is out of time*: Marie has been running from an anxiety deep in her being, rushing along with no time to spare; she is now running out of time. She is also *outside time*. Was she ever able to rest, to be contained, within time? Again we return to the earliest mother-infant relationship where desire is given opportunity to form within one's deepest being, the psychesoma (Winnicott, 1971). This development of self requires time and timing.

A relationship to temporality takes shape initially in relation to the maternal body (Bornholdt, 2009). The infant comes to live in time to the rhythms of the mother's embodied care, held, swaying dreamily, as if in a hammock. Desire gestates within this matrix. This maternal container is essential in our ability to live with, and in, time. Spontaneity, creative vitality, desire, each rest on an embodied relation to time: "Temporality is like an underground fountain whose water con-stantly flows throughout development and the psychoanalytical process" (p. 110). Human development is inseparable from our relation to time.

Marie has been rushing herself along her entire life. It is not surprising that the invitation from the analyst and of the treatment would have terrifying undertows into emotional life suppressed since earliest childhood. As her driven work persona fails, an underlying void in Marie's personality is revealed and she panics; she has no true internalization of a core sense of self – a sense of being real rather than a self in reaction. With so much pressure to achieve, any time to desire, for sponta-neous contact with a lively inner self, has been obliterated. Any change in this brittle existence would be intensely threatening.

What might we expect for a woman such as Marie in her treatment? She might flee; that is her history when brought into contact with her desire. She might develop a strong negative transference, full of fury and resentful withdrawal in order to ward off dependent longings and yearning for contact, especially in rela-tion to the maternal transference figure. Alternatively, she might accept the "seduction" of the treatment setting and dive deep into Eros in a manner that would likely be de-stabilizing for Marie and possibly quite challenging for her analyst as well. She might open to a sense of self previously unfound, not even looked for, where genuine experiencing might unfold.

Psychoanalytic treatment places Marie in the space and time of the analyst's mind, represented by the frame and the space it contains. The therapeutic setting would hopefully establish, possibly for the first time, a potential space for contact with a self that can desire – the true self (Winnicott, 1971): "In a tantalizing way many individuals have experienced just enough of creative living to recognize that most of their lives they are living uncreatively" (p. 65). Winnicott emphasizes that this variable is directly related to the quality of experiencing in the early relation with the mother: "one must study the fate of the potential space between any one baby and the mother-figure" (p. 100). "It can be looked on as sacred to the individual that it is here that the individual experiences creative living" (p. 103). False self efforts have been running Marie ragged in compliance to some internal dictate to succeed in business and never stop for a moment to look back or within. But can she let go, feel held and access a potential space for a spontaneous gesture to arise? We can expect patients such as Marie to be terrified of this invitation, fearing it to portend catastrophic change (Bion, 1970). Having little prior experience of being held, safely contained, Marie may feel she is falling off a cliff.

Yet, we see with her first affair, a spark bursts forth into flame; something is under her frozen surface, however frightening. Treatment as well, especially one of analytic depth, may bring to the fore desires that have remained unexplored, even unrecognized – revealing an erotic path not taken, with associated feelings of de-vitalization having undermined a capacity to actualize desire in a deeply felt manner. Marie both *craves* her female analyst's attention and fears immersion in this maternal sea of desire. This realm of opened erotic space is fraught with potential torments that are disturbing to many in one manner or another. Yet, along with the terrors and conflicts are the potential benefits of being able to access, rather than repress, erotic life at multiple levels of development. In the experience of erotic aliveness, including and especially in relation to the analyst, a patient has the opportunity to get to know a passionate part of the self, as well as all the conflicts that may accompany (Elise, 2002, 2015b). A patient such as Marie may have the sense of discovering herself, contacting a valuable and surprising aspect of her being, her desire.

Psychoanalytic treatment can provide for both participants a potent(ial) space for creative elaboration of desire. As clinicians, we hope to help each patient access and elaborate their own unique expression of desire. Clinical engagement with patients' passions is challenging. We must appreciate that, in engaging desire, we are entering dangerous waters of longing and loss. Such a transformative journey is central to the development of the mind, the personality, and one's erotic life. Milner (1969) describes a force within people "to do with growth, growth towards their own shape" (p. 384) that breaks down false inner organizations – "something which can also be deeply feared, as a kind of creative fury that will not let them rest content with a merely compliant adaptation; and also feared because of the temporary chaos it must cause" (pp. 384–5). For Marie to travel such a path may wreak havoc in her marriage, her family, her sense of self. She will wonder whether such a journey is worth the risks. She will have to decide if she is willing to find out for herself.

References

Bion, W. (1970). *Attention and interpretation: A scientific approach to insight in psychoanalysis and groups*. London, UK: Tavistock.

Bornholdt, I. (2009). The impact of the time experience on the psychoanalysis of children and adolescents. In L. Glocer Fiorini and J. Canestri (Eds.) *The experience of time: Psychoanalytic perspectives*. London: Karnac, pp. 97–116.

Elise, D. (2000). Woman and desire: Why women may not want to want. *Studies in Gender and Sexuality*, 1: 125–145.

Elise, D. (2002). Blocked creativity and inhibited erotic transference. *Studies in Gender and Sexuality*, 3: 161–195.

Elise, D. (2012). Failure to thrive: Shame, inhibition, and masochistic submission in women. In D. Holtzman and N. Kulish (Eds.), *The clinical problem of masochism*. New York: Jason Aronson, pp. 161–185.

Elise, D. (2015a) Eroticism in the maternal matrix: Infusion through development and the clinical situation. *Fort da*, 21(2): 17–32.

Elise, D. (2015b). Reclaiming lost loves: Transcending unrequited desires. Discussion of Davies' "Oedipal Complexity". *Psychoanalytic Dialogues*, 25: 284–294.

Freud, S. (1905). Three essays on the theory of sexuality. *S.E.*, 7: 130–243. London: Hogarth Press, 1953.

Kristeva, J. (2014). Reliance, or maternal eroticism. *Journal of the American Psychoanalytic Association*, 62: 69–85.

Laplanche, J. (1997). The theory of seduction and the problem of the other. *International Journal of Psychoanalysis*, 78: 653–666.

Milner, M. (1969). *The hands of the living God: An account of a psycho-analytic treatment*. New York: Routledge.

Winnicott, D.W. (1971). *Playing and reality*. London: Tavistock.

PART II

Ambition

6

FEMALE AMBITION

Psychoanalytic perspectives

Frances Arnold

> Ambition is the loving, passionate pursuit of what you most fervently want to become, with perseverance and focus, despite the odds.
>
> *Dorothy Holmes (2015)*

Introduction

Personal meanings of ambition vary enormously, perhaps more so for women now than in any previous generation, particularly given that many experience more possibility and choice than previously imaginable. At the same time many barriers remain, both personal and sociocultural, that make up "the odds." Possibility is inaccessible to some American women and to many women around the globe – a reality our profession cannot afford to disown. While the choice to "lean in" may be out of reach for some working women, "leaning out," or worse, being "left out," offers no advantage. This chapter will explore what makes ambition a successful and passionate pursuit, and also its barriers, drawing from a psychoanalytic lens that views the psyche, culture, politics and body as interrelated.

These are interesting times to consider the topic of female ambition. Hillary Rodham Clinton won the popular vote, but lost the 2016 election, narrowly missing the opportunity to become America's first female president. As we worked on this book, our country was rife with division and reeling from efforts to make sense of our political landscape. For those who supported HRC, particularly the women and girls invested not only in her qualifications and political positions but also the possibility of a female president, the election upset was followed by mourning for "what might have been" (Kattlove, 2017). Many had thought, at last, a woman would break the ultimate glass ceiling, and yet, this remains out of reach. Opinions differ about the role of gender, character and strategy in the 2016 election outcome. However, the vitriol that marked the political race reminds us that fear and dread often accompany an ambitious, female challenge of social power structures. We believe that our topic of women and ambition cannot easily be de-linked from its larger generational and historic context, what has been referred to as "the social third," and with the narrow miss of a first female U.S. President, this argument seems more prescient than ever.

What makes the pursuit of one's dreams and ambitions possible and rewarding? How does one discover and follow what one wants to become, despite the barriers? A few years ago, I attended an art exhibition of Henri Matisse's "Cut Outs," which Matisse created in his 80s, during a time of hardship as he was suffering from blindness, decreased mobility, and a series of losses – all occurring during the Nazi occupation of his homeland, France. Amidst his bold and vibrant images, Matisse's artistic spirit strikes the viewer as indomitable. His irrepressible drive to create against all odds raises the question of "why some people are able to develop and sustain passionate pursuits, despite all odds, while others are not?" Some develop interests easily and with pleasure, while others become disengaged, suffering work inhibition, or an inability to seek, imagine or try out possibility. For those who are able to pursue creative interests, there is typically a strong correlation with psychological wellbeing, resiliency and engagement with the larger world, even during challenging times.

Drawing from our psychoanalytic work with female clients, we will explore how ambition develops and what creates the freedom to pursue it. We will consider what is essential for healthy female ambition and how we might understand its derailment or more pathological forms. Among women who are vulnerable to inhibition, some experience difficulties launching into adulthood, becoming stuck in their 20s or 30s, sometimes developing chronic dissatisfaction and often depression. Other women have difficulty re-launching after loss, rejection, or narcissistic injury, even if previously able to actualize goals. Such difficulties may be marked by a primary inability to define or sustain passionate interests, or a secondary disengagement from ambitions initially followed. Their psychological experience may include the following: lack of an internal subjectivity regarding interests and aspirations; difficulty accessing imagination and personal agency; conflicts or inexperience with self-authorization or initiative; toxic experiences of envy and competition; inability to make creative, flexible and adaptive use of identifications; or avoidance of risk and new experience. Family and social systems are implicit and deeply influential factors, which can promote and/or inhibit the growth and actualization of ambition, and often define the terms under which ambitious pursuit may be thought about and imaginatively constructed.

Central to our topic is the question of whether contemporary psychoanalytic theory adequately addresses female ambition. Psychoanalysis has a long history of looking at deficit rather than determinants of success. Indeed, female ambition has long been associated with the extremes of either deficit, or excessive power and potential destructiveness, Hillary Clinton's presidential run being a powerful example of both. Her favorability polls dropped every time she announced her ambition to run for government positions, only to rise again when she assumed the role for which she had been striving. This fluctuation happened during her senate race, her nomination for Secretary of State, and, again, during the democratic presidential nomination – and we will never know her potential popularity had she been elected president.

Once a woman is in the role of power, she is more easily valued. But, when challenging social power structures, women risk being viewed as either threatening or deficient. Hillary worried, painfully, about her presentation, her appearance, and her expressiveness, and attempted to rewrite her performance into something she imagined constituents wanted. In contrast, her opponent threw likability to winds and gave free rein to the unrestrained and unfiltered, as well as the offensive and the outrageous, which unbelievably led to his win.

An obvious consideration is that "women" are not a monolithic identity group, a factor often unaddressed in psychoanalytic theorizing. Early psychoanalytic ideas about women were full of implicit bias and written largely from the perspective of white male experience, assuming a white audience, and/or an audience of color presumed color blind. Social nuance often remains unaddressed in psychoanalytic literature. Relevant to our topic is evidence that black women may be "more ambitious" than white women, yet struggle with disturbing invisibility around significant leadership positions (Marshall and Wingfield, 2016). Along these lines, we might consider the impact of Hillary Clinton as an elite, white female candidate. Did her whiteness make a difference in an election heavily impacted by racial and class identity? Clearly, the perception of her as a disconnected elitist had an enormous impact. Did a white woman with an elitist education and social positioning create more anxiety than an elitist white man (a scenario we take for granted)?

In this chapter, we will explore the history of psychoanalytic ideas about female ambition, and focus on contributions by several women analysts whose writing illuminates the unfolding, psychoanalytic narrative of "women and what they want." While prescient and rich with ideas, these works reflect their historical times and are blind to many social and identity complexities. To bring our topic to life from a postmodern perspective, our introduction will be followed by a clinical case example and discussions of this example by three contemporary women analysts: Dorothy Holmes, Dionne Powell and Nancy Kulish.

Our mission in writing this book is both intellectually driven and deeply personal. Both Stephanie and I were raised by ambitious and successful mothers – forces of nature who were, in many ways, ahead of their times. My own mother never completed her college degree, although she was talented in math and political science. She married at the end of World War II, accepting my father's proposal on the eve of Hiroshima and leaving college to follow my father's legal career, partly wooed by the political milieu of his family. A divorce and re-marriage later, my mother found herself the sole provider in challenging circumstances. With a natural, if not educated, talent for business, she was successful and passionate about her profession and became more than able to energetically nurture and provide for three children, although not without conflict and difficulty, leaving us with the enigmatic task of unraveling "who was this force field mother?"

Looking back, it is not surprising that I would complete a graduate degree and become a psychoanalyst. Initially, I assumed this was a natural legacy from my intellectual father, but now assign equal importance to my mother's ambition, unfinished business, and unshakable faith in her daughters' competence. She would not have chosen my particular career for herself – we were very different in terms of talent and sensibility – yet she was wistful about her educational ambitions cut short by the more conventional marriage plot. A woman of her times, the binary splits she experienced were complex and intensely felt. On the one hand, she was deeply gratified by her pursuits, and on the other, she was burdened by the stereotypic (and ungratified) assumption that she would be more at peace if provided for by a male partner, reflecting the social and psychological construction of her 1950s white, privileged, predominantly heterosexual, middle class suburban life. Holding the paradox of her internal desires and ambitions was not easy for her, nor for those who wished to understand her. For my curious and energetic mother, ambition was empowering. Yet as a woman of her post-World War II generation, she struggled with a nagging sense she was missing something more conventional and valued, her often disowned wish for provision and caretaking. My mother, who had many chapters to her paradoxical life, was in later years "provided for" by a partner, only to feel that this offer, given by a loving man, created a chapter in which she deeply missed many of her relinquished pursuits. In many ways, the divide between our generations (those who came of age during World War II versus the Vietnam War) is profound and representative of the change that has unfolded in psychoanalytic theory about gender, and women in particular.

Psychoanalytic ideas about women and ambition: early history and social activism

Psychoanalytic theory has always had an ambivalent history regarding women and ambition since its inception with Freud. The birth of psychoanalysis occurred following the European and American women's suffrage movement of the late 1800s and early 1900s, and during a time of enormous social upheaval and activism in the United States, Europe and other parts of the world, spanning both world wars. Essential to the women's movement was the insistence that women have a voice, a vote, an impact on social and political process, and later, control of their basic personal and bodily rights. Female ambition and activism were at the forefront of both early feminism, and the second and third waves of the women's movement – and influenced parallel changes in psychoanalytic ideas about "women and what they want."

In early twentieth century Europe, psychoanalysis was a field that, in practice, included and promoted women, while in reality it embraced a theoretical canon that was phallocentric and binary, relegating female experience to a lesser version of everything "masculine." In an alluring, but contradictory fashion, classical psychoanalysis offered the promise to help women actively "become what they most fervently wished to be," yet theoretically was diminishing and limiting of women's capacities and opportunities, casting women as lacking or passive. Moreover, as in many professions, psychoanalysis was sometimes guilty of "ghosting" or appropriating the contributions of its most gifted, female contributors.

Much of classical psychoanalytic theory pathologized female assertion and agency as defensive and compensatory. From this analytic perspective, a woman's ambitious "wanting" was rooted in envy. Wanting what she could not have, a woman's pursuit of competence and mastery was based on insecurity, absence and compensating for what she lacks. The theory implied that unless a woman's resolution was to relinquish her ambitions by choosing passivity, with agency channeled toward reproduction, she faced the dissolution of her competitive strivings into neurosis and thwarted ambition. In this early model, penis envy was the theoretical construct constituting female, motivational bedrock, suggesting that female ambition and frustrations are propelled by an envy that must be domesticated. If a woman was able to actualize her ambitions, she was viewed as "masculine," or as having "masculine strivings." If she was blocked, and troubled by an inability to achieve goals or actualize her ambitions, she was likely masochistic. Either way, she was in an unenviable bind and her actual, subjective experience was unacceptable.

Despite its paradoxes and limitations, however, classical psychoanalytic theory played a critical role in new understandings of gender, and women in particular. For example, in *Three Essays on the Theory of Sexuality*, Freud (1905) presented groundbreaking ideas about gender and identity, opening up radical possibility for male and female development. Using the construct of bisexuality, Freud argued that men and women might have both masculine and feminine identifications, at least in early development. Undeniably prescient, Freud's suggestion has taken more than a century for psychoanalytic theory to deconstruct and redefine. Only recently have the meanings of gender identifications been understood in non-binary terms and rooted in the individuality of psychological experience. As a result of these postmodern efforts, feminine and masculine identifications are no longer linked to the binaries of passivity or activity. There has been a de-linking of gender with the experience of agency, activity or ambition, as well as a general de-linking of sexuality with gender identifications. These shifts have been transformative, with implications for how we think about female ambition in particular, and gender at large.

Classical psychoanalytic theory about women and "what they want" was known for its illumination of the psychological experience of the body, even if its conclusions were confounded. Indeed, the view of female sexuality and desire as being about "absence" has been recognized as capturing legitimate features of some female experience. Rather than discussing "lacking" or "absence," however, we are now more likely to talk about what is unconsciously, or consciously, "hidden" about a woman's sexuality and passionate wishes. The body and embodied experience remain important subjects for postmodern gender theorists, despite the trend toward a relational or attachment focus. Presently, the postmodern tension between the centrality of the physical body and the transcendence of body (including the de-linking of gender from the body as bedrock) is a subject of important debate, as is the recent plea for more focus on sexuality and embodied experience.

Joan Riviere, Karen Horney and Sabina Spielrein: Early voices and the search for recognition, authorship and authority

Overview

Female voice, recognition and authorship are closely connected to the successful pursuit of a woman's ambitions. By the 1920s, female analysts had become important contributors to theories about women's development, calling for recognition of a female subjectivity, particularly regarding "what women want." We will highlight the work of three voices from this classical period of psycho-analysis – Joan Riviere, a British psychoanalyst, Karen Horney, an American psychoanalyst, and Sabina Spielrein, a Russian psychoanalyst. Each is surprisingly modern in her thinking, and for each, their contributions were marginalized by complex enactments within our field. These pioneers have been re-discovered by contemporary writers who have illuminated their visionary understanding of female ambition from an inside/out perspective that captures the subjectivity of female experience. Riviere, Horney and Spielrein are important not only for their ideas, but for the story their lives tell of our profession and of the trajectory of female ambition itself. Our history of transgressions is a painful psychoanalytic legacy, influencing what is recognized versus dissociated from our psychoanalytic gaze. The narratives of female analysts such as Riviere and Spielrein are important reminders of the impact of our transgressions and of our inter-generational, pro-fessional trauma.

Joan Riviere

In 1929, Joan Riviere, a training analyst and founding member of the British Psy-choanalytic Institute, also an activist in early suffragist and divorce reform movements, wrote a watershed paper, "Womanliness as a Masquerade." Riviere describes a certain type of ambitious woman who wishes to be like a man, but experiences anxiety and conflict about intellectual performance, particularly its public exhibition. Defensively, Riviere's woman conceals the dread which follows her ambitious performance by flirtatiously seeking male sexual reassurance that she is, indeed, "womanly," and therefore, not a challenge to male authority (Riviere, 1929).

Riviere takes up a number of themes that are startlingly modern. Exploring the issue of identifications, she suggests that the ambitious woman is not only male or father identified, but also strikingly feminine. However, such a woman uses her "womanliness" as "a masquerade" to conceal anxiety about the excitement and power that follows an exhibition of competence and authority. Riviere touches on complex issues about the construction of competition and power in relationships between women, as well as between an ambitious woman and her male audience. Riviere's striving woman is highly rivalrous with other women, and driven to establish herself as superior in all domains, including the domestic. After laying out a series of compelling, subjective conflicts, Riviere emphasizes that such an ambitious woman turns to a father figure in order to avoid competition and maternal aggression, in a sense capitulating to prevailing psychoanalytic ideas of her time and seeming to enact her own theory (Harris, 1997).

Particularly prescient is Riviere's use of "performance" as a psychological construct that explains how gender is portrayed or communicated and how the experience of ambition, competence and power are managed with regard to the intersection of private experience, and public or social contexts (Harris, 1997; Butler, 1995). Riviere's ambitious and successful 1920s woman must creatively, and simultaneously, own and disavow her experience of competence and power, including its accompanying excitement and pleasure. She does so through a "masquerade," which at once reveals and conceals her ambition and success. Riviere's creativity can be appreciated in light of her context of the 1920s worlds of psychoanalysis and British society. Some have speculated that Riviere's paper on womanliness is autobiographical, suggesting she is describing a "masquerade," useful to her and perhaps inhibiting her from embracing what she "most fervently wanted to become."

Riviere's first, formal contact with psychoanalysis began when she undertook her own, personal analysis with Ernest Jones, following a depression that was linked to the death of her father in her early 30s. Records indicate that her treatment was marked by a tenacious erotic transference as well as by what would be considered boundary transgressions by Jones – allegedly, he allowed her to stay in his country home, care for his dog and converse with him about his marriage. Reaching an impasse, Jones referred Riviere to Freud, with whom she completed a second analysis. Despite her inhibitions and self-concealments, and her troubled first analysis, Riviere went on to become a substantial contributor in the British Psychoanalytic Society. Her personal experience illustrates not only the compromises of female ambition within the history of psychoanalysis, but also transgressions ongoing within contemporary psychoanalytic institutes. Sexual transgressions are typically understood as arising from the inability to contain and analyze erotic countertransference. We might consider whether an analyst's sexualization also reflects concealed aggression, or non-recognition, toward female competency and striving – a sexualization of power and ambition, and also of the female patient's inherent conflicts about such experiences. Riviere was deeply interested in psychoanalysis and was in treatment with Jones at a time when her aspirations to learn and develop her own ideas were likely in full force.

It has taken psychoanalysis nearly a century to re-discover and re-interpret Riviere's work, a feat accomplished primarily by women psychoanalysts. Postmodern gender theorists have embraced a number of Riviere's central ideas, particularly her ideas about female ambition and her understanding of gender as an individualized psychological "performance," not necessarily linked to body. Riviere's story is also interesting to consider in light of the #ME TOO movement which has spotlighted exploitative sexualization of female ambition and forced us to reckon with the ways larger social constructions undermine female power and assertion.

Karen Horney

Karen Horney is an American, and formerly German psychoanalyst, whose seminal paper, "Flight from Womanhood: The Masculinity Complex in Women, as Viewed by Men and Women," was published in 1926, just prior to Riviere's, "Womanliness as Masquerade" (and six years after women won the right to vote in the United States). Horney had been one of the founders of the Berlin Psycho-analytic Institute, leaving Germany as Nazis were coming to power and her relationship with Freud had cooled following a series of debates about female development. In her seminal paper, Horney directly challenges Freud's thinking about female development. Using the work of the German sociologist, George Simmel, she debunks many of Freud's basic assumptions about women that were based on a male developmental model. Horney is breathtaking in her risks, and simultaneously gracious, allowing for Freud's male perspective as understandable while masterfully deconstructing the logic of his position. Horney argues that the sociocultural re-contextualization of psychoanalytic ideas about female experience is essential in order to create a psychological theory of women based on a female model of development and representative of female subjective experience. Taking classical theory to task for failing to grasp the importance of this lens, Horney suc-ceeds in deconstructing Freud's phallocentrism, and in creating a female "presence" rather than absence in psychoanalytic theory about gender and development.

Horney notes that, from the classical and phallocentric perspective, women become the "deposit for all the desires and disappointments of men" and have "adapted themselves to the wishes of men," leaving them feeling this "adaptation (is) their true nature" (Horney, 1926, p. 326). Horney underscores the inherent contempt in the perspective that inadequate achievements are viewed as "femi-nine," while distinguished achievements by women are often called "masculine." Horney introduces the idea that the girl takes flight from womanhood through identification with her father and because of her anxiety and guilt about sexuality and oedipal relations, rather than penis envy. She views the motives for this flight as reinforced by actual social subordination of women, which leaves women with fewer outlets for achievement and fewer reasons to identify with their mothers.

Horney's critiques of Freudian theory led to her resignation from the New York Psychoanalytic Institute, in 1941. The intensity of the schism, between Horney and her New York colleagues, is captured by Susan Quinn in her biography, *A Mind of Her Own: The Life of Karen Horney:*

> On March 13, 1940, a New York psychoanalyst named Fritz Wittels wrote a long, angry letter to fellow members of the New York Psychoanalytic Society. "Freud's psychoanalysis achieves remarkable success in America," Wittels began. Nevertheless, the New York Society, the first and most influential in America, was threatened with "pending disintegration" because of the dis-ruptive influence of one of its members, a fifty-four-year-old German born analyst named Karen Horney. Not only had Karen Horney "with one

sweeping gesture refuted most of the fundamentals of psychoanalysis" but she had done it "in a book written in a demagogic style and avidly read by social workers, politically minded laymen and by the critics of the New York Times," with the result that "forty years of patient scientific work were thrown to the dogs." The issue, as Wittels saw it, came down to "Freud or not Freud." Either Dr. Horney should return to "Freud's principles" or she should give her doctrine a new name and teach it somewhere else, with "an educational staff of her own." Wittels' letter was the opening salvo in a battle that was to rage within the New York Society for a year, culminating, in the spring of 1941, in a report from the society's education committee. The "published writings and contentions of Dr. Karen Horney," the committee declared, were resulting in "preliminary indoctrination with theoretical and emotional orientations which are contrary to the fundamental principles of psychoanalytic education." The committee therefore recommended that Horney be removed from her training and supervisory role. For Karen Horney, a founding member of the Berlin Psychoanalytic Institute, who had been teaching psychoanalysis longer than anyone else in the New York group at the time, there could be only one response to such an affront. On April 29, 1941, after the membership had voted to demote her, she got up and walked out of the New York Psychoanalytic Society, never to return.

(Quinn, 1988, pp. 56–57)

Not easily deterred, this same year, Horney co-founded and co-edited the *American Journal of Psychoanalysis*. She also established the Association for the Advancement of Psychoanalysis, whose focus was the role of culture in shaping personality. Horney remains a central figure in American psychoanalysis – more recognized than either Riviere or Sabina Spielrein, and credited as the foremother of a psychology of women. The challenges raised by our first women analysts, such as Horney, are an important part of why psychoanalysis widened its gaze to consider the influences of sociocultural power structures. That said, it took psychoanalysis decades to fully appreciate the influences of social theory which have expanded and transformed ideas about "women and what they want."

Sabina Spielrein

Born in 1885, Spielrein was a Russian psychoanalyst who was only marginally known, mostly for her reputation as the institutionalized young woman who had an affair with Carl Jung, her psychoanalyst while she received treatment at the Burgholzli Psychiatric Clinic in Zurich. Many know this story from its dramatization in the 2014 film, *A Dangerous Method*, but few know her intellectual contribution to psychoanalysis. Spielrein's professional history and substantial contributions were recently unearthed and brought to life by Coline Covington (2003) in her book *Forgotten Pioneer of Psychoanalysis* and by Adrienne Harris (2015) in her paper, "Language is There to Bewilder." As Harris reminds us, Spielrein pursued medical training and became a psychoanalyst despite her history of a psychiatric hospitalization, her complex love relationship with Carl Jung, and the backdrop of the World War II. Tragically, Spielrein and her two daughters were murdered during the Nazi invasion of Rostov, Russia. Spielrein wrote on subjects ranging from human sexuality and destructiveness, to child development and cognitive psychology, and is thought to have had a significant impact on major psychological theorists, including Freud, Jung, Piaget, whom she analyzed, and Vytgotsky.

Spielrein's 1911 (Spielrein, 1995) paper on "Destruction As the Cause of Coming into Being," was presented in Vienna, shortly after she left Zurich (and Jung), and is referenced by Freud (1920) in *Beyond the Pleasure Principle*. Indeed, Freud credits her with helping him with his own ideas about the death drive. Spielrein's paper is uncanny in its articulation of a woman's fear and ambivalence about reproduction or creation. Early in the paper, she writes, quoting Jung:

> Passionate longing, e.e., the libido, has two aspects: It is the power that beautifies everything, and in certain cases, destroys everything. Often one cannot recognize the source of this creative power's destructive quality. A woman who, in today's society abandons herself to passion soon leads herself to ruin. One need only contemplate the current bourgeois state of affairs to understand how a feeling of unbounded insecurity occurs in those who unconditionally surrender to Fate. To be fruitful provokes one's downfall; at the rise of the next generation, the previous one has exceeded its peak. Our descendants become our most dangerous enemies for whom we are unprepared. They will survive and take power from our enfeebled hands. Anxiety in the presence of erotic Fate is completely comprehensible, for there is something immeasurable within it. Fate usually contains hidden dangers. The wish not to wrestle in the dangerous struggle of life explains the continual hesitation of neurotics to take risks. Whoever relinquishes experiencing a risky undertaking must stifle an erotic wish, committing a form of self-murder. This explains the death fantasies that often accompany the renunciation of the erotic wish.
>
> *(Spielrein, 1995, pp. 154–155)*

Spielrein proceeds to elaborate her own thoughts about passionate dilemmas. She writes about sexuality as a union that brings both the joyful feeling of "coming into being" alongside a sense of disgust and ambivalence, or even of death, just at the point of sexual union (Spielrein, 1995). Ambition seems to have been on Spielrein's mind, as much as her passionate attachment to Jung – during the time of their involvement. Not only did she regain her psychological health, but she completed medical school and wrote papers about psychoanalysis. According to some accounts, Spielrein worried that her preoccupation with Jung might interfere with her ambitions for a serious career.

Spielrein pursued her passionate and ambitious intellectual interest in psychoanalysis, against extraordinary odds, yet her voice was "ghosted," and only recently re-discovered. Harris's mission has been to bring Spielrein back from invisibility and to re-establish her authorship, as well as her recognition as a contributor to psychoanalytic discourse (Harris, 2015). Likely, there are numerous reasons why Spielrein was "disappeared" over the years, including her relationship with Jung, their triangle with Freud, and the devastating impact of World War II, cutting short her life. That said, Spielrein's story is representative of the kind of appropriation that can happen to female authorship. As with Riviere's story, this history raises the question of whether boundary transgressions often reveal hostility and misogyny – perhaps, as Spielrein might contend, a destructiveness present in all of us, and most apparent at the point of ambition or creation. Harris's effort to bring to life and re-authorize Spielrein's work is a postmodern feat of revisionism that corrects the lines of intellectual creativity and authority, of a highly ambitious woman (Harris, 2015).

Modern and postmodern psychoanalytic ideas about women and ambition

The movement within psychoanalysis from a classical to a more modern perspective of gender theory parallels the second wave of American feminism. This movement, spanning the 1960s to 1980s, was centered on cultural and political gender inequities, including the psychological ramifications of political and societal power structures. American women were fighting for control of their bodies, for reproductive rights, and for equal access to education and work. American psychoanalysis was deeply affected by this period of social change, entering what is considered a more "modern" theoretical period. Within gender theory, specifically, this was known as an "essentialist" period, characterized by efforts to explore what was unique, different and essential about female versus male development and experience. Women were theorized to be more intrinsically "relational," remaining attached to their mothers into adulthood, whereas men were considered more intrinsically focused on independence, paying the price of disowned vulnerability around their more traumatic separation from maternal caregivers.

Marcia Angell (2014), the first woman editor and chief of the *New England Journal of Medicine*, offers an account of the social changes during the 1960s, which had life altering impact on women, their passions and their ambitions. Angell reviews the 1960s social revolution and the introduction of the birth control pill, arguing that with the advent of The Pill, sex was suddenly untethered from pregnancy. Women could now freely have multiple partners. She notes that the median age of women's first marriages went from 21 in 1960, to 27 in 2011. Women had more time for education before having children. By the 1980s, more women were able to enter the work force, supporting themselves and their children, if they wished or needed to do so. Marriage itself became uncoupled from sexuality and progeny. Female ambition took off in new directions. Angell notes that, unlike earlier generations, a woman's security and status were no longer necessarily tied to marriage, and her source of power was not limited to the granting or withholding of sexuality. This social revolution was a critical backdrop to modern shifts in psychoanalytic ideas about women, including the psychology of female ambition. The change in opportunities for women was groundbreaking: women were no longer dependent on marriage for financial security, nor (therefore) emotional security. Women were no longer limited to attachment to male privilege in order to secure stability for themselves and their children. Looking back at psychoanalytic literature from the 1960s, it is striking that more attention was not directed toward the liberating impact of these unfolding, historical shifts.

Dawn Skorczewski (2012), a psychoanalytic scholar and a Professor of English, has written about the psychoanalytically oriented treatment of the poet, Anne Sexton, during the late 1950s and early 1960s. Skorczewski's (2012) "biography of a psychotherapy" offers a rare glimpse into the life of gifted writer, with serious psychological issues, who was revolutionary in breaking artistic boundaries, at the historical cusp of social change and emerging feminism of the 1960s. Sexton's story is heartbreaking and illustrates the ways psychiatry, and a psychodynamic psychotherapy, let her down (including physical boundary violations and culminating in her suicide). It also documents Sexton's profound artistic ambition and creativity, as she became a prolific, female poet. It is a story both of a deeply troubled woman and one who was, in many ways, ahead of her peers, and ahead of psychiatry and psychoanalysis at the time.

During the 1970s and 1980s, as more women began to enter the fields of psychology and psychoanalysis and to contribute to the new field of gender studies, analytic writing shifted to include a female vantage point. This was a watershed change for psychoanalytic theory and for the culture at large. Female psychological experience was no longer objectified and studied from the outside/in, through a male psychoanalyst's gaze. Instead, women's experience was given an internal voice and subjectivity. Female sexuality and femininity were finally recast as primary and active, capable of agency and intentionality. Female development was no longer about penis envy and masochism, as these concepts became irrelevant to the "inherently feminine." These shifts heralded a sea change regarding how female striving and ambition are experienced and understood.

The postmodern period of psychoanalytic thinking, beginning in the 1980s roughly coincided with third wave American feminism and leads to the current time. Postmodern gender theory is centered on the deconstruction of the binary of masculinity and femininity, understanding them as dialectical categories that are constructed by political, social and individual experience. Given the current increase in women's participation in every aspect of American society, mirrored by changes in psychoanalytic thinking about gender, as well as new conceptualizations of our familial and social lives, we might wonder if we have now entered a new wave feminist movement – one that is further redefining American psychoanalytic thinking about gender and "what women want." Such a shift might share reciprocal influence with broad sociopolitical and cultural changes, the near election of a female president being one example and the #ME TOO movement being another.

Engaging the body, identity and multiplicity: New modernists and postmodernists – Chodorow, Balsam and Harris

Overview

In this section, we will consider the work of several modern and postmodern analysts who have addressed female ambition from important vantage points. With her background in sociology and psychoanalysis, Nancy Chodorow brings a double lens to her consideration of the determinants and barriers to female ambition, holding the tension between individual and social influences. More recently, Chodorow has moved to the position that the primary use of psychoanalysis is its capacity to elaborate and understand the individualized meanings of either internal or social influences.

From another perspective, Rosemary Balsam explores the centrality of female embodied experience, re-working psychoanalytic theories about female development with an eye for what has been "vanished" and how rediscoveries and new recognitions might change not only our theories, but our experience with our patients. Balsam's exploration of the psychoanalytic "masculinizing" and "disappearing" of the female body sets the record straight and calls for rethinking the association between the female body and the capacity for agency and power. Her work suggests that the necessary and vital precursors to the capacity of ambitious pursuit include a woman's sense of agency – beginning with embodied experience, followed by recognition from self and others, including the analyst and the psychoanalytic "field." Implicit in her work is the idea that psychoanalysis needs to be aware of its own disavowal of female embodied experience.

We will also consider contributions by Adrienne Harris who explores the complexities of envy and identification between women, including mothers and daughters, sisters and peers, and across generations. We will conclude with consideration of postmodern psychoanalysis and its impact on how we think about gender and sexuality and the binaries and dualities that have marked earlier thinking.

Nancy Chodorow

Nancy Chodorow defies simple categorization as her writing spans several decades of psychoanalytic theorizing. Chodorow (1979) has discussed the role of "the social," including its impact on over-arching female ambitions, such as the "reproduction of mothering." Reflecting back on her writing (Chodorow, 2000, 2004), and re-thinking the tilts of her ideas, she has called for a less "social" and more intra-psychic perspective, mirroring her own movement from a more sociological to a psychoanalytic lens. While her early work reveals her as a modern essentialist, addressing the unique differences between female and male development, over the course of her career she has placed increasing emphasis on the psychoanalytic individualizing of meaning-making (Chodorow, 1979, 2012). She draws from intrapsychic and object relations perspectives, weaving back and forth from the intrapsychic to the social, but more often privileging the former.

Chodorow's (2002) chapter, "Glass ceilings, sticky floors, and concrete walls: internal and external barriers to women's work and achievement," speaks directly to women and ambition. In it, she considers the barriers to female strivings and work promotions, suggesting that as psychoanalysts we "can really only contribute to an understanding of the ways that glass ceilings are still – though in more complex ways than 'fear of success' – also internal" (p. 18). She notes that psychoanalysis can help to explain some of the external, often unnoticed or indirect, assumptions and practices that make up the external barriers. However, she makes an important case for how the internalization of the external sociocultural "third" may differ greatly for each individual, arguing for the psychoanalytic "individualizing" of issues that relate to ambition and success, and their inhibitions. Chodorow's contributions hold and explore the tensions among internal, individual experience and sociocultural influence.

Rosemary Balsam

Psychoanalysts often work with women whose curiosity and pursuit of interests are inhibited by an inability to make something happen. Such women may have difficulty locating or owning a sense of personal agency, self-initiative or a capacity for self-determination. They may be able to imagine what they wish to become, yet be unable to connect their dreams with realistic possibility or the capacity for agency on their own behalf. While possible determinants in individual lives vary, this feeling of impasse is often accompanied by a dissociation from embodied experience.

Balsam places the female body, and embodied experience, on the psychoanalytic map. She invites us to consider how its presence and accurate representation change psychoanalytic portrayal of female experience. She does so by drawing from rich, close process and clinical vignettes. Writing in a style that radiates exuberance for her subject, she illuminates the relationship of embodiment to the capacity to imagine and engage in passionate possibilities. Balsam's work demonstrates a dramatic shift in psychoanalytic perspective, a movement from the absence of female subjectivity to its vibrant, powerful and embodied presence.

In "The Vanished Pregnant Body in Psychoanalytic Female Developmental Theory," Balsam (2003) traces the ways that psychoanalysis and early medical science failed to accurately represent the pregnant body, erasing a powerful creative aspect of female capacity. She suggests that the pregnant body, with all its plasticity, and ability to change shape and function, may be highly problematic, for both men and women to contemplate. She also connects its erasure to unconscious fear and dread of its power and changeability (Balsam, 2003).

Balsam underscores the clinical importance of paying close clinical attention to embodied experience, and its related representations. Through this lens, a woman's pursuit of passionate interests is rooted in visceral experience and its associated meanings. Reflecting on her work with a female artist, who works with her hands, something that has great meaning in relation to her mother's own, haggard, "working class hands," Balsam writes:

> the body is a window upon encoded internal perceptions, and as a route to unconscious fantasy, lends renewed interest to separate body parts: how they relate to a whole configuration; what is registered as asset or liability; how they become gendered. From such a viewpoint it becomes more problematic to make global statements such as, "The patient turned away from her femininity," or, as was frequent in the older writings, to conceptualize a woman's ambition to work outside the home as necessarily "masculine."
>
> *(Balsam, 2003, p. 1172)*

Balsam concludes that with a more nuanced developmental theory about women, one that takes into consideration an accurate representation and appreciation for female bodily experience, analysts will be better positioned to apprehend unconscious and unformulated, experiences, particularly bodily experience and its meanings for our female patients.

In "Women Showing Off: Notes of Female Exhibitionism," Balsam (2008) explores the idea that exhibitionism may be a prototypic female behavior, related to the pleasures of showing off the power inherent in a woman's body. Again, she privileges the body, with its varied associations and meanings, viewing "showing off one's stuff" as representative of a primary experience of pleasure about basic female capacities and power. This view might be contrasted with that of Joan Riviere, or social constructionists, such as Louise Kaplan, who view female exhibitionism as socially determined, and often defensive or performative, aimed at concealing underlying "masculine" ambitions – a perspective that is reflective of a more binary lens.

Yet, there is always a potential, public dimension of our physical selves, or always social conditions of embodiment (Butler, 1995, 2005). To give an example, abortion and reproductive rights, and their sociopolitical context, demonstrate ways in which the female experience of embodiment is influenced by social construction. Indeed, bodily agency and self-determination are complex issues, sometimes irreducible to individual embodiment.

Adrienne Harris

Harris is a prolific contributor to the development of postmodern thinking about gender and sexuality, and about female ambition in particular. By bringing to life the contributions of marginalized female psychoanalysts, such as Riviere and Spielrein, Harris (1997, 2015) has also re-established integrity and authorship in the history of psychoanalytic ideas, particularly the ideas of women analysts. Throughout her work, she demonstrates a keen ear for the social, historical and other regulatory forces that impact both psyche and the body – predicated on viewing the body as emergent, impacted and constructed in relationships and in context with the social third. Particularly relevant to the topic of ambition, Harris reminds us that to answer the question, "What does a woman want?" we have to ask, "What woman, where, and in what historical epoch" (Harris, 1997).

Whereas Balsam's concentration is on restoring the disappeared female body, and embodied experience, Harris focuses more on restoring the female mind and authorship. Both thinkers explore identity, its fluidity and multiplicity. Harris's breadth is remarkable as she is aware of the intersections of class, race and gender, particularly their impact on internal and intrapsychic experience (Harris, 1997).

In "Aggression, Ambition and Envy: Circulating Tensions in Women's Psychic Life" and "Mothers, Monsters, Mentors," Harris (1997, 2002) develops some of her complex, postmodern views about ambition and its detractors. In the former, Harris begins by acknowledging her identification with one of her female patients, resonating with the price of "drudgery and the yoke of debt" that, in her patient's experience, must be extracted and are preferable to the experience of ambition, striving and achievement (Harris, 1997). Harris is aware that enslavement by time and debt can seem safer than anxiety stimulated by ambition. In sharing her own experience, Harris demonstrates the degree to which identification can be central to the work of female analysts with their female patients. Harris also reveals the pressures and complexity of such clinical work as we try to stand with our patients in shared, unstable spaces.

Harris's writing style interweaves both the scholarly and personal, including disclosures about her own personal identifications and history. At first read, it can seem that Harris uses autobiographical scenes primarily to illustrate and enliven her ideas, but more is at stake. Her style literally parallels therapeutic action. Through her disclosures and acknowledgment of her identifications, Harris humanizes her patients' experiences by finding commonality with her own vulnerability. This resonance is a hallmark of the relational approach and a moving force in Harris's clinical work, which also leaves room for necessary moments of disruption and dis-identification.

As Harris notes, a woman's dread of her own ambition, her fear of hurting others, makes for powerful and multi-generational bastions of dissociated ambition and competition – perhaps the most important result being a potentially corrosive envy between women and across generations. Elaborating further, Harris notes that a woman's retreat from ambition may be part of a depressive tie to a maternal figure, as well as an idealization of male power which serves to keep her own authority safely out of reach (Harris, 1997).

Given that Harris's paper on "Aggression, Envy and Ambition" was written 20 years ago, we might wonder about socio-political change, along gender lines, since that time. In 2002, Harris writes,

> It is rare for a woman to feel and use a connection to a maternal imago that is full and rich or to a real-life mother who seems authorized and fully subject and who can therefore be safely killed in fantasy and so outdone or joined with in reality.
>
> (Harris, 2002, p. 284)

More than a decade later, we might ask, "have things changed?" Maybe they have, for some women, yet recent sociocultural events suggest that we are in the midst of an unprecedented and incendiary challenge to what we thought had been achieved.

Harris calls "envy" "the outsider's disease," or the "province of the powerless and immobilized." Her definition of envy is interesting to consider in light of recent, political misogyny. One might wonder if the 2016 election aftermath reflects the process Harris describes – a kind of female (internalized) misogyny, as well as a general misogyny of disempowered outsiders (Harris, 2002, 2017). In "Mothers, Monsters and Mentors," Harris (2002) considers the paradoxes inherent in the mother-daughter relationship around the developing girl's sense of power and agency, and capacity for creativity – particularly the relationship of these capacities to envy, as it exists between mother and daughter. She takes up both the power associated with being the female object of envy, including envy's hidden or "shadowy" presence of desire, and the ways in which, too often, the maternal imago cannot "underwrite mastery, effort, agency, goals and projects" (Harris, 2002, pp. 288–289). Central to the concern about mothers, daughters and generational disempowerment or envy, is the potential disruption of a daughter's capacity to draw inspiration and confidence around creativity and self-assertion from maternal identification.

In "Gender as Soft Assembly: Tomboy's Stories," Harris (2000) takes up the meaning and creativity inherent in gender explorations, making a plea for flexibility and multiplicity. Drawing from her own tomboy history, she suggests that "tomboy" is often a creative in-between space, an area for critical, developmental "play" that contains and generates multiple identifications and meanings. The tomboy can represent a "doubling of identity," "sanctioned motility," or, a space to move imaginatively and "less anchored to binaries" (Harris, 2000, p. 277). For many of us who have known or worked with women who suffer from a rigidity and lack of imaginative capacity around gender identifications, Harris's work is a breath of fresh air, demonstrating ways to move, or open up, what might become an airtight "bell jar."

Harris uses the tomboy narrative to explore the relationship of aggression and bodily experience to self-assertion and ambition. Turning to her own, personal story, she describes her experience of petitioning the University of Michigan Men's Lacrosse Team to allow her to play, in 1970, a time when athletic departments were adjusting to the impact of Title IX. In her account, Harris describes her feat of joining the men's team and then of "having to play." She shares her experience of (literally) bumping up against the world of male contact sports, with all its physicality and aggression, and concludes that this experience created an enduring connection between mastery and bodily resilience:

> The concept of mastery came to have a highly physical cathexis for me. I felt in possession of a body image formed and streamlined away from the objectifying male gaze that stains and maintains so much in female subjectivity. Body

imago and self-state were focused and delineated by the impact of flesh on flesh, muscle to muscle, the body mixup and shocks that do not usually arrive for women outside the funhouse or the bedroom. I had never understood the exhilaration and power of physical contact sports, despite a lifetime of those more distal rather than proximal competitions, that is, tennis or those earlier forms of women's basketball where you could not move or make physical contact. I understood as never before how much the physicality of sport was another instance of Winnicott's (1950) concept of the power of well-managed aggression. This kind of pleasurable aggression can be vicariously felt in any viewing of the current version of professional women's basketball or soccer or women's boxing, but 30 years ago it was a revelation.

(Harris, 2000, p. 224)

The implications of her story are rich. In many ways, it is a story about the potential vitality and resilience that comes with being hit, knocked down, bruised, winning and losing and getting up to play again. It stands in stark contrast to the view of women as pulling their punches, dismissing ambitions and hiding "their stuff." This is not to say that such physicality and athletic experience is a necessary condition for healthy ambition. Yet, Harris's story captures both the importance of embodiment and the experience of taking aggressive risks.

The social third: Layton, Dimen and current debate – women and wanting it all

Overview

Two contemporary psychoanalysts, Lynne Layton, a critical theorist, and Muriel Dimen, an anthropologist and cultural theorist, are foremothers in their recognition of sociopolitical influences, or "the social third," a contextualization that psychoanalysis has often dismissed. If we consider Freud's (1930) *Civilization and Its Discontents*, we are reminded that the beginnings of psychoanalysis were never exclusively about individual, interior life. Indeed, psychoanalysis unfolded during one of the more destructive historical periods and its theoretical beginnings recognize this history. That said, even in present discourse, a binary divide persists between analysts who privilege interior experience and those who believe in the force of exterior cultural/sociopolitical influence.

Layton

As an astute observer of political process and its impact on the psyche, Layton and colleagues (2006) chronicle the rise of heightened and anxious individualism in the United States. Layton's ideas are prescient and timely, especially considering recent (2016) U.S. election and its subsequent political fall-out, including attacks on women's rights. She points out that when we dissociate individuals from their social context, an inclination that may be particularly American, we end up "severing the mind's capacity to fully think" (Layton, Hollander & Guttrell, 2006, p. 107, Layton, 2004a). She underscores that our ideas are not solely our own, but rather given to us by sociopolitical structures, or "the social third." Moreover, she suggests that changes in the external sociopolitical field create actual internal psychic shifts. The latter may seem radical, particularly for psychoanalysts who hold exclusively to universal "truths" of the individual psyche.

Layton explores the dualities and splits in sociopolitical discourse that impact the psyche, noting (leading up to the early 2000s) a movement away from recognition of interdependency and containment of vulnerability, toward binary splits (individualism/dependency and attachment; doer/done to, etc.) (Layton, 2004a, 2004b). She suggests that, in the United States, our "manic society" has privileged activity in a frantic effort to ward off insecurity and to preserve individualism, through narcissistic defenses. In essence, she identifies a singular narcissism in American culture.

In this context, Layton explores the history of women's efforts to combine work with sustained, personal satisfactions. In her paper, "Working Nine to Nine: The New Women of Prime Time," Layton (2004c) draws from popular TV to deconstruct contemporary discourse about women and work. Contrasting her conclusions with early, essentialist assumptions, that women are solely relational, Layton argues that contemporary portrayals of women suggest something different; women are pulled toward defensive autonomy and over-extension, working constantly and warding off the need for attachment and relationship. According to Layton, women of this generation may over-value identification with the traditional male work ethic and undervalue our relational needs. Many psychoanalysts may be drawn to interpret such observations in light of individual psychodynamics, but she suggests that to do so would miss a critical, sociopolitical variable which she believes reflects the impact of the stalled women's movement, at this time period (Layton, 2004c, Hochschild and Manchung, 1989):

> What we are witnessing, I think, is a transition stage in which white, middle-class women are caught between two psychic structures that are products of white, middle-class, heterosexist splitting: the submissive relational female and the defensively autonomous male. The relational female that was an outcome of the gendered public-private split had difficulty establishing a public, agentic self because there was no social location for such a self. The public-private split that functioned so well for earlier stages of capitalism and patriarchy created a system of gender socialization that kept capacities for agency split off from capacities for maintaining intimate relations. Now that high-achieving middle-class, white women do the same work as their male counterparts and do it in the same work environments, they face the same difficulty finding time to tend relationships that men do. Some women who can afford to do so quit work to resolve this dilemma or work part time, thus serving the interests of a traditional patriarchal capitalism that prefers to have male and female functions split in this way.
>
> *(Layton, 2004b, p. 366)*

An important caveat, Layton is largely talking about white, heterosexual, middle class women. Moreover, writing in 2004, she is focused on a particular context and time period, mostly the 1980s and 1990s. As she says, the "stalled women's movement" of this period was focused on equality for women, but not the familial and workplace changes necessary to achieve such progress, the effect being that the pressure was placed back "on middle class women's psychic structure instead" (Layton, 2004c, p. 33).

Slaughter and Sandberg debate

The more recent debates between Anne-Marie Slaughter (2012) and Cheryl Sandberg (2013) re-examined the credo, "women can have it all." Ignoring issues of race and class, Slaughter and Sandberg focused primarily on privileged, high-achieving women. Drawing from her decision to leave her State Department position, in order to be with her family, Slaughter (2012) critiques "having it all," calling for significant re-evaluation of work and family structures. Slaughter describes an earlier generation of women who experienced pressure to separate their personal lives from their professional personas, in order to protect against discrimination for a lack of work commitment. In the process, these women sometimes ended up fetishizing their walled off professional lives (Slaughter, 2012). On the other hand, Sandberg, Facebook's COO, asks that women "lean in" to close the ambition gap by believing in one's own capacities, rather than pulling back from challenges, and by seeking the support of partners who are willing to truly share in work/family life. Needless to say, the debate sparked national interest. The areas of overlap for Slaughter and Sandberg include the call for creative and flexible boundaries between the private/familial and public/work domains.

Dimen

Like Lynn Layton, Muriel Dimen concentrates on the influences between the social third and individual and intersubjective experience, exploring "women and what they want" in this intersectional space. Dimen originally trained as an anthropologist and was deeply influenced by contemporary cultural theory. In *With Culture in Mind* (2011), she serves as the editor and a commentator for a collection of essays from a writing group focused on "locating the psychic and the social in a single clinical moment" (Dimen, 2011a, p. 2). Dimen describes how such moments might examine "transference and countertransference (or an enactment); a symptom or a facet of a personality; a newspaper headline or a cultural event or a war" – all representing an "opportunity and means to reflect on that familiar binary of mind versus culture, on the relationship between internal and external, psychic interior and sociopolitical surround" (Dimen, 2011a, p. 2). Dimen's book is a collective enterprise, based on dialogue among its contributors and centered on "speaking to others" (Dimen, 2011a). Describing this structure, Dimen makes the following point:

What happened in the group is a microcosm of what is beginning to happen more widely in the psychoanalytic world. Analysts are acknowledging that the orthodox ways of analyzing people are insufficient. Usually analysts don't consider social forces. Over time, they came to understand that their grasp of clinical problems needed more than the historical psychoanalytic focus on family narratives, patterns of relating, and attachment or sexual problems. In each case, they saw it made sense to consider psychoanalysis' conventional subject – interior life – as steeped in sociopolitical forces, that psychic life is made equally of inner and outer worlds, and they have found ways to talk about it that sacrifice neither dimension. Their novel approach, in turn, dovetails with a changing construal of clinical process.

(Dimen, 2011a, p. 3)

Dimen lays out this postmodern perspective, inclusive of the social third, with clarity, inviting us to move beyond the viewpoint that psychoanalysis is solely about either individual, psychic interior, or limited notions of intersubjectivity. She describes concepts that are critical to her way of thinking, particularly the idea of "discourse," which has the power to delimit both how we think and what we think. As she puts it, "discursive formations … are power structures. They are networks of socially located ideas, beliefs, attitudes, behaviors, and action patterns that systematically fashion and inform subjectivity and its practices" (Dimen, 2011a, p. 5).

"Interpellation" is another concept central to Dimen's thinking – a concept drawn from the work of Louis Althusser (French Marxist, analyzed by Lacan), which names the process by which subjectivity comes into being (Dimen, 2011b, p. 3). This process is everywhere and outside of us, and can both determine and potentially constrain subjectivity, which is governed by prevailing discourse. In this model, freedom and change are founded on the capacity to make different meanings or "resignification." Dimen writes:

Interpellation, as an idea, argues that our collusion and our oppression are constructed of the same stuff. It entails a paradox: one becomes a subject of oneself, an autonomous and sovereign being, only by becoming subject to the Law's sovereignty, to discourse or society itself. In other words, one becomes authentic – intelligible to oneself – only by recognizing the authority of discourse to render one's being intelligible. Even before one comes into being, one is always already constructed as a subject: even before birth, for example, parents-to-be will imagine relations with that other subject, now a fetus who, once born, will be their child and is, and will be, intelligible only as a separate center of subjectivity-to-be. If intelligibility is also key to integrity and sanity, however, one's freedom and capacity to change depend on "resignification", on the capacity to endow old enchainments with new meaning – which one may define as a principal goal of psychoanalysis, not to mention struggles for political and cultural liberation.

(Dimen, 2011a, p. 6)

According to this model, meaning making, or resignification, grows out of the capacity of patient and analyst, together, to assign new meaning to shared experiences that intersect at the crossroads of the intrapsychic, intersubjective and the social third. Tracing the history of psychoanalytic ideas about "women and what they want," we are suggesting that explanations of female desire and ambition require standing in this transitional space.

A call for diversity and deconstruction of women as a monolithic identity

Leary

Postmodern psychoanalysis offers us increasingly complex understandings of identity, including ethnicity, race and class. Identity is experienced in relation to others and particularly around perceived difference. Describing a heated clinical moment about competition and power between a black female analyst and black female patient, Leary (2000) notes that "race does not in any meaningful sense speak for itself," but "is instead a complex negotiation within persons as well as a complex negotiation between persons" (p. 649). Leary illuminates a flash point of power and competition, and its underbelly of loss and shame, as experienced between two black women who, not surprisingly, have varying histories and identifications within their racial experience.

Leary suggests that

> race occupies a transitional conceptual space (cf. Dimen, 1991; Leary, 1995, 1997, 1999) and that it is a material reality, pertaining to the real world, as well as a social construction with meanings shaped by the cultural milieu and like gender, an identity that can be negotiated and "performed."
>
> *(Leary, 2000, p. 649)*

She points out that racial enactments can raise issues such as "the dialectics of deprivation and domination, powerlessness and control and privilege and rejection," all of which may touch on historical and traumatic unformulated experience (Leary, 2000, p. 640). Leary's observations seem to have important implications for any clinical exploration of female ambition and its attendant experiences of competition, power and their inverse of shame and rejection. Clinical deconstructions of racial/class enactments open up the meaning and experience of ambition that become linked with fear, guilt, invisibility, envy and mis-recognition – as opposed to more hoped for feelings of agency, power and pride. All of these feelings can be re-conceived in the consulting room, with the potential for more injury or possible transformation for both patient and analyst.

Leary (2007) describes how race functions as a "closed system" in which everyday "racial relations are defined by the resolute denial of particularity" (p. 541). She takes up how, through stereotyping and social construction, "the social fact of being 'raced,' rather than race itself," controls social engagement. She writes: "To be raced is to be implicated in a system of cultural weights and measures that a priori aims to specify, stabilize, and fix who one is and who one may become" (Leary, 2007, p. 541).

Perhaps now, more than ever, there is a call for analysts to engage with women of diverse backgrounds, with whom we have much to learn about different personal meanings of ambition and what different women want, and the particular internal and social barriers to becoming who they most fervently wish to be. Such engagement might require difficult conversations, and also lead to unanticipated discoveries about ourselves and our field. Presently, the inequality divide is far too great for our field to remain on the sidelines, or trapped in staid theories that fail to address diverse experience.

The need for perspectives that account for mutual growth and agency

Another missing piece in psychoanalytic literature on women and ambition is a focus on the positive and mutual identifications and experiences between daughter and mother(s), or daughter and father(s). In addition, psychoanalysis overlooks the role of peers and mentors, particularly their role of helping women develop broadening, horizontal identities. A postmodern perspective might assume that the developing girl, young woman and adult daughter may have an ongoing, positive and mutually rewarding relationship with key figures of identification (and even dis-identification) and that these relationships might be bi-directional and include mutual impact.

A contemporary writer on identity and diversity, Andrew Solomon (2012) explores the issue of identity, particularly horizontal identity, as it develops with peers and surrounding communities rather than vertically from family. This is a particularly important issue for children who differ significantly from key family members and who need the support and identity that comes from "like communities." Solomon's thesis has implications for our topic about women and ambition. While psychoanalysis focuses on the impact of identity as it develops within one's family, it is less concerned with identity development in other, or developmentally later, contexts. This is surprising, given that psychoanalytic training is, itself, about professional, adult identity development and its connection to ongoing psychological growth. Indeed, we might consider psychoanalysis as more reflective about professional identity formation over the life span, than many other professions.

Consider the following, simple interchange: a young, female medical student, who has been excelling in her clinical experiences, finds herself in a new rotation with a female preceptor. The student is impressed by her preceptor's knowledge and leadership, but shaken by the challenges and risks the rotation demands. The student struggles with moments of inadequacy, along with wishes to excel, connect with her preceptor, and master the rotation. Although anxious, the medical student and preceptor discover a coincidence – the preceptor was, herself, trained by two women physicians, known to the medical student and influential in the student's decision to enter medicine. Although the medical student must master her anxieties about her training, both she and her preceptor are more open as they recognize their common identifications and history. The medical student ends her rotation challenged, inspired and also identified with her preceptor, and senses that this is a mutually influential experience.

Clearly, good teachers and mentors find ways of embracing difference and diversity around developmental paths and identifications, as do resilient students, but finding these positive identifications and role models remains an important part of development. The most crucial part of becoming a psychoanalyst is one's "training analysis," the several years of one's own analysis that occurs simultaneously with classes and clinical immersion. Identification with one's analyst is thought to be a critical part of professional development, as well as a lifelong anchoring professional force. The flexibility for professional differentiation and dis-identification is an equally important part of a good training analysis experience. In fact, the most important aspect of this identification experience may be the flexibility, curiosity and freedom to try on multiple, imaginative possibilities.

A drawback of psychoanalytic theory is that it tends to be deficit focused, with an eye for the troubling aspects of relationships and identifications, rather than the capacities for agency and ambitious pursuit. These perspectives tend to be bidirectional only in so far as they explain what is problematic, rather than what fosters growth. While we need ways to understand deficit and stalled growth, an explanation of what fosters healthy pursuit of ambition must take into account what goes right, or extremely well. There is much in the literature about intergenerational trauma, challenge and impasse, but less about resilience, the factors that make up the success stories, or the capacity to transform challenge into growth.

We might wonder if our field's tendency to take up female doom and gloom is a continued enactment of its original ideas about female lacking and absence. Does it remain uncannily problematic to think about what is forceful, positive, and transformative about mother/daughter relationships in particular? A scan of the literature reveals a tilt towards uncovering the problematic, rather than the live force field of mutual impact. Envy can be corrosive between women, but we can refocus our attention toward desire, a vital and welcome part of envious experience. Too often, our female patients collapse into dead ends when envy arises, and when such experience might be clarifying or contain the seeds of curiosity, desire and ambition. As has been suggested, envy is sometimes the "fig leaf of desire" (Gerhardt, 2009, p. 267).

As psychoanalysts, our mission is to help our female patients "transcend limits and barriers and meet challenges boldly," making use of potential power and agency, all the while holding multiple perspectives and possibilities (Richards and Spira, 2015, p. xix).

Bibliography

Angell, M. (2014). Women At the Top. *New York Review of Books*, March 20.

Balsam, R.H. (2003). The Vanished Pregnant Body in Psychoanalytic Female Developmental Theory. *J. Amer. Psychoanal. Assn.*, 51(4):1153–1179.

Balsam, R.H. (2008). Women Showing off: Notes on Female Exhibitionism. *J. Amer. Psychoanal. Assn.*, 56(1):99–121.

Butler, J. (1995). Melancholy Gender—Refused Identification. *Psychoanal. Dial.*, 5 (2):165–180.

Butler, J. (2005). *Giving an Account of Oneself.* New York: Fordham University Press.

Chodorow, N.J. (1979). *Reproduction of Mothering.* Berkeley: University of California Press.

Chodorow, N.J. (2000). Reflections on The Reproduction of Mothering—Twenty Years Later. *Studies in Gender and Sexuality*, 1(4):337–348.

Chodorow, N. (2002). Glass ceilings, sticky walls and concrete floors: Internal and external barriers to women's work and achievement, in *Constructing and Deconstructing Women's Power*, Selig, B., Paul, R., Levy, C.B. (Eds.), London and New York: Karnac.

Chodorow, N.J. (2004). Psychoanalysis and Women: A Personal Thirty-Five-Year Retrospect. *Ann. Psychoanal.*, 32:101–129.

Chodorow, N.J. (2012). *Individualizing Gender and Sexuality: Theory and Practice.* New York, London: Routledge Press.

Covington, C. and Wharton, B. (eds.) (2003) *Sabina Spielrein. Forgotten Pioneer of Psychoanalysis.* Hove and New York: Brunner-Routledge.

Dimen, M. (1991). Deconstructing Difference: Gender, Splitting, and Transitional Space. *Psychoanal. Dial.*, 1(3):335–352.

Dimen, M. (2011a). *With Culture in Mind: Psychoanalytic Stories.* Relational Perspectives Book Series, Vol 50. New York and London: Routledge.

Dimen, M. (2011b). With Culture in Mind: The Social Third Introduction: Writing the Clinical and the Social. *Studies in Gender and Sexuality*, 12(1):1–3.

Freud, S. (1905). Three Essays on the Theory of Sexuality (1905). *The Standard Edition of the Complete Psychological Works of Sigmund Freud, Volume VII (1901–1905): A Case of Hysteria, Three Essays on Sexuality and Other Works*, 123–246. London: Hogarth.

Freud, S. (1920). Beyond the Pleasure Principle. *The Standard Edition of the Complete Psychological Works of Sigmund Freud, Volume XVIII (1920–1922): Beyond the Pleasure Principle, Group Psychology and Other Works*, 1–64. London: Hogarth.

Freud, S. (1930). Civilization and its Discontents. *The Standard Edition of the Complete Psychological Works of Sigmund Freud. Volume XXI (1927-1931): The Future of an Illusion, Civilization and its Discontents and other Works*, 57–146. London: Hogarth.

Gerhardt, J. (2009). The Roots of Envy: The Unaesthetic Experience of the Tantalized/Dispossessed Self. *Psychoanal. Dial.*, 19:267–293.

Harris, A. (1997). Aggression, Envy, and Ambition: Circulating Tensions in Women's Psychic Life. *Gender and Psychoanalysis*, 2(3):291–325.

Harris, A. (2000). Gender as a Soft Assembly: Tomboys' Stories. *Studies in Gender and Sexuality*, 1(3):223–225.

Harris, A. (2002). Mothers, Monsters, Mentors. *Studies in Gender and Sexuality*, 3(3):281–295.

Harris, A. (2015). "Language is there to Bewilder itself and others": Theoretical and Clinical Contributions of Sabina Spielrein. *J. Amer. Psychoanal. Assn.*, 63(4):727–767.

Harris, A. (2017). Discussion Group: Women and their psychoanalytic experience of competence, ambition and leadership, APsaA Meetings, New York City.

Hochschild, A.R. and Manchung, A. (1989). *The Second Shift: Working Parents and the Revolution at Home.* New York: Penguin.

Holmes, D. (2015). My Journey to become my ambitious self. Invited Presenter for Discussion Group on Women's Experience of Competence, Ambition and Leadership, American Psychoanalytic Association Meeting, New York, NY.

Horney, K. (1926). The Flight from Womanhood: The Masculinity-Complex in Women, as Viewed by Men and by Women. *Int. J. Psycho-Anal.*, 7:324–339.

Kattlove, S. (2017). Personal Communication, Boston Psychoanalytic Society and Institute.

Layton, L. (2004a). Dreams of Americana/American Dreams. *Psychoanal. Dial.*, 14:233–254.

Layton, L. (2004b). Relational No More: Defensive Autonomy in Middle Class Women. *Ann. Psychoanal.*, 32: 29–42.

Layton, L. (2004c). Working Nine to Nine: The New Women of Prime Time. *Studies in Gender and Sexuality*, 5(1):351–369.

Layton, L., Hollander, N., and Gutrell, S. (Eds.) (2006). *Psychoanalysis, Class and Politics.* New York and London: Routledge.

Leary, K. (1995). Interpreting in the Dark. *Psychoanal. Psychol.* 12:127–140.

Leary, K. (1997). Race, Self-Disclosure and Forbidden Talk: Race and Ethnicity in Contemporary Clinical Practice. *Psychoanal. Q.*, 66:163–189.

Leary, K. (1999). Passing, posing and "keeping it real." *Constellations*, 6:85–96.

Leary, K. (2000). Racial Enactments in Dynamic Treatment. *Psychoanal Dial.*, 10(4):639–653.

Leary, K. (2007). Racial Insult and Repair. *Psychoanal. Dial.*, 17(4):539–549.

Marshall, M. and Wingfield, T. (2016). Getting More Black Women into the C-Suite, *Harvard Business Review*, July 1.

Quinn, S. (1988). *A Mind of Her Own: The Life of Karen Horney.* New York: Summit Books (Kindle edition 2011).

Richards, A. and Spira, L. (Eds.) (2015) *Myths of Mighty Women: Their Application in Psychoanalytic Psychotherapy* (Psychoanalysis and Women Series). London and New York: Karnac Books.

Riviere, J. (1929). Womanliness as a Masquerade. *Int. J. Psycho-Anal.*, 10:303–313.

Sandberg, C. (2013). *Lean In: Women, Work and the Will to Lead.* New York: Knopf.

Skorczewski, D. (2012). *An Accident of Hope: The Therapy Tapes of Anne Sexton.* New York and London: Routledge.

Slaughter, A.M. (2012). Why Women Still Can't Have It All. *The Atlantic*, July/August.

Solomon, Andrew (2012). *Far From the Tree.* New York: Simon & Schuster.

Spielrein, S. (1995). Destruction as Cause of Becoming. *Psychoanal. Contemp. Thought*, 18 (1):85–118.

Winnicott, D.W. (1950). Aggression in relation to emotional development. In: *Collected Papers: Through Paediatrics to Psychoanalysis.* New York: Basic Books, 1958.

7

ELIZABETH

A story of ambition

Frances Arnold

Introduction

The following case example describes the psychoanalytic work with Elizabeth, a female patient who presented with primary issues around work conflict and inhibition. Elizabeth's narrative highlights the experience of a minority woman in a male dominated field. Her story also raises important questions about the impact of complex intellectual and work identifications on female ambition, including how this might be addressed in psychoanalytic treatment. Competition and authorship, as well as shame and inhibition, are central themes in Elizabeth's clinical presentation. Our three discussants, Dionne Powell, Dorothy Holmes and Nancy Kulish, were invited to respond to the case, with these themes in mind, and to consider the following challenges, central for women navigating ambition: competition and envy, authorship versus disavowal of agency and ambition, the impact of multiple competing identifications, the impact of non-recognition, and the mercurial issue of defining achievement, success and a meaningful life.

In Chapter 8, Dorothy Holmes discusses the case of Elizabeth from multiple perspectives, with particular focus on how a woman's ambitions can be derailed, clouded, corrupted, or "othered." Dr. Holmes begins her discussion with consideration of Elizabeth's complex familial identifications, which Elizabeth held with sadness and ambivalence, and that may have led to her success neurosis. Drawing from a variety of works, including her own, Holmes also explores the dark forces impacting women and their pursuits, that are particularly important when considering derailed ambition in a minority woman, or woman of color, in academia. Holmes emphasizes that there are numerous historical and cultural factors that limit a woman's ambitions and that a psychoanalytic treatment is often incomplete if it does not address their specific impact. Holmes makes a strong case for the importance of considering the role of our "American Identity," especially our cultural practice of "othering" women, and women minorities in particular.

In Chapter 9 Nancy Kulish takes up ambition from the perspective of a woman's pursuit of rank, power and fame, and the achievement of a particular goal. Kulish notes that, despite changes, the modern woman is still plagued by inner inhibitions, passed down by generations, and that power, in particular, remains unreachable for women. Kulish explores several theories about female inhibition, including the notion of the "unconscious saboteur," pre-oedipal mother–daughter issues, and the "Persephone" (or female oedipal) complex, which contribute to the daughter backing away from success and fulfillment of her ambitions. Particularly important, Kulish emphasizes the importance of agency, or the capacity to make things happen, as critical to the capacity to actualize ambition.

In Chapter 10, Dionne Powell discusses the case of Elizabeth from both personal and clinical perspectives, with a particular emphasis on the unique challenges for minority women, whose stories are often excluded in psychoanalytic literature. Powell recognizes, and calls into question, the compromises and sacrifices women, especially minority women, often make in order to recognize, and be recognized, for their full potential. Powell also takes up the failure of the psychoanalytic profession, and our society at large, to adequately address racial, ethnic and gender biases as they apply to female ambition. Drawing from her clinical, as well as personal experience as an African American psychoanalyst, Powell notes the ways in which a woman's pursuit of her ambitions may be dismissed, objectified or hijacked by the surrounding culture and its biased patriarchy.

Elizabeth

When I first met Elizabeth, I was struck by her natural beauty and obvious warmth. She arrived at my office in her attractive athletic attire, her long hair draped loosely around her shoulders. The session began with her cheerful curiosity. How did I like my profession? What was it like to see patients all day? Was it difficult to listen to patients for so many hours? Elizabeth wondered if psychoanalysis might be very different from what she did every day as a scientist. She smiled often and graciously as she spoke, leaving me to wonder how I would find a way to ask, "How can I be of help to you?"

When I did ask, Elizabeth teared up. She explained that she had become consumed with a difficult work situation, now causing terrible anxiety and insomnia, and creating conflict with both her advisor and her husband, a scientist in the same lab. Both men felt she was overreacting and should redirect her energies to completing her research publications.

The unfolding story was of a complex and upsetting work situation. Elizabeth explained that both she and her husband were completing research training at a well-known neuroscience lab. The source of Elizabeth's distress centered on a conflict that erupted involving the use of her research data by an adolescent

Russian girl, whose father had financially contributed to her lab. Like a number of financial contributors, the young woman's father represented a biotech fund which had supported the lab's research. Elizabeth found this father and investor's role complicated, but was particularly surprised by his request to add his daughter's name to Elizabeth's research papers, with the explanation that his daughter was a budding scientist in need of research exposure. Elizabeth felt pressed to agree to something that did not feel right and attempted to defer her response, but eventually acquiesced at her advisor's request.

Elizabeth struggled with her decision, only later to hear that the "budding scientist" won a prestigious science scholarship. Indeed, Elizabeth discovered that her own research had been used, by the adolescent girl, in the scholarship competition. Elizabeth believed her research was being mis-represented as the girl's *own* findings, for a project that the adolescent claimed to have worked on, when in fact, she had never visited Elizabeth's lab.

Distressed about what seemed like blatant plagiarism and misrepresentation, Elizabeth contacted the girl's father who responded, "How could you make a big deal out of this, you know what it is like to be a minority and try to get ahead in this country! Also, as a woman in science, you should be eager to help my daughter get ahead."

Stunned by the conversation, Elizabeth turned to her husband and her lab director. Both responded similarly, with sympathy and support, but downplayed what Elizabeth viewed as a serious misrepresentation of her own research. They viewed the story as about the indiscretion of an adolescent girl, whose father had been supportive of their own, larger research efforts, and suggested to Elizabeth that she drop her grievance and re-focus on her own work.

Struggling with her reaction, Elizabeth turned to her own father, a neurosurgeon, who likewise suggested, "these things happen," and recommended she not to waste her professional time. Like her husband and her advisor, he suggested she focus on her own publications.

Elizabeth found it difficult to follow this advice. She became anxious, unable to sleep and continually preoccupied by the young Russian woman, who she felt had plagiarized her work. She found it impossible to think of anything else and became obsessed with finding out everything she could about this young woman. Elizabeth was also troubled by her feelings of distance and disappointment with the important men in her life. Since the incident erupted, she felt removed from her husband, who had always been her most loving support. At the point of coming to therapy, Elizabeth felt her mind was no longer her own and that her capacity to think had been hijacked by constant intrusion of thoughts about this disturbing experience. She even worried she might be going crazy.

This story unfolded in rapid sequence, over the course of Elizabeth's first treatment hour. The easy casualness, that marked the beginning session, was eclipsed by a barrage of torment and helplessness. I was struck by the effort and restraint Elizabeth must have put into her initial presentation, how quickly this gave away, and also, how smoothly she regained her composure before leaving my office. At some point, we discussed whether medication would be helpful, particularly given her acute anxiety and sleep disturbance. Not wanting to alter her thinking capacities, she declined medication, readily agreeing that talking would probably be most effective.

So began a two-year treatment, often at twice weekly frequency, that covered a range of issues. The story of her ideas being stolen and misrepresented emerged as a central traumatic event to be elaborated and understood. We entered into an exploration of what this event might represent to her, assuming that there would be layers of story and meaning.

Elizabeth's first associations went to her father, an understated, Indian man and the son of a rural farmer. According to family history, he was exceedingly smart and hardworking, and because of these qualities, won opportunities and financial support to pursue advanced education. The latter culminated in combined M.D. and Ph.D. degrees from a prestigious American university. From there, he built a highly successful neurosurgery department and was involved in scientific research.

Elizabeth was struck by two important differences between her own father and that of the budding scientist who misrepresented her work. She saw her own father as a humble man who had worked extraordinarily hard to gain his professional position and had done so honestly, without self-promotion beyond the observable success of his own scientific work. In contrast, the adolescent girl and her father seemed dishonest, calculating and self-promotional. Secondly, Elizabeth's father had been a more removed parent, in contrast to the adolescent's over-involved father. While Elizabeth's observations about her father's integrity and humility aroused considerable anger toward the young scientist, her observations about the businessman's involvement with his daughter evoked sadness about her own experience. As we continued to unpack the story, Elizabeth found herself experiencing a confusing envy toward this daughter whose father was so over-involved that he seemed to highjack his daughter's intellectual autonomy.

As the treatment progressed, Elizabeth began to realize that she wished her own father had been more involved, while also experiencing complicated feelings about the pressure she felt to pursue science and math. Particularly painful, Elizabeth realized that although she and her father shared the world of science, she has little recollection of conversations about her father's work or intellectual interests.

Also important, was Elizabeth's awareness that she had been more rejecting and rebellious toward parental pressures, than this adolescent girl who seemed so overtly compliant. When Elizabeth attended college, she stopped speaking to her parents for an extended time, partly in response to the continued pressures she felt around selection of her courses and area of academic concentration. Furthermore, she had experienced difficulty, during her freshman year, having over-challenged herself with demanding science courses while contending with her parents' threats to pull her out of school in response to a precipitous drop in her grades.

Elizabeth and I spoke about her complex professional dilemma, which presented a deep challenge to her ability to hold and express her own perspective. As I thought about Elizabeth's story, I felt drawn to respond with outrage. I also wanted to explore her recourse to action, despite her lack of external support. Thinking about these pressures, I wondered what Elizabeth and I might be enacting as the drama unfolded. How would we come to understand the various pressures that were building between us, as we both reacted to various components of her narrative? I wondered about my urge to step in or speak up on her behalf, particularly in light of her seemingly silent mother, a stay at home mom who struggled with the English language. I felt an urgency to help Elizabeth consider whether she preferred to let this situation drift into the background, or assume more agency and action. From the outset, Elizabeth agreed that her reactions to this drama had great meaning for her and would help us to understand what had been troubling for some time.

Elizabeth settled on the importance of seeking an outside point of view, agreeing that I could be her therapist, but was not in a position to consult around the ethical issues. Eventually, Elizabeth sought advice from someone who consulted on ethical matters and indeed was surprised by consultant's conclusion that this was a very serious ethical situation. Over the course of several meetings with this person, Elizabeth explored various courses of action, weighing these possibilities against her wish to preserve and protect her academic career and her hard earned professional relations.

Following the consultation, Elizabeth went to her advisor and pressed him to take some protective action. As a result, the fund contributor was pushed to give up his involvement with the research team. A few months later, Elizabeth told me about how she had gone to her advisor and said, "I want to discuss two things – I want you to take some action on my behalf about this ethical issue and secondly, I want you to know that my goal is to pursue a tenure track teaching and research position." The latter was a significant clarification of her ambitions, directed at an important authority figure, and put on the table just as she took steps to protect herself from plagiarism.

At this point, the meaning of the young adolescent scientist began to deepen. While this infuriating incident of stolen intellectual work presented a complex dilemma, it also pushed to the fore Elizabeth's own aspirations in a way that she had not previously experienced. Indeed, it seemed to catapult her into identifying and claiming her own ambitions. We discussed at length how complicated it felt to express her intentions so boldly and clearly given this was not consistent with her personality and usual manner of relating. As she put it, "I felt like, if this young girl could steal others' work and promote herself so unabashedly, I should be able to claim my own aspirations."

Elizabeth's pathway, from her research fellowship to running her own neuroscience lab, was not easy. Competition was fierce, she struggled with concerns about her limited number of publications and she also worried about her ability to present herself in a forceful and clear way, particularly in interviews and presentations. During this time period, Elizabeth, again, found herself obsessed with following Google alerts about the adolescent scientist, especially after hearing that she had gone on to win a number of other prestigious honors. Interestingly, Elizabeth also began Google tracking the adolescent daughter of *The Tiger Mother*, who, in contrast to the young scientist, Elizabeth felt was "the real deal," intelligent, thoughtful, funny and seemingly very much herself, in contrast to the adolescent scientist whom she saw as an "impostor."

I was struck by the extremes of the two adolescent figures who seemed to become important transferential figures for Elizabeth. One was a younger adolescent who was astoundingly successful, albeit seemingly colonized by her father, and the other was an intelligent, apparently honest young woman raised by an infamous Chinese American mother and author, who ignited a debate about child rearing practices and the tendency of American parents to hold back from rigorous expectations and goals.

As things progressed, Elizabeth experienced a withdrawal and loss of interest in her work, just as she was facing competition and difficult choices around future job options. I was mindful of how it had taken her a long time to complete her graduate degree and that now she seemed to pull back just when she needed to push forward. Elizabeth spoke about her advisor's international fame, which made him less available to his lab and to her. Elizabeth had found it difficult to capture his attention, a particularly daunting goal when she had a small daughter at home and an advisor who was known to hold office hours late at night. On the one hand, Elizabeth seemed to passively withdraw, and on the other, she became intensely envious of peers who seemed to have more visibility or were being rewarded with prestigious academic positions. In hindsight, Elizabeth wonders if her withdrawal was related to the complexity of holding and framing her own ambitions as she and her husband jointly applied for positions, a situation that is not uncommon for academic women, who often have academic partners. There was always an underlying sense that they would move to where her husband was offered tenure, but that an offer of tenure for her alone would not be acceptable.

This situation intensified, as the careers of Elizabeth's peers took off around her, including her husband's as he secured a coveted, tenure track position. Applying jointly, the university that offered her husband a position, also offered Elizabeth the opportunity to develop her own lab. Although not a tenure track position, this university vowed to re-consider the tenure issue at a later time. As these circumstances unfolded, Elizabeth's feelings ran high. She felt like she was just becoming aware of the extent of her ambition, and the extent to which she felt like she had held herself back during the earlier years of her training. She had felt shy and insecure as a young graduate student and overcoming this had taken several years of further training, some psychotherapy, and more awareness of her own wishes.

Elizabeth's treatment came to an end as she moved to another state to pursue her new research position. Both of us were saddened by the premature termination. In the final weeks of her treatment, Elizabeth returned to the issue of her lack of adequate publications. She was particularly upset that several of her colleagues were assured of completing more papers before leaving the lab in search of permanent positions. She also focused on her sadness about her past rebelliousness toward her parents and their high expectations, viewing this as both a necessary reaction to feeling colonized and also a detour that cost her time and opportunity.

Shortly before ending her treatment, Elizabeth arranged several meetings with her advisor to review the status of her papers and to establish a way of completing her publications. She associated to her father's success, as well as to his remoteness and her difficulty engaging him in substantive dialogue. She talked about how she wished she had known more about her father's work and impressive publications, which she stumbled upon as a graduate student. Finally, she also talked about the confusing, but liberating, shift in her aging parents, who are now less focused on their adult children's achievement, just as she is becoming aware of the extent of her own ambition.

Elizabeth is a patient who lingers on one's mind, as does her story. She is an impressive woman who possesses the unusual qualities of appreciation and graciousness, combined with extraordinarily high expectation and ambition. Moreover, her capacity to hold her ground, even when she felt unsupported or that her grievances were driving her crazy, was striking. Remarkably, Elizabeth rarely lost the capacity to question her own reactions and to search for the personal meaning held by the events and people surrounding her. Not surprisingly, I later learned that Elizabeth went on to secure a tenure track position and that her traumatic work experience had faded to the background.

8

COMMENTARY ON ELIZABETH

A case of the othering of a woman's ambition

Dorothy Holmes

I am privileged to have the opportunity to comment on the case of Elizabeth. The narrative introduced me to her as a young scientist who was at an advanced point in her studies. She had strategically placed herself in a prestigious laboratory to be able to write and publish scientific papers that would help her be competitive for a tenure-line university appointment.

Notable factors surrounding her in her academic world included that she was in a male-dominated field and that her husband, with the same standing in his career development and aspirations, worked in the same laboratory. Her advisor was also male. It was additionally critical for my thinking about Elizabeth that she was describe as "being a minority female in a male-dominated field." The ambiguity of the statement aroused my curiosity about what was meant by "minority." Did the word "minority" modify "male-dominated," or did it refer to her racial and/or ethnic status? Two points in the narrative clarified that the meaning of "minority" included racial and/or ethnic status: one was a reference to Elizabeth's mother as a "more silent … stay at home mom who struggled with the English language." Secondly, Elizabeth was scolded at one point by the man she held responsible for stealing some of her research data, a fact on which I focus below. He said to her, "How could you make a big deal out of this, you know what it is like to be a minority, and try to get ahead in this country." In preparing to comment on this case I also noted that Elizabeth's father was described as a distinguished physician-researcher in the field of neurosurgery. Clearly, Elizabeth admired him and in setting her own professional course, had identified with him. Elizabeth and her father shared mutual admiration, but throughout her life, Elizabeth had painfully experienced her father as aloof.

Elizabeth presented for treatment in crisis at a critical point in her career advancement. The crisis was precipitated when the lab director, Elizabeth's advisor, allowed the adolescent daughter of one of the lab's financial backers to plagiarize some of Elizabeth's data. Launched by that unethical appropriation, the adolescent girl went on to "win" several prestigious academic honors.

Historical and current trends in researching the psychology of women

My interest in how a woman's ambition can be derailed, clouded, corrupted, or "othered" was first expressed in a scholarly journal article published in 1976, entitled, "Emerging truths on the psychology of women: as through a glass darkly" (Evans, 1976). In that article, I reviewed a collection of papers written as the Zeitgist for inquiry about the psychology of women was beginning to change from works being heavily influenced by sex role stereotyping – that is, women looked at through the dark glass of sex role stereotyping – to a more objective, open inquiry. I opined that the lens through which we looked at women was made dark by:

> the place women have occupied and by the historical place women have occupied … [and] by the fact that the inquirers, be they men or women, are products of the very sex role stereotyping we seek to investigate and to clarify.
> *(Evans, 1976, p. 60)*

Fast forwarding to this era, and to Elizabeth's narrative, I am certain that we do see issues of the psychology of women, including their ambitions, more clearly. From the early 1970s until the present, numerous writers have advanced our thinking about how historical and ongoing cultural factors have limited women's ambitions, and about ways of working clinically with women to free them to express their ambitions. Examples of these contributions include but are not limited to: Janeway, 1971; Schafer, 1984; Seelig, Paul & Levy, 2002; Holmes, 2002, 2006, 2015, 2016a, 2016b; in press a, in press b.

A conceptualization of ambition and family contributions to it becoming conflicted

The case of Elizabeth is especially rich in showing that we still deal with dark forces in play as ambitious women and as scholars and therapists trying to understand and ameliorate those forces. Elizabeth allows us to bring light to those forces in a particularly important arena – academia – in which the ambitions of women have not been widely investigated. To begin my discussion of Elizabeth, I want to share with you my definition of ambition: For me, it is, "the loving, passionate pursuit of what you most fervently want to become, with perseverance and focus, despite the odds" (Holmes, 2015). Obviously, Elizabeth's pursuit of the fulfillment of her ambition was waged against the odds. As I see her, there was a dispiriting melancholy attached to her academic ambition. It was developed out of her identification with her father, but that identification was ambivalently held with elements of sadness. Though the case narrative does not develop the point, I wonder if she came by her scientific aspirations and ambitions as a way of developing and enriching a personal and emotional relationship with her father, a variant of "if you can't lick 'em, join 'em," but it was not to be. That is, the distance she felt between them was not reduced by her following in his footsteps. Further, the failure of this hypothesized fantasied hope for connection with her father was compounded when he, along with her advisor and her husband, proposed that she overlook the blow she experienced when her data were appropriated. She sought treatment, in part, because she thought she was losing her mind. In a sense, that is what was threatened in that the failure of the most important men in her life to understand the centrality and core importance to her of her data was experienced by her as their being complicit with "mind murder." It would take us far afield to speculate too much on the seemingly easy alliance the men formed to negate her intent to stop the theft of her data. I will offer, however, from my own 38-year career in academia, including my own successful but challenging path towards tenure, that in matters of academic advancement for women, it is not unusual for unfair or unscrupulous treatment of women to be minimized or dismissed. Janeway's wisdom, articulated in 1971, that it is a man's world in which women place second still holds true in a variety of settings, including academia, especially if the woman seeks to join the men in the first rank, which tenure still represents. It is particularly maddening in the case of Elizabeth because the men seemed to be in cahoots to permit an adolescent girl at the hands of her father to steal data and "advance" on that basis, which is, of course, to endorse a notion that a woman cannot make it on her own merit. No wonder Elizabeth felt she was going mad!

I hope there was an opportunity in her treatment to de-pathologize her "madness" and help her express it as appropriate anger to be judiciously used to fuel her efforts to reclaim her proper place. Clearly, she needed treatment to do so. As the narrative points out, the treatment helped her to gather herself and make proper demands on her advisor to protect her from the predatory actions of the lab's "benefactor." It seemed to me particularly exploitative and manipulative that the benefactor, himself from a minority group, tried to shame Elizabeth into submission to his plot by saying to her that as a minority she should be okay with his plot, since it is so hard for minorities to advance. He seemed to argue for a kind of corrupt identification with the aggressor along the lines of, "since they cheat us of opportunity, it's okay for us to cheat, too." This push to get ahead, no matter how you do it, is a corruption of ambition. Perhaps we could best call it a malignant form of ambition. The racialized element in this case will be further discussed later.

Why did Elizabeth stall out for a while during treatment, after regaining traction, including having successfully gotten her advisor to sever his ties with the corrupt benefactor? I find it necessary to explicate conflicted elements of her ambition to answer this question. I think the narrative makes clear that her ambition to become a successful scientist was an important part of who she was, but I think her ambition to become loved by her father in a way she had not felt loved by him was also important. In addition, the fact that her mother was a shadowy, silent figure was most likely implicated to some unknown degree in her temporary withdrawal from the stage, i.e., becoming silent. The provided narrative does not elaborate the family influence on Elizabeth's ambition. I speculate that as she became self-animating, including her gathering her voice to speak up in her own interest and in the interest of ethical practices, a conflict ripened between her competing longings. This aspect of her identity formation, rooted in family dynamics, would be an important focus in her treatment. It would permit access to, and the possibility for working through the various layers of attachment she felt to her father. These layers included her wish to have had a more emotionally rich relationship with him, and the necessity of mourning its unavailability. Also, I think the full animation of herself in the world of work would require Elizabeth to differentiate herself from her shadowy, silent, stay at home mother. I hypothesize that in the midst of those working through processes, she blinked, as it were, taking one more time to look over her shoulder for her father and to become free to say, "look ma, no hands," before she could transform those conflicted aspects of herself into a fuller, passionate engagement of her own work.

Treatment enabled Elizabeth to free up her full capacity for ambitious work. In that regard, I found it important and wise on her part that she declined the use of psychotropic medication in her treatment, believing that it would further cloud her mind, which she did not want. I take her to have meant, at least implicitly, that she knew the powers of her own mind and wanted to control its functioning and expansion as much as she could with her own powers. This attitude towards her own mind reminds me of two points of view. One was expressed by Ruth Simmons, the woman who became the first African-American to head Smith College and then, Brown University. She was born and reared in Texas during Jim Crow, the daughter of sharecroppers. She said that in the community of her youth, she was taught not to expect to go very far. However, on the occasion of her installation as President of Smith College, she said that those community forces notwithstanding, "I knew my mind could take me anywhere" (Holmes, 2006).

The second point of view is one expressed by Freud (1930), in *Civilization and its Discontents*, in which work, Freud said (p. 80):

> No other technique for the conduct of life attaches the individual so firmly to reality as laying emphasis on work; for his work at least gives him a secure place in a portion of reality in the human community. The possibility it offers … lends it a value by no means second to what it enjoys as something indispensable to the preservation and justification of existence in society.

Elizabeth needed her treatment to build on her intuitive sense of the central, organizing and animating value of her own mind and to invest fully in it to take her as far as her intellectual gifts and ambition would permit so that she could do her most productive work.

Ambition, othering and prejudice in academia: gender dynamics and minority status

Having examined familiar family dynamics as a contribution to Elizabeth's success neurosis, I now want to explore more closely the role of societal forces, particularly the potentially crippling contradictions in our American identity as they find expression in various ways. For Elizabeth those ways include the prejudices that play out in academic settings, gender dynamics and minority status. What do I mean by American identity? I define it as the unstable amalgam between our country's highest ideals and our equally available and often ascendant base tendencies. Our founding principles, as provided in the Declaration of Independence, include:

> that all men are created equal, that they are endowed by their creator with certain unalienable rights; that among these are life, liberty, and the pursuit of happiness; that to secure these rights, governments are instituted among men, deriving their just powers from the consent of the governed.

It does not take much thinking, if one is open to thinking about these matters, to be acutely aware of how much breakdown there has been among us culturally since the founding of our country, to the point that we have often played out a narrative of "My Country 'tis of We and Them." From its inception, we have sought ways around application of the principles to *all*. Men meant men. So, from the beginning there has been the cultural practice of othering women, i.e., devaluing them as outside the dominant, controlling group (Holmes, 2016b). Of course, the same was true from the beginning in terms of Blacks. As we know, these exclusions have been perpetrated brutally across our entire history. In the case of Elizabeth, we see modern day applications of this dysfunction in our American identity – when base tendencies took over in her academic setting. As previously illustrated, examining the breakdown in terms of familiar family dynamics and their impact on her was necessary. Now it is necessary to examine the breakdown in terms of her gender and her minority status as played out in academia.

The narrative does not make clear how factors of gender and minority status were addressed in her treatment. It is hard for me to see how her treatment could be as thorough as it needed to be without the factors of her femaleness and her racial and/or ethnic identity being addressed. If not addressed, I would consider the treatment to be incomplete in the same way I would consider a treatment to be incomplete if it did not deal with maternal and paternal transferences, or if a patient's conflicts about aggression were left unaddressed. So, how can I bring those factors into focus? First, to emphasize the importance of exploring how a woman can be adversely affected by how society regards her femaleness and the necessity of treating those effects, I will offer the wisdom of Schafer (1984). He said (p. 404),

> De-idealization of unhappiness that is often accomplished through psycho-analysis tends to bring with it an increased readiness … for women [to develop] lively critiques of our sexist world and adequately assertive means to resist and combat the seductions into suffering with which they are constantly surrounded.

Schafer went on to opine that society resists these changes. I propose that we, as psychoanalyst members of our society also at times resist applying our craft on these issues. We, too, can become immobilized by historical and current societal influences on us. We need to think deeply about how to open Elizabeth's treatment to consider how her femaleness played a role in what happened in the lab. She needed particular help to examine the uniform collusive agreement by the three most important men in her life not to address the plagiarism and their discouraging her to do so. Of the multiple important levels on which this matter should be queried, I proffer that male dominance and male fear of a woman's uncompromised expression of her competitive ambitions have a role. If Elizabeth had conceded to the men's wish that she set aside her concerns about the plagiarism, it would have kept their male dominion in place and would have silenced Elizabeth and established an even more corrupt image of a woman's success, i.e., that it cannot be earned, but, as manifested in the adolescent girl, it is stolen. Hopefully, that girl found her way to treatment at some point in her life to rescue her real self from the false self into which she was molded. One could argue that Elizabeth found her voice without focusing on the dynamics and cultural history of gender bias. My rebuttal to such an argument would be that the most complete resolution of her challenges to achieving conflict-free ambitiousness requires work on the level of culturally-imposed gender bias to build and preserve resilience, given that our society's inescapable history and ongoing intention is to hold to or revert to gender bias and to forcefully project it into women.

In Elizabeth's narrative, her minority status remains the most elusive. As noted earlier, there were three references to it – one in the introduction to the narrative in which she is referred to as a "minority female in a male-dominated field," the reference to her mother's failure to master the English language, and the Machia-vellian manipulation of her by the father of the adolescent girl when he chastised her for pushing back against his stealing of her data for his daughter, with: "How could you make a big deal out of this, you know what it is like to be a minority and try to get ahead in this country"! Here, too, I think deep and thorough work would require this material to be unpacked, probed, and worked through. What stands out for me is the deep cynicism of the lab benefactor father's position, in his impassioned representation that the system is so rigged against minorities that the only way a minority person can get ahead is by cheating. What a spirit-killing, mind-numbing point of view. To the extent that his approach was not Machia-vellian, what else could it reflect? Perhaps if one is injured enough by our society's practices that work against you as a minority, the minority person can become hopeless about working within the system. Rather, that minority person can develop a point of view that you cannot expect something that makes sense for you within the system, and that all that is left is to out-trick the system. To the extent that the lab benefactor father's approach was Machiavellian, it could represent a malignant form of identification with the dominant culture aggressor in which you beat him at his own debased and debasing game. If I were the therapist, I would be curious about these considerations and about how Elizabeth experienced her own minority status and how that experience was affected by the benefactor father's minority status claims. I do take note here that the therapist conceptualized Elizabeth's view of the father in terms of family dynamics (e.g., did Elizabeth envy the close connection between the corrupt father and his adolescent daughter). My point here is that *in addition*, the work would benefit from examining racial/ethnic dynamics per se. My rationale for this recommendation is in part the same as for looking at gender bias: our society, in our various expressions of our American identity, insists on bringing these dynamics forward. Also, for both gender and minority status, one cannot achieve wholeness without claiming and finding an affirming expression for all of who we are, including our gender and our racial/ethnic aspects.

Conclusion

In conclusion, the case of Elizabeth is a complex one with many layers and dimensions. It has the usual individual and family dynamics that are familiar to all psychodynamic clinicians. In addition, it offers rich material for looking at a woman's ambitions through the lenses of societal values and American identity, and their various derivatives, which often promote our growth, but also can, in certain manifestations, impede our growth. It is imperative that the psychoanalytic clinician examine the patient's functioning from all relevant perspectives and offer treatment that addresses all relevant factors. Of course, what is sufficiently at the surface to be worked with varies among patients and within a given patient over time. While acknowledging such variation, my own experience is that the major limitation to the scholarly and clinical examination of factors affecting women and the full expression of their ambitions is the continuing pressure from our core cultural selves to stick to limitations that have been present from the beginning of our country. From the beginning, our high principles (all men are created equal) were operationally defined to apply the principles only to men and only to white men. The progress we have made and can make on this front, in my view, is not to eradicate this cultural tendency. I believe it is permanent. However, as psycho-analytic thinkers and clinicians, we can ameliorate the harmful impact of our attraction to our exclusionary, othering tendencies by finding their expression in the treatment situation and committing to working with them. Elizabeth is a very good case example of the possibilities for doing such work. I appreciate having had the opportunity to write a commentary on her life story and her treatment experience. In doing so, I have tried to open our psychoanalytic thinking and its clinical applications to working with Elizabeth's individual, family and societal factors as key to a robust resolution of interferences to her full expression of her ambitious self. There are many more Elizabeths in our world. As psychoanalytic thinkers and practitioners, let us do our best, in our commitment to human liberation, to give them their due!

References

Evans, D. (1976). Emerging truths on the psychology of women: As through a glass darkly. *The Journal of Counseling Psychologist*, 6, 60–63.

Freud, S. (1930). Civilization and its discontents. *Standard Edition*, 21, 59–145. London: Hogarth.

Holmes, D. (2002). "Glass ceilings": their origins, psychodynamic manifestations, and consequences in women. In B. Seelig, R. Paul & C. Levy (Eds.), *Constructing and Deconstructing Woman's Power*, London, New York: Karnac.

Holmes, D. (2006). The wrecking effects of race and social class on self and success. *Psychoanalytic Quarterly*, 75, 215–235.

Holmes, D. (2015). My journey to become my ambitious self. Invited Presenter for Discussion Group on Women's Experience of Competence, Ambition and Leadership, Ambitions and Power, American Psychoanalytic Association Meeting, New York, NY.

Holmes, D. (2016a). "I knew that my mind could take me anywhere"; psychoanalytic reflections on the dignity of African Americans living in a racist society. In S. Levine (Ed.), *Dignity Matters*. London: Karnac.

Holmes, D. (2016b). Come hither, American psychoanalysis: Our complex multicultural America needs what we have to offer. *Journal of the American Psychoanalytic Association*, 64, 568–586.

Holmes, D. (In press, a). Reflections on Hollander's "Hegemonic Mind" and how to treat it. *Psychoanalytic Dialogues*.

Holmes, D. (In press, b). My psychoanalytic self: Discovery, embrace, and formation. In L. Hillman, & T. Rosenblatt (Eds.), *Becoming a Psychoanalyst, a Life-long Pursuit: Fifteen Stories on Finding One's Analytic Voice/Identity*. London: Routledge.

Janeway, E. (1971). *Man's World, Woman's Place*. New York: Dell.

Schafer, R. (1984). The pursuit of failure and the idealization of unhappiness. *American Psychologist*, 39, 398–405.

Seelig, B., Paul, R. & Levy, C. (Eds.) (2002). *Constructing and Deconstructing Woman's Power*. London, New York: Karnac.

9

THE CASE OF ELIZABETH

A discussion of ambition

Nancy Kulish

Ambition, according to the dictionary (Gove, 1976), is defined as: "an ardent desire for rank, fame or power" or "the will or the desire to succeed or achieve a particular goal." Given this definition, it is not difficult to understand why ambition might be a particular problem for women. The achievement of rank, fame or power is not easily attainable for women in many parts of the world. Even as opportunities have begun to open up for women, inner inhibitions passed down through the generations still have a hold on modern women. As Harris (1997) puts it: "gender inscription attaches to ambition and strivings and achievement" (p. 292). The desire for *Power* is especially conflicted and unreachable for women.

Thwarted and unresolved ambitions become the subject for psychoanalysts, who try to understand and alleviate internal inhibitions in women and girls they see for treatment. Numerous case studies spell out the underlying factors that impede or influence a woman's ambition. Wrye (2006), for example, describes the "unconscious saboteur" and internal unconscious narratives, which constrain the expression of female ambition. Wrye describes how aspects of the pre-oedipal relationship with the mother, rife with envy and fantasied or experienced abandonments and rejections, inhibit ambition. She also cites the male abrogation of female capability and society's denigration of ambition as "unfeminine." In her brilliant and thorough discussion of this topic, Harris (1997) outlines several important factors that affect female ambition: negotiation of issues around separation and rapprochement, anxieties about aggression, identifications with the mother. She elucidates the unconscious dynamics of an all-powerful maternal imago that crushes the daughter's desires and ambitions. I would emphasize the unconscious triangular or oedipal/persephonal conflicts with the mother that often cause the daughter to back away from success and fulfillment of ambitions.

Several other writers (Lachman, 1988; Schecter, 2006; Shane, 2006) offer similar explanations of female inhibition of ambition. Lachman, for example, emphasizes that girls and women often suffer from conflicts between attachments and ambitions. For many girls, these authors argue, ambitions and aggression threaten object ties and closeness and raise the specter of object loss. This is so because of the different patterns of object relationships for girls versus boys in development (Chodorow 1978). Because in the typical patterns of family constellations, girls must separate from the same sexed object – the mothers, they are more susceptible to struggling with issues around separation. At the same time, as documented in clinical and sociological research, they tend to value relationships and closeness more than boys. These needs and related conflicts about closeness with their mothers then shape later triangular (oedipal/persephonal) relationships, so that worries about separation add anxiety and guilt to feelings of competition with their mothers (Kulish and Holtzman, 2008).

Moreover, girls typically handle aggression differently from boys (Holtzman and Kulish 2003). For females, aggression is not socially sanctioned and often pathologized so that they must find different, perhaps more indirect or veiled means of its expression. For example, typical female defenses against aggressions are to become manipulative or to turn the aggression upon the self. Thus, ambitions for power or rank can become unconsciously disguised or even disavowed.

This brings us back to the definition of ambition, which rests on the sense of agency. I would underscore the importance of the sense of agency in actualizing ambition. To have the will or the desire to succeed, one must first own up to one's desires, and have a sense of agency over making them happen. The sense of agency entails the conscious will to act, as well as underlying unconscious conflicts, fantasies and narratives. And here lies a recurring problem in many of the women I see clinically. Their sense of agency is inhibited for many reasons, including the major factors cited above. "Oedipal" or triangular issues are frequently involved. Girls and women come to fear their competitive feelings toward their mother, as they fear their mother's disapproval and the loss of the caretaker on whom they depend. Thus, a common defensive outcome of such conflict is to abrogate their ownership of their desire or will. Elise (2012) describes inhibitions in the sense of agency in women that take the form of masochistic surrender as a result of the narcissistic injuries in the triangular, oedipal phase. This "laying low" becomes an unconscious defense, a characterological way of meeting the world.

And when we speak of the will to succeed, we need to specify succeed at what. Women may not have the will or desire for success in the business world, for example, but want to achieve in the *domestic* realm – to bake the best cherry pie; or, to catch a good husband. I once had a patient whose mother arduously sewed a new wardrobe for her before she set off to college so that she might find a suitable and wealthy husband. Such desires in circumscribed areas may be allowed or encouraged, although these too may become conflicted and accrue dangerous meanings if competition with other women is a source of conflict or guilt.

Inhibitions in a sense of agency are connected with one's identifications. If there are models for a girl of people who themselves have a sense of agency and assertiveness then she may take similar attitudes into the self. Benjamin (1988) points out that it is hard for girls to acquire a sense of active subjectivity in the sexual sphere because they do not see their mothers as active subjects over their desires. What is true for sexuality may well be true for aggression and ambition. If girls and women have appropriate identifications, they are better able to own and actualize their ambitions for success in the wider world. Girls often lack internal and external models of an achieving mother who encourages and also facilitates a girl's ambitions in the outer world.

These generalizations about girls and women may or may not obtain in any given case, as theorists such as Chodorow (1994) and Harris (1997) have warned us. So, not holding too tightly to our generalizations, let us now turn to the individual case of Elizabeth. When we first meet Elizabeth we find that she is a step ahead of many young women in realizing her ambitions. She has already achieved considerable success in her career as an academic scientist. We are told also that Elizabeth had showed some spunk. In college she had rebelled and for a time not spoken to her parents, which I suspect is rather unusual in a young girl of her ethnic background. Given this evidence, Elizabeth does seem to have a sense of agency that has allowed her to get as far as she did.

But it was Elizabeth's running into trouble in achieving her goals that brought her into psychotherapy. Her ultimate goal to have her own laboratory seems to be stymied; she was told that she needed a certain number of publications to do so, but her scientific work was appropriated by the daughter of a powerful man, whose money was funding the scientific laboratory of Elizabeth's advisor. At this point, Elizabeth was not able to master this very complicated challenge and to muster the necessary aggression to stand up for herself – that is, to stand up to the people who stole her work, or who were allowing it to be stolen. When she appealed to her advisor for help and her husband and father, both scientists, for support, she was rebuffed and she became depressed.

Let us pause here. The situation in which Elizabeth found herself was akin to many obstacles that confront young women in their quests toward achieving academic and/or career goals. Many women often find themselves up against men who abuse their power through sexual harassment of their supervisees, students, advisees, or employees, or as Wrye (2006) states, through the literal abrogation of female capability or output. Many of my female patients report such incidents in their schooling or careers. These incidents often put women in impossible dilemmas; if they speak up they are unsupported or get into worse trouble. Often a male teacher or supervisor steals a female's ideas or research; here it was a powerful, influential male stealing a woman's research in the name of his daughter. Elizabeth was the victim of abuse of power and generalized corruption that involved the powerful and unscrupulous donor, his dishonest daughter, and the advisor. The advisor was complicit as his research was partially funded by this man so he coerced the patient into adding the name of the patron's daughter to her research. Her father, her husband, and her advisor – all important men in her life – told her to lie low and concentrate on doing more work, publishing more papers. That is, they told her to be a "good girl," do her homework, and not make trouble. The men ducked responsibility for their roles in the corruption by blaming the "indiscretions" on the donor's adolescent daughter. This is the same sad story of what many bright girls have faced. No wonder Elizabeth became depressed. Happily the story did not end there for Elizabeth. Luckily she found a supportive therapist who helped her find her voice and will to stand up for herself.

We might speculate that in this case we find an example of Wrye's "unconscious saboteur" which reflects the internalized voices of parents and other important figures from the past. Elizabeth may have internalized her father's unconscious anxieties about confronting authority. He told her that she was over-reaching. We are told he was a hardworking, humble man, who had worked himself to his current success from a humble background. The mother is described only as "quiet"; we do not know more about her. Surely identifications with these figures, the *humble* hard working father and the *quiet* mother represented identifications that shaped Elizabeth's own personality and her response to this crisis. She was told *to be humble and to be quiet.*

Nevertheless, it is perhaps because of her strong but conflicted assertiveness and ambition that Elizabeth did so well in her relatively short psychotherapy, which ended when she moved away from the therapist for her new and better position. Her progress reflects her own motivations to overcome her inhibitions and what appears to be good and thoughtful work by her therapist, as well.

The therapist wonders about her wish to step in and actively help Elizabeth in this situation – to speak up on her behalf. It is not surprising that a therapist would feel this way. This countertransferencial need to help is in response to the patient's need for support, in lieu of a silent mother and non-supporting father. I would argue that someone had to step in somehow, if not directly, then at least more quietly and indirectly with a sense of understanding and acknowledgement that Elizabeth was in the position of a victim. This pull is similar to the therapeutic situation in which therapists listen to female patients talk about childhood sexual abuse, or adult sexual harassment. One needs to acknowledge or, as Poland (2000) writes, "witness" the reality of the trauma before one can help the person deal with it herself. I think this therapist did just this by negotiating thoughtfully around her self-awareness of the countertransference to take the place of a parent. She was able then to guide the patient to an expert who advised her that what she was facing was indeed a serious ethical breach.

Other countertransferences may have been at play, as they usually are, when female psychotherapists or analysts try to help their female patients around problems of ambition. Surely therapists, who are themselves career women, have struggled with similar internal conflicts and have faced similar external obstacles. And as they can easily identify with their female patients, they may project their own wishes, dormant conflicts, resentments and values onto them. Or on the other hand, a therapist may back away from these areas and push the patient in the opposite direction. Male therapists too are influenced by their own conscious and unconscious biases and values about female ambition. In the early part of my career as an analyst the current theory about female development was tilted toward the idea of helping a woman sublimate and renounce her "masculine" ambitions and perhaps be satisfied with roles of wife and mother.

We are not told much about the transference in Elizabeth's therapy. (Certainly, in this short non-intensive psychotherapy there was not much opportunity to explore the transference.) In addition to the pull in the countertransference to take care of this young woman suggesting an underlying maternal transference, there are glimpses of attitudes toward the therapist that suggest that Elizabeth was yearning for a female after whom she could model herself as a married career woman. The first session began with the patient's "cheerful curiosity" about the therapist: how did she like her profession? We know that such innocuous remarks at the beginning of therapy are loaded with meaning. I wonder whether the patient was asking about how it felt to be a professional woman. Elizabeth asked another question: was it difficult to listen to patients for so many hours? Do we have here a transference, which echoes Elizabeth's childhood experience of a tired mother whose attention was hard to get or had to be shared? We learn that the cheerfulness was a thin cover for her need for help.

We can only really understand unconscious conflicts with mother, that often lie beneath inhibitions in women, through uncovering of the transference. These deeper maternal dynamics become alive in the transference–countertransference interplay. I think of a woman in analysis many years ago, a teacher who had long cherished secret ambitions to be a known writer of fiction. She had felt that her mother, a controlling and domineering woman, took over and took credit for her achievements; in reaction, she had always held herself back in her need for self-autonomy and as a secret triumph over her mother. After much work on her inhibitions in the analysis, the patient was able to write and finish several novels. However, at that point she froze and was not able to do anything further to try to get them published even though she had gotten a lot of positive feedback on them. In my countertransference I felt frustrated and had to resist the urge to push her to move forward. This was a replay of the mother/daughter situation: the patient felt I would take "credit for her writing" as a sign of the success of the analysis and she rebelled as she had always done by stifling herself.

Questions of Elizabeth's identifications and deeper conflicts with her mother as described in the literature could not be explored further in this relatively short treatment. As it was, however, Elizabeth was able to overcome her inhibitions and make very good use of the psychotherapy and the relationship with her therapist.

References

Benjamin, J. (1988). *The Bonds of Love*. New York: Pantheon Books.

Chodorow, N. J. (1978). *The Reproduction of Mothering: Psychoanalysis and the Sociology of Gender*. Berkeley, CA: University of California Press.

Chodorow, N. (1994). *Femininities Masculinities Sexualities*. Lexington, Kentucky: University Press of Kentucky.

Elise, D. (2012). Failure to thrive: Shame, inhibition, and masochistic submission in women. In *The Clinical Problem of Masochism*, eds. D. Holtzman and N. Kulish. New York: Roman & Littlefield, pp. 187–195.

Gove, P. B. (1976). *Webster's Third International Dictionary*. Springfield, MA: G & C Merriam.

Harris, A. (1997). Aggression, envy, and ambition: circulating tensions in women's psychic life. *Gender & Psychoanalysis*, 2: 291–325.

Holtzman, D. and Kulish, N. (2003). The feminization of the female oedipal complex, part 2: a reconsideration of the significance of aggression. *Journal of the American Psychoanalytic Association*, 51: 1127–1151.

Kulish, N. and Holtzman, D. (2008) *A Story of her Own. The Female Oedipus Complex Reexamined and Renamed*. New York: Jason Aronson.

Lachman, F. M. (1988). On ambition and hubris: A case study. *Progress in Self Psychology*, 3: 195–209.

Poland, W. S. (2000). The analyst's witnessing and otherness. *Journal of the American Psychoanalytic Association*, 48: 17–34.

Schecter, R. A. (2006). The universal nature of gender subjectivity and unconscious saboteurs: A discussion of Harriet Kimble Wrye's paper "Deconstructing the unconscious saboteur: Composing a life with ambition and desire." *International Forum of Psychoanalysis*, 15: 81–84.

Shane, E. (2006). Girls, their fathers, and their mothers: Patterned links to ambition and prohibition in women. *International Forum of Psychoanalysis*, 15: 99–108.

Wrye, H. K. (2006). Deconstructing the unconscious saboteur: Composing a life with ambition and desire. *International Forum of Psychoanalysis*, 15: 70–80.

10

ELIZABETH

Appropriated ambition … a narrative

Dionne Powell

Elizabeth's story, shared by her therapist, draws our attention to multiple themes from the basic to the most complex. In this chapter I will share both personal and clinical perspectives regarding ambition and women, with emphasis on the unique challenges for minority women whose stories are often excluded in the literature. Not only are women like Elizabeth trying to break through 'glass ceilings,' but they often are striving forward on foundations built from hard fought efforts for achievement that precipitously turns to quicksand. Similar to many minority women, Elizabeth is not the queen of her own castle, or in this case, her lab and career. As a minority woman her position and title are abruptly stripped away as she is reduced to 'the help,' in the service of a young white woman who has not paid her academic dues but profits from her wealthy Russian father. These themes of opportunities lost, and ambitions derailed are frequent in my clinical work with women. This tenuousness of place and belonging requires appreciation and acknowledgment by the treating clinician for all women, but particularly women of minority ethnic, racial, religious affiliations or gender preference. There continues to be an uneven playing field that is more uneven the further you are from white male hetero-normative archetypes.

Elizabeth's story reminds me of my own, and the lengths and depths that women will travel to recognize, and to be recognized for, their full potential, along with the 'compromises' they are pressured to 'accept' both internally and externally. Early in my psychoanalytic training I excitedly attended the winter meetings of the American Psychoanalytic Association at the Waldorf Astoria hotel. I was enthralled by a particular panel presentation in the Vanderbilt ballroom. Wanting to continue the conversation, but feeling too naïve and intimidated to approach the microphone, I lingered behind hoping to have an opportunity to ask my question to the panelists. As the presenters continued speaking to each other and members of the audience I followed them into the lobby; having rehearsed my question, it was finally my moment to act. With my nascent analytic ambition, curiosity and desire taking the lead I walked, unaware in my determination, right into the men's restroom off the lobby of the Waldorf Astoria hotel. Quickly recognizing that I had crossed an implicit boundary made manifest, this experience captures the boundaries that women face whether in the boardroom, the conference hall, the laboratory or the restroom, where women are ambivalently tolerated, explicitly and subtly prevented to venture. Elizabeth's story exposes us to the barriers and obstacles to being the subject of our own stories, especially when our ambition is far beyond societal expectations based on gender and racial stereotypes. Despite tremendous advances these biases are most entrenched at the highest levels of achievement: a woman scientist with her own lab, a woman chair of a university psychiatry department, or a woman president of the United States.

Elizabeth draws on several overlapping themes that center on women's ambition and require further exploration:

1. Ambition for selfhood, struggle for subjectivity.
2. Ambition to be treated equally like the others (men) in Elizabeth's life.
3. The author's ambition to narrate a story of Elizabeth's ambition, not ensnaring the reader by privileging the objectified roles of 'mother' or 'wife.'
4. Ambitions denied: Elizabeth's 'forced' return to maternal identifications.
5. Ambition to free herself from the immigrant's fate of passive submission, remaining silent in the face of injustice and unethical treatment.
6. Women to women: How do we speak to our ambition within the patient–therapist interaction?

Schafer speaks to the multiple narratives that our patients bring, that are discovered and constructed during the course of treatment (Schafer, 1983). The author shares a particular narrative about Elizabeth to the reader. We discover at the outset that Elizabeth is a highly accomplished, intelligent, attractive and capable scientist who disarmingly conceals any signs of pain, discomfort or distress. The emotional landscape of expressed ambition, anger or pain in the professional world, continues to be verboten for women. Thus when her female therapist inquires 'how can I help,' we are not surprised at the affects expressed, allowing with this abreaction for an exploratory process to begin. That simple question seemed woefully absent from Elizabeth's major supports in her chosen profession: her advisor, husband, lab director and father. Elizabeth was abandoned by those who shared her ambition, with the only common feature to their neglect being their gender (male), and perhaps their race (white). Did these features contribute to their inability to empathize with Elizabeth's predicament?

Jessica Benjamin has described the complex journey of women finding their own subjectivity in her book *The Bonds of Love*. Particularly relevant to Elizabeth is her chapter on 'Women's Desire' (Benjamin, 1988, pp. 85–131). Benjamin's opening paragraph to this chapter captures the essence of Elizabeth's dilemma:

The discussion of erotic domination has shown how the breakdown of the tension between assertion and recognition becomes associated with the polarization of gender identity. Male and female each adopt one side of an interlocking whole. This one sided character of differentiation evolves in response to the mother's lack of subjectivity, with which the girl identifies and the boy disidentifies.

(Benjamin, 1988, p. 85)

While Elizabeth is in a similar field as her father and the exact field of her husband the crisis that Elizabeth confronts, alone, exposes the boundary between her and her male colleagues. That her academic integrity and pursuits can be so summarily dismissed as though her research was never hers to 'own' speaks to her male supporters' inability to empathically engage across gender lines. At this moment of crisis she becomes objectified not as a scientist who was plagiarized, but as if she is a betrayed spouse who needs to get over her husband's cheating ways, because 'these things happen.'

At the time of this writing the United States was in the midst of one of the most vitriolic election cycles of modern memory. Awakened in women throughout the country, if not the world, are the various injustices and corruption of power against women politically, sexually and professionally (Healy, 2016). The Presidential election served as an illuminating study of women's desires, and their various subjectivities. While many women were supportive and identified with Hillary Clinton's strides toward the highest office in the free world, others were equally repelled by the notion that a woman would be our leader, with the frequent objection to her presidency being: 'yes, we want a woman president, but not this woman!' Unlike any other democratic process of modern history this election dynamically captures the challenges women face with how their ambition, desire, intelligence and strides for achievement are experienced by men and women in modern society. It is a complex situation, indeed.

Accepting the familiar immigrant promise of success coming from hard work, and having her father as a professional role model, Elizabeth pursues with vigor and passion the best in education. Elizabeth accepts and believes in the idea that she can write her own story. However even the immigrant story as primarily told is a particularly patriarchal one, similar to those who aspire to become President of the United States.

Throughout my career I have worked with women like Elizabeth at various stages of achieving academic or professional success, experiencing major reversals, often being blamed, along with self-blame, for their downfall. Sudden reversals of ambition can have severe psychological consequences. I can personally recall (echoed by several of my female patients) family members sympathetically stating: 'I'm glad you're smart because you'll never get married and have children.' For a young brown-skinned girl, in a family that privileged the lighter-skinned girls and women, these words were a double assault. If I failed in my academic pursuits I was less smart and deserving of my downfall due to my hubris. Embedded in my failure was the opportunity for empathic resonance with other female family members who had jobs supporting their families, but not careers. While if academically or professionally successful I could not have a partner and children, too. My academic success would be my sole comfort. Otherwise I would have acquired too much, far beyond what is expected and acceptable for an African American woman from limited means. Most women who have gone beyond familial, societal and cultural expectations have a similar narrative of what one can rightfully claim as a professional, career or academic woman. I include in this category those women who have established their own businesses or used a given skill or gift for advancement. These unexplored narratives can become fertile ground to an academic acquiescence, or suspension of ambition, based on feelings of guilt and being an imposter to your 'true nature' as a woman. Thus Elizabeth's specific story becomes a relatable theme for most women. These challenges are wrenchingly depicted by Niamey Wilson (2017), a surgeon, in the book *The Status of Women*.

Women's identification with men while climbing the aspirational ladder, a type of modeling due to the paucity of women in their chosen field, can prove harmful when a woman needs to ask for help and the familiar casual arenas where men make these requests are closed off to women (men's room, pub, golf course, sporting events, locker room). These hidden borders can quickly derail a woman's career, as my patient Michelle experienced. Michelle a woman who had reached the apex of her global company dominated by men found herself unable to seek help from her superiors when her marriage fell apart. Michelle's identification with her father's success, both during and after divorcing Michelle's mother, provided a framework that she emulated and ultimately led to her professional demise. For Michelle asking for help, a brief leave of absence was experienced by her as a demonstration of 'weakness' to be avoided at all costs. Michelle quit the company instead of receiving the assistance that in retrospect would have been freely given based on the quality of her work, if she had only asked.

Like Elizabeth and Michelle, women's attempts to be a silent team player in their professional lives, accompanied by their strong paternal identification, contribute to a closeting of maternal attributes, such as asking for help, seeking advice and nurturance. These restrictions are further enforced in fields and professions where there are few female mentors. To seek out help and demands of justice continue to be experienced negatively when women speak up in predominantly male fields.

Elizabeth's narrative suggests that her lab director was passively encouraging Elizabeth to accept the Russian investor's daughter's plagiarism. The lab director's *bartering for dollars* at Elizabeth's expense is similar to the dowry, of payment as relief from removing a female child from the paternal nest. As Hillary Clinton referenced at the third 2016 presidential debate, this form of devaluation 'women are very familiar with' (October 19, 2016). Unfortunately men are very familiar with this too, and are silent conspirators, thus no outcry from other members of the lab, including her husband.

The absurdity of the request starkly uncovers the devaluation by the lab director of his minority female scientist. One suspects if this was a white male, the lab director would never place him in this compromised situation, and would find a creative mechanism to involve the investor's daughter without plagiarizing any-one's work. At that moment of Elizabeth's 'agreement to go along with the ruse' no one could appreciate or empathize with her ambivalence or with her academic sacrifice. This sacrifice by Elizabeth, from the perspective of the men in her life, became a part of the larger pantheon of sacrifices that women make, and therefore normative, an allegiance to the accepted *passivity* of women. From lab director, to advisor, father or husband, all felt Elizabeth should 'go along,' without apparent reflection or insight. At that moment race and gender were sacrificed for financial gain. Elizabeth's hard fought self-esteem, based on her considerable academic gifts and accomplishments in a predominantly male world, was suddenly reduced to the level of her devalued mother. Elizabeth no longer was the subject of her own life. She was being extruded from the men's room!

Elizabeth's crisis speaks to the precariousness both of her academic position as a woman, and the tenuous bond of those men purportedly available to protect her interests as embodying the larger academic institution. If rape is an outgrowth of power and control, how do we experience Elizabeth's crisis as other than the rape of her intellectual property? Although we can consider the Russian father's and daughter's behavior appalling, the devastation to Elizabeth's subjectivity culminat-ing in her inability to think and fears of going mad were the result of the more intimate crime of her supporters. Elizabeth was no longer an equal amongst her peers, precipitously reduced to her mother's position, a position without a voice that she had striven hard to escape.

Benjamin describes the girl's identification with father beginning in the pre-Oedipal phase as a means of separation from the maternal stronghold. Traditionally it is the father who goes out into the world and has adventures that children of both genders emulate. Elizabeth's having followed a similar field as her father is further reinforcement to her striving for independence in spite of being an immi-grant, a minority, and a woman. Finally as an academician the act of writing becomes another signifier to Elizabeth's subjectivity and identity. In academia 'publish or perish' is the assured path to academic success. Thus for Elizabeth adding someone's name, plagiarizing her own work to credit someone who had no part in its creation, is anathema to the field. This is not one of those 'things (that) happen.' Elizabeth acquiescing becomes a self-betrayal to her own legitimacy. This type of behavior, or to use a phrase from the recent 2016 presidential election, passive submission to *locker room talk*, reduces Elizabeth to an expendable object. The scene of the crime, in this instance the research lab, is highly variable but the objectification of women is uniquely recognizable regardless of the locale of the offense.

Elizabeth's treatment: rediscovering self

The therapist's (author's) role is remarkable for her struggle to define her function for Elizabeth: to remain her therapist, and not attempt to compensate for the lack of support by the men in Elizabeth's life by providing advice. Patients like Elizabeth challenge the woman therapist's own ambitions to have a fulfilling professional academic life. It can often become complicated. Jocelyn, a tirelessly hardworking master negotiator, with advanced degrees, had secured her position at a major financial institution. While at home she struggled to find her voice, acquiescing to her husband's bullying to the point that her middle school children began to wonder: 'Mom what is your opinion. Do you have anything to say that's separate from Dad? What do *you* want, Mom?' The questions her children were asking were similar to my own, reflecting the disjuncture between her professional and domestic worlds. Attempting to discover Jocelyn's authentic self and desires became the basis of treatment. Guilt and shame surrounding ambitions in the work place, frequently lead to the surrender of the same woman's voice of authority at home. This compromise can lead to challenges at work and home as each aspect of self becomes rigidly concretized, as each reflects a false polarized self.

By the therapist clearly defining her role, Elizabeth could remain the subject and not a victim that the therapist must rescue. Seeking separate consultation on the ethical and professional violation created a protective layer for the treatment to unfold so Elizabeth and her therapist could explore the numerous self and relationship challenges that this crisis simultaneously illuminated.

As importantly the therapist kept the focus on Elizabeth's crisis of subjectivity; not as a wife or mother or daughter, but as a scientist who felt manipulated and coerced to submit to male authority figures. There remains a professional misperception that a woman's ambition takes her away from her *rightful* place at home tending to her children and spouse. That one's career is secondary to domestic gender roles. This binary becomes an added pressure for women that are less evident for men. Essentially if women choose to follow their ambitions they have to prove that they can effectively keep one foot in both places, home and work. The challenge that women, like Elizabeth, face is one that forces them to choose between a maternal response, therefore being accommodating and potentially losing professional stature, or standing one's ground, a stereotypically male response, and bearing the derogatory wrath from co-workers. There is potential loss regardless of the choice. Negotiating and illuminating these dilemmas is pivotal in working through the paralytic stalemate which our patients present.

As Benjamin points out the male and female child is drawn to the father, traditionally as the one who goes out into the world and has adventures. In addition the paternal presence disrupts and allows triadic relationships, as the child advances developmentally toward greater independence. Therefore Elizabeth's continued identification with her father, a fellow academician, is not surprising considering the lure of his success and relative aloofness in Elizabeth's life. Who would not choose to explore the desires of the mind freed from the demands of domestic life?

Elizabeth's yearning to follow the path of her father who is successful, brilliant and yet remote and mysterious is similar to several of my professionally successful female patients, including Michelle that I described earlier. However in both Elizabeth's and Michelle's situation when they needed the support of male figures, especially their fathers, there was a sharp abandonment. By the time Michelle entered a four times per week analysis, unemployed and divorced, she no longer trusted the functioning of her own mind, insisting that I recite verbatim comments made during previous sessions to validate what was real in her own mind. Elizabeth's and Michelle's fears of losing their minds followed the loss of support and their objectification by their male supporters. Elizabeth's therapist provides a framework that Elizabeth can recognize and give voice to her desire and ambition to no longer be under the shadow of her father, lab director, advisor and husband. Similarly with Michelle as she reclaimed the veracity of her own mind, she became less reliant on me as the arbiter of 'reality.' Both women felt less as if they were losing their mind the more they were able to find their voice and reclaim their subjectivity.

This rediscovery of Elizabeth's voice concomitantly brought meaning back to her early adolescent rebellion as an opposing dynamic to her fascination with the Russian teenager and Tiger Mom's daughter, allowing Elizabeth to re-experience the freedom she established earlier in her youth as contrasted by these two young women who are heavily influenced by their parents. What initially was a source of envy, the strength of parental involvement in both the Russian father and Tiger Mom, became a pivotal point of pride in her independence in being able to speak her mind. Working through and separating out her ambitions and desires, along with her complicated ambivalent feelings regarding parental and gender roles, led to Elizabeth's successful statement of her needs.

As a minority woman Elizabeth had been accustomed to 'flying under the radar,' in the shadows of her famous father in a field close to her own. The need to shrink in the face of male competition is familiar to most women, but especially evident with women of color due to latent and overt racial and ethnic discrimination. bell hooks' book *Ain't I a Woman* explores the near total erasure of African American woman in the pursuit of social justice and civil rights in American history (hooks, 1981). hooks captures the tension that minority women face, being excluded as primary figures in both the struggle for civil rights and women's rights. Similar to the history of civil rights in this country, the roles of African American women and other women of color in the history of women's rights have been excluded from history. However the tentacles of racism and sexism continue to affect modern society, especially for minority women.

For those who supported the plagiarizing of Elizabeth's research, there is an implicit bias that the desires and pursuit of a Russian teenager are equivalent to those of a PhD female, minority researcher. As best exemplified by the Russian father's words: 'How could you make a big deal out of this, you know what it's like to be a minority and try to get ahead in this country!' Clearly this wealthy father of economic privilege is emphasizing how Elizabeth, as a minority woman, should automatically provide room for his daughter. That Elizabeth remains a second class citizen despite her academic credentials. The withering effects of these flagrant devaluations toward minority women remain a common occurrence in the professional community.

Increasingly women in science and the professional ranks are finding their voice. As Elizabeth found hers through treatment she was able to appreciate how she undervalued her own career by not speaking up, placing everyone's aspirations before her own. In finding her voice Elizabeth could now speak to her ambitions and a desire for a lab of her own. This was made very evident in my psychiatry residency at Cornell Payne Whitney Clinic. As one of the few minority residents and the only African American in all four years of my training I was asked by our residency director to apply for a minority fellowship. As I discussed the possible opportunities of applying for the fellowship I wanted to ensure that if awarded I would be able to use some of the financial award to support having an African American supervisor for my psychotherapy patients. This, I believed, would be an important adjunct to my education, as I had taken an extensive course in Black Psychology while in medical school at the undergraduate university. The fellowship was intended to support a minority resident in their training. When told 'no' that if I were to secure this fellowship I could only use the funds to create a course on diversity for the other residents I decided not to apply. This was not the response my residency director expected, but like Elizabeth, my education was not subject to a form of bartering where I would be compromised as a result. Speaking up and leaning into the discomfort of not going along with racial or gender bias is a chronic challenge for women, especially ethnic and racial minorities, to be considered and treated fairly. As therapists we need to assess our own biases when working with women from traditionally underrepresented and discriminated minority groups. Only then can we help minority women become the subject of their stories, and fully and equally contribute their tremendous talents to their professional careers.

References

Benjamin, J. (1988). *The Bonds of Love. Psychoanalysis, feminism and the problem of domination.* New York, NY: Pantheon Books.

Healy, J. (2016). She never spoke of it to her husband. Then she heard the Trump tape. *New York Times*, October 21.

hooks, b. (1981). *Ain't I a Woman. Black women and feminism.* Boston, MA: South End Press.

Schafer, R. (1983). Narration in the Psychoanalytic Dialogue. In *The Analytic Attitude*, pp. 212–239. London: Basic Books.

Wilson, N.P. (2017). A woman surgeon: her story. In V. Pender (Ed.), *The Status of Women. Violence, identity and activism*, pp. 1–14. London: Karnac Books.

PART III

Leadership

11

LEADERSHIP AND WOMEN

Opportunity mobilized

Stephanie Brody

A new wave

My mother was wistful as she told me how much she loved to run, moving fast on the green grass. She remembered the long expanse of lawn, the feeling she had of play, of running with her brothers, 90 years ago. I can see her in my mind's eye, her thick dark curls and rosy cheeks. My mother, sandwiched between two brothers and many cousins, did not recoil from effort and athletics. She could swim in Sheepshead Bay in the summer, and chase down the neighborhood kids who called her names. She knew she would be an artist as a child, remembering the pleasure in drawing that was already taking hold. Her talent was exceptional. Her idyllic youth, untouched by the Depression, was disrupted suddenly by the death of her father and the war. Though my mother loved to paint, she attended an art school that would prepare her for employment. Commercial artwork offered security and my mother's natural creative talent, design skills, and graphic sensibility made the transition to advertising an obvious choice. Throughout the war, she worked, finding her place in a man's world, increasingly relied upon for her excellence and reliability. She and my father settled in suburban New York and both commuted on a daily basis. Unlike many mothers of the 1950s and 1960s, my mother was employed outside of the home. She went to her advertising job on a daily basis, juggling the responsibilities of a family with her demanding job.

I knew no other experience. Though I missed my mother, I was very proud of her. She was different from the other mothers. When my grandmother became ill and could no longer care for us, my mother trusted that we could manage the afternoons on our own. My sisters and I learned self-sufficiency, relying on each other, with ongoing communications to my mother's New York workplace. She was given some flexibility and two days a week, worked from home on a large flat table where tracing paper, pads, triangles, rulers, pencils and special erasers were laid. Off to the side, there was an easel with an oil painting in progress, a portrait, landscape or abstract.

The large block size New York City department store where my mother was art director became a landing place of sorts for me, an iconic center of gravity as I learned to navigate through the urban landscape. The open loft space overlooking Madison Avenue was my mother's office, an area never seen by the shoppers. There, my mother managed a group of young employees: setting type, creating fashion layouts and drawings, designing, correcting, setting in motion the advertisements for print media. As the art director, her creative vision would be plastered over every advertisement, newspaper, catalogue and sign. Her imprint was all over the store. In the bustling Manhattan crowds, I would see the shopping bags that my mother designed. Her handwriting was the logo of the store, as familiar to me as if she had personally set her pen to every ad. Her reach was broad. To me it seemed she was all over the city.

Despite her creative impact, occasionally she would voice frustration. When the Mad Men series arrived on mainstream television, she viewed it as an accurate representation of the New York advertising world. Though she never claimed personal harassment, her authority was often subjected to managerial incursions; always men, they co-opted her ideas as their own, crediting her for the execution, but not the creative genius. When she reported these moments to me, I was outraged. But my mother did not feel it would be wise to undercut someone specifically, and seemed to find consolation from an unshakable self-confidence; a conviction that she had always been the most talented creative artist in any setting, with any group of men and women. This seemed unfair to me, and I often urged her to be combative, to resist. She demurred.

In the department store world, she had escaped the intensity of the advertising agency culture. Her male counterparts, the ones who had attended art school with her, ran the agencies that she had foreclosed so she could have a family. Being female, and in department store advertising meant that her salary did not come close to that of her male counterparts, but it was a compromise she was willing to accept. Her staff adored her, and she mentored young female college graduates, though many of them came to her with few credentials besides intelligence and a desire to learn. She enjoyed teaching them the trade. They were loyal. On her platform she was a dominant force, highly respected, always in control of her product and the people who implemented her orders and creative ideas. I think of her now, as we write this book on women, and I wonder about where her talent could have led her if she had been born in my generation, how far she would have run along the great green expanse of career potential.

As we turn now, to the question of women and leadership in 2018, we look back in our American history, to present times, and wonder if the gains that were taken for granted in 2016 were that secure. The 19th Amendment to the US Constitution, a woman's right to vote, was ratified in 1920, three years before my mother's birth. Only another 35 years had passed before the baby boom. In that period, though women could be elected to higher office, representation of women in Congress did not reflect the population of women. Gender stereotypes in post-World War II America held sway, followed by protests of the 1960s. Birth control, Roe v. Wade, and sexual freedom seemed to reflect a growing respect for the rights of women to make their own choices. The expectation that women would be "stay at home" moms was replaced by other goals: work-life balance, "having it all" and "leaning in." Though in some sectors, it looked like women could find entry into new spaces, large swaths of women were left out. Sensitivity to issues of race, class, gender, education and politics exposed painful realities regarding embedded bias and privilege.

The expectation of a female President was followed by the ascendency of a television personality/salesman to the country's highest office. Whatever one's political alliance, now it is next to impossible to avoid the persistence of disrupting information and the intensity of a divide. My generation is sandwiched between the aspirations of our mothers, the second wave of feminism and the efforts of the third wavers, a confusing mix of generational differences and diversity galvanized by the impact of political forces and an unexpected disorder of the norm. The post-election reality is about resistance: waves of protest that reflect a rising up, of voices, of numbers and of action. Taking to the streets, grass roots movements reveal a willingness to act, to seize the airwaves, the podiums and the ballot boxes. Running for election, defying stereotypes of age, gender, race and class, women seem empowered. At first it was the Women's March, then #MeToo and Time's Up. Adolescents responding to school shootings became a force to be reckoned with, wielding power that arrives unbidden, when the dodged bullet defines the fragility and gift of life. Bystanders have turned into activists. Former activists are activists once more, marching with grandchildren who have the sudden influence derived from the power of the vote. Alongside the declarative voices, insistent on change, there are the voices of denial, dismissal and denigration. No one, on either side of the increasingly divided field, has been immune. Difference has turned into "other," and we are each confronted with the painful realities of our divisions, our privilege and our failures. If there is excitement in the intensity of protest there is also a sense of danger. Our threat antennas crackle when the danger that we feel tells us that the storm is already upon us. Now we must calculate how to survive without too much damage. It is easy to wonder about the "what ifs." What would it be like to live in a world that *had* elected its first female president? It is an interesting challenge to consider how the election of a woman might have triggered a change, in how women are viewed, in how power is distributed, in how women exert their presence when legitimized with the authority of the Constitution. And yet, there is a profound irony in this surge of activism: would women have been so mobilized if the election had gone the other way?

As I write this chapter, it is important for me to share this disclaimer: I do not regard myself to be a leader, not in the terms that define leadership to me. In point of fact, it is my preference to avoid leadership roles: governance and by laws have no appeal, and I do not relish political dynamics or situations where there are fights for power; I have not been a part of corporate hierarchies, or government bureaucracy, managerial crises or performance evaluations. But I admit to personal fantasies that my limited platforms of writing, speaking and teaching may inspire kindred spirits to find new paths for the beliefs and convictions that I hold dear. In this way, I do not believe I am alone in this alternative version of leadership aspiration: the wish to have an impact, or to inspire others, in small but meaningful ways.

And in the privacy of my consulting room, women share their stories of desire, ambition and leadership – their big ideas and germinating wishes. They dream: of being center stage, the important person who commands attention and respect. They dream: of being a headliner, and game changer in the close quarters of their universe. They dream: of finding others who also need to make a difference. And they question and struggle. Are the goals they seek grandiose dreams, compensations for emotional loss, or are they examples of courage, fortitude and persistence? And what if the wish to have an impact is a result of a personal history of denigration and despair – would the goal be any less worthy in the broad landscape of a community, social action or political arena? They seek my help to uncover the sources of their frustration and unhappiness, the fear of conflict or rejection that inhibits their freedom to represent themselves fully. They engage deeply in the therapeutic process to understand, to transform, and to change. They explore the dimensions of the intrapsychic and family systems. But their pragmatic and cynical observations convey the significant reach of the external context: of gender bias, discrimination, conflict and exclusion. No exploration of unconscious processes can foreclose the existence of concrete examples of suppression. Inequities represented in salary disparity and promotional disadvantage remain present in the larger world, in medical settings, business, academics and service industries. Workplace safety remains an issue, with ongoing complaints of harassment. Unfair practices and workplace abuse remain a significant factor, and in too many settings, power is wielded in the form of threats and belittlement – effected through shaming tactics, indifference, or threat of termination. Though many women speak aspirationally, about the roles they may take to exert impact, they are still having problems attaining positions of power. They do not often express optimism regarding roles in public places.

More recently, the atmosphere in my consulting room has taken on a new turbulence. The political climate has become a platform for personal history. Memories of bullies and harassers intersect with news stories of domestic abuse and disparagement of individuals based on gender or nationality. Facts discredited, liars rewarded, are all reminders of the past, and trigger anger, helplessness and, at times, a wish to withdraw. Relationship conflict, family dynamics and parenting challenges are fraught with past conflicts, compromises and fear of loss. Finding love remains central, a universal longing. Clinical hours are spent trying to tackle the unsettling meaning of the world, as we now know it. Though I have been privy to powerful achievements and leadership stories, there remain painful impediments. Too often, the path to safety is riddled with foreclosures of opportunity. For women who wish to lead, for those who have the need to stay quiet, and for those who think about leading for the first time, it has not been easy to disentangle the present from the past, or if that kind of deconstruction is even possible in these times.

In training sites, discussions regarding the relevance of external events and the impact on clinical work are ongoing. Questions about analytic identity attach to debates about the clinical relevance of current events that intrude, sometimes daily, into the clinical dyad. Clinicians find themselves on opposite corners, not just divided by theoretical orientation, but by politics. Within this environment, where the free press is under attack, climate change is dismissed, immigrant families are separated, and dictators are praised, does a discussion of leadership and women matter? Would it make a difference if a woman were to have the biggest voice at the table, to set the agenda, to assume authority? To write a chapter on the topic of women and leadership remains a challenging task. Each time words are set down, new events transpire. My content reflects an effort to corral my wishes, my fears for the future and my hope for change. It has been hard to get words on the page, to assess what is useful, or what is relevant. Time passes. When the idea for this book was proposed, the world was a different place. Or was it?

Women's leadership in psychoanalysis: absence

In the context of psychoanalysis, perhaps it should not be a surprise to discover that our research into leadership in our library of analytic theory bore little scholarly fruit. A search of Psychoanalytic Electronic Publications (pep-web) provided few articles in which the words "women" and "leadership" were connected meaningfully. Believing that our poor yield was due to limited reference skills, we enlisted the assistance of the librarian[1] at our Institute who seems (always) to be able to locate anything we need. She too came up with a painfully small number of references[2] and one, very odd item: a letter donated to the Boston Psychoanalytic Society and Institute archive from 1968.

It documents a correspondence that took place between Ruth Grossman, a Boston social worker, and D.W. Winnicott. Ms. Grossman makes an inquiry about several papers[3] she has read where Winnicott suggests that (her words): "both men and women hesitate to vote women into positions of power because we have been helpless at the hands of a powerful mother" (Winnicott and Grossman, n.d., letters/donation description, 1968). Intrigued, Grossman sent Winnicott a letter, inquiring if he might provide some thoughts about Golda Meir. Winnicott wrote back, stating, somewhat surprisingly, that he "seemed not to have heard of her." Grossman reminds Winnicott that Meir is the newly elected, female Prime Minister of Israel. Winnicott responds to Grossman in a second letter, and provides this description of Meir: "she has come right through womanhood and come out the other end practically a man. I shudder ... a woman who is a man could be ruthless in some special sort of way" (Winnicott and Grossman, n.d., letters, 1968). In these letters, Winnicott seems to be citing himself from an obscure paper: "Some Thoughts on the Meaning of Democracy" (Winnicott, 1950/2017, p. 416).[4]

Within a list of topics that Winnicott himself questions his authority to consider (e. g. the definition of democracy, the secret vote, creation of a democratic society) is a subtitle: *Person – Man or Woman*. Noting that women occupy increasingly responsible posts in government, Winnicott asserts that it is only men who will be elected into leadership roles. He hypothesizes that an unconscious process is at work. Returning to the earliest parent child relationship, Winnicott describes the "double dependency" (ibid., p. 416) factor that exists for all children and leads to a universal fear of women: though all healthy individuals require the mother for survival, this "dependence" has a double edge. The mother's loving devotion imposes an ironic irreconcilable "debt" onto her child: a humiliating awareness, unconsciously embedded, that survival is dependent on a mother. "The original dependence is not remembered, and therefore the debt is not acknowledged, except in so far as the fear of *woman* represents the first stage of this acknowledgement" (ibid., p. 416). The mother's love and devotion is received and transformed in the mind of the child and becomes cemented into the unconscious with a veil of paranoia. Processed as an ongoing threat, Winnicott argues that the need to disavow the dependency, shame and vulnerability leads to a widespread mistrust of *all* women, whether they assert influence politically or not. The reason is simple: when women wield power, the earliest experience of helplessness is revived. . Symbolically then, all women are mothers who are not only capable of exerting power, but would do so in a form that would control and enfeeble. Winnicott regarded this reaction to women as a "universal fear of domination" by the "all-powerful woman of fantasy" (ibid., p. 417). Cruelty towards and bias against women is regarded as a "powerful agent in society structure" (ibid., p. 416) and sounds like an explanation for and justification of misogyny, though Winnicott never uses the word. He even goes so far as to conclude that the rise of dictators originates from this inextinguishable universal fantasy: were women to have power, they would wield it without love and therefore, must be controlled. The dictator is empowered by the "compulsion to deal with this fear of women" (ibid., p. 417,). That followers (voters?) may:

> accept or even seek *actual* domination is derived from a fear of domination by *fantasy woman*. This fear leads them to seek, and even welcome, domination by a known human being, especially one who has taken on himself the burden of personifying and therefore *limiting the magical qualities of the all-powerful woman of fantasy* (italics added) to whom is owed the great debt. The dictator can be overthrown, and must eventually die; but the woman figure of primitive unconscious fantasy has no limits to her existence or power.
>
> *(Ibid., p. 417)*

According to Winnicott, we are all helpless because we have all been mothered. Our helplessness does not produce comfort, soothing, or satiation of hungers. We are not bathed in the wellbeing of security. Rather, we are in the grips of a malevolent mother who will withhold; a mother who embodies danger, and threatens victimization because she alone has the power to maintain survival – a woman who can control whether you live or die. In this archived letter, every woman has the potential to be regarded as the *bad* mother, especially if, in other contexts, she expresses symptoms of her power. If a woman aspires to leadership, has ideas that might shape the future or seeks authority, she is suspect. Generalized to all women, the universal unconscious memory of being mothered exerts an inextinguishable negative impact. It is a reason for the gender disparities that encumber all women. Winnicott was not alone in his idea. Chasseguet-Smirgel (1976) voices a similar argument: the denigration of women by men is necessary to manage the inadequacy and helplessness activated in early male sexual development (ibid., p. 283).[5] Riviere also described women's need to masquerade their power in order to avoid the intensification of male insecurities (Riviere, 1926).

Though Winnicott notes a "first stage of acknowledgement" (Winnicott, 1950, p. 416) for this "inevitable" fear, he offers no second stage, or ideas regarding the fallacy of this belief. Nor does he offer a possibility that maturity results in an alteration of this unconscious misperception. Nor does he argue that this is a myth. He does not suggest that this belief is *a developmental problem that will be outgrown, or a fixation that requires clinical attention.* Only in his paper, "This Feminism," does Winnicott state that "the awkward fact remains, for men and women, that each was once dependent on woman, and somehow a hatred of this has to be trans-formed into a kind of gratitude if full maturity of the personality is to be reached" (Winnicott, 1964/2017b, p. 110). It is still unclear how Winnicott believes we will reach this gratitude for the mother's role and then convert it into the acceptance of women's power and women's leadership or what happens if that developmental step is never attained. Winnicott's disclosure, his ideas about women, appear to reverse his ideas about mothers as nurturers and consolidators of developmental milestones. Instead, Winnicott seems to argue that women must be safely con-trolled. Though the natural and biological world of Winnicott's era offered few alternatives – mothers could only be women. It is clear that Winnicott thought that women should only be what nature had given women the capacity to be. Winnicott's views are an argument for sexism and though we live in times where babies can be created without the presence of a mother, and women can opt out of motherhood, Winnicott suggests that no woman can escape the negative regard if she should enter a wider sphere of influence, authority or control.

Do we need a theory to explain the rejection of women in powerful roles? May we reject Winnicott's perspective, or is there too much evidence for his claim? If Winnicott is to be believed, there is an eternal phenomenon that can never be altered as long as women are mothers: repetition recreates the fear of dependency and danger, activated in the parental incubator and nurtured in subsequent generations. This idea would explain the strong reaction to female leadership in politics and boardrooms, in families and relationships. Winnicott's "good enough" (Winnicott, 1953, p. 94), devoted mother, can never do enough to overcome this burden that attaches to her role. That D.W. Winnicott, an icon of psychoanalytic theory, has played a role in the creation of another, more sinister layer in the archetype of women is a disturbing revelation. But does it apply to all nations, or just to America? Does this explain why Americans could not elect a female president?

Stories of women in power

Long before Freud, Shakespeare described the roles of women, documenting his view of history and dynamics that, for many, reflect an essential cultural, political and gender tradition from Western civilization. Dame Harriet Walter, a Shakespearean actor of renown, explains that, from *The Taming of the Shrew* to the tragic figures of Juliet, Desdemona, Ophelia and Cordelia, the Bard described women in ways that continue to resonate in our consciousness: women are schemers, temptresses, sexual manipulators and victims. Even though Shakespeare wrote during the reign of the great Queen Elizabeth, his dramas placed female monarchs in precarious positions. Those who survived, even those who were smart enough to analyze the treacherous landscape, eventually ended up exiled or dead. Their leadership qualities only served to secure the legacy (or safety) of their children, or to promote the ambitions of husbands. In the dramas, women would fret over the peculiar behaviors of their beloveds, caught in the crossfire of betrayals, competition and exploitation, and though crucial, women played secondary roles. According to Walter, Shakespeare's women generally did not drive the narrative, and emerge only in the context of men. The plays, she claims, are likely to fail the Bechdel test[6] (Mead, 2015, p. 32). She notes that:

> when the greatest playwright – so considered – in the English language leaves women out of the picture so much, it has a bad effect on your sense of worth, because the culture that followed in his shadow has reinforced that. It does have an effect on us.
>
> *(Ibid., p. 32)*

Tina Packer (2015), a highly regarded expert, notes that the Bard seemed to understand the universal resistance to women in leadership roles, in the theatre and on the world stage. Packer states that: "Because women are such potent ingredients of men's imaginations, we see how much power men feel women have over them, and how women must be suppressed, defanged, or idealized in one way or another" (ibid., p. xv).

Packer has a decidedly analytic stance: the unconscious influence of fantasy leads to a curtailment of women in many walks of life. It's about the power. Packer suggests that women colonize the fantasy world of men, and like Winnicott, she believes that men find women's power intolerable. So preoccupied by a need to defeat, adore or control women, men never feel free. Even after the battle has been fought, even after victory has been declared, there is no relief.

Note the recent article in the *New York Times*, months after the 2016 election. Frank Bruni (2017) notes that Donald Trump still seems to be obsessed with

Hillary Clinton. Ongoing speeches to Boy Scouts, tweets about Benghazi or the legality of the election, continue to prove that he cannot get her out of his mind: "Trump is still hauling his vanquished opponent out for public ridicule and marching her towards the stockade". *He cannot let her go*, "desperate to keep her at the center of every page" (ibid., p. A23). Ruminating, perseverating, Trump reveals himself to the country like the boy who crushed on the girl who was out of his league, haunted by a girl who had other important tasks, who couldn't be bothered by the schoolyard bully who obviously craved love, but wasn't worthy of her attention. Unable to get her out of his mind, her presence still organizes his thinking. She is the center of his universe, and he can't help but circle her, hoping she will notice that he's still there. He is tied down by her power, and even though he defeated her, he acts like she was the dominatrix who tied him up in knots, while she was able to walk away. He cannot get over *her* defeat, knowing somewhere deep inside that she is still important to him. This is the extreme example of Winnicott's meme. The man who cannot bear that at one time, he relied on another for survival. This cannot be what happens for all men, but for women who aspire to leadership status, it cannot help to run into an obstacle like this. But this is still the phallocentric lens, the world that men fear when they imagine women in power.

Going further back, the historian Mary Beard (2017) notes that the voices of many women, over centuries of history, are represented in the first book of Homer's Odyssey, a 3,000-year-old poem – in one brief scene. Penelope, who has been waiting for her husband Odysseus to return, is increasingly encroached upon by suitors who co-opt her home and consume her food and wine as if they already own her. In an attempt to protect herself from the assaults of unwanted suitors, she enters the common space of her own home and tries to speak. Her son, Telemachus, himself disempowered because of his father's long absence, dismisses her. Telemachus tries to reclaim his compromised authority over other men, by asserting power over his mother. Though publicly silenced she secretly sabotages the shroud whose completion will require her to marry. Quietly, she weaves, and then undoes her work. The endlessness of her task is a protection against being acquired (but it doesn't give her space for other missions). This is a metaphor. As Mary Beard eloquently states: "we want to understand – and do something about – the fact that women even when they are not silenced, still have to pay a very high price for being heard ..." (p. 8). Homer, Shakespeare, Winnicott, and Freud's stories about women are compelling, but they are phallocentric. It is worth trying to understand and undo the cemented-in bias, but it is also important to remember that this particular representation of women is really about men: how *men* think, how *men* feel, and how *men* position women in their affective world. It is important to remember that women must contend with corrosive branding on a daily basis. Women must learn how to reject real derision, dismissal, and denigration. Women must inoculate themselves against the destructive potential that bias has on their well-being, on the freedom to think and act. Women must question rigidified expectations and stereotyped restrictions that are embedded in another's mind. But there are many examples when women refused to comply with an interpretation set by others and instead, were compelled to defy or assert an alternative plan. I have run across a number of moments like this lately and in the past, where the attempts to silence or roadblock a woman, impediments that might have led to setbacks, instead became galvanizing missions – opportunities for change and for impact. It is possible, and serves as a model for us all.

The gauntlet

Ben Barres, a neuroscientist and advocate for women in science, illustrates the point. Dr. Ben Barres was born Barbara Barres, assigned female at birth, a transgender man in his 40s. As an undergraduate MIT student, prior to transitioning, he solved a math problem that the rest of his (all male) class had been unable to solve. Bringing the solution to his professor, his work was dismissed. The professor accused Ms. Barres of lying – stating that someone else, probably a boyfriend, had come up with the solution that he was attempting to pass off as his own. Dr. Ben Barres often spoke of this moment, and reflected on the difference between being treated as a woman *and* a man. His unique experience confirmed that gender bias was high in his field. When Larry Summers, Steven Pinker, and Peter Lawrence explained that the disparity between men and women in the STEM world[7] was a result of intellectual disparities, Barres took issue, calling out the "Larry Summer's Hypothesis" as lacking credibility, wholly discriminatory, and sexist. He argued instead for the "Stephen Jay Gould Hypothesis" (Barres, 2006, p. 134):

> We pass through this world but once. Few tragedies can be more extensive than the stunting of life, few injustices deeper than the denial of an opportunity to strive or even to hope, by a limit imposed from without, but falsely identified as lying within.
>
> *(Gould, 1996, p. 50).*

It wasn't that women didn't have the intellectual talents, it was that they were being muted, and that is what needed to change. Barres stated that: "I am suspicious when those who are at an advantage proclaim that a disadvantaged group of people is innately less able. Historically, claims that disadvantaged groups are innately inferior have been based on junk science and intolerance" (Barres, 2006, p. 134). Ben Barres made it his mission to mentor female colleagues, a response to the memory of disempowerment and sexism, his experience of being a woman. "The question is not whether male or female brains are different, but why society insists on labeling male brains as better" (Genzlinger, 2017).

Kathe Kollwitz was a prolific artist of the early 20th century, the granddaughter of a radical Lutheran pastor, who was raised on social duty and egalitarianism. The death of her son in World War I turned a life of mourning into art and social activism. Her work is often described as a "testimony," not only of her life, but the ravages of war on women, on mothers and on Germany. Kollwitz depicted women as activists, breadwinners and mourners of the dead. She turned the death of her son into a memorial for all mothers who lose children. Her art was meant to incite, to stimulate public rebuke for the arrogance of war – of its fraud and idealism. Ripping off the veneer of nationalistic propaganda, she revealed the pain and grief of women in times of war, calling out the role of authorities, those who stir conflict and destruction. Reflecting on her art, Kollwitz said:

> when I was drawing I cried along with the fearful children, I felt the burden I was carrying. I felt that I could not withdraw from the task to be an advocate. I shall speak up about the suffering of people, which never ends, and which is mountainous.
>
> *(Kollwitz, 1988, p. 96)*

Among her projects, she championed abortion rights, revealed domestic abuse and alcoholism, hunger and exploitation. She became the first woman elected and appointed professor to the Prussian Arts Academy and founder and director of the Women's Art Association, until 1933, when she was forced by the Nazis to resign her post and to never again exhibit her work.

Educated at Wellesley College, Marjory Stoneman Douglas became a writer and journalist with causes that included civil rights and the environment. Though she described herself as "untutored" in environmental laws, policy and practices, she is best known for her focus on the "river of grass," her name for the Everglades (Douglas, 2017). Her exhaustive journalism for the *Miami Herald* revealed the growing efforts by commercial developers to make extinct the vast acreage of the Florida Everglades. Douglas describes a precious waterway, an irreplaceable natural environment, whose loss would be tragic. Douglas confronted corrupt powers that sought personal financial gain over the benefits of maintaining a pristine habitat, unique to the planet. Environmentalists argue that her efforts led to the restrictions that were ultimately enacted to protect the Everglades. But though she was relentless in her determination, Douglas was unable to totally weaken the dominant corporate and governmental agencies that worked to drain the land of its unique value. Yet she remained resolute. She describes her growing sense of mission:

> The Everglades were always a topic, but now they promised to become more than that. They promised to become a reason for things, a central force in my existence at the beginning of my 80th year. Perhaps it had taken me that long to figure out exactly what I was able to contribute, and for me to marshal my forces.
>
> *(Douglas, 2011, p. 224)*

On the Eastern edge of a levee that was constructed to divert the natural water flow of the "river of grass," the city of Parkland, Florida was established. On February 14, 2018, a group of activists were born, when a school shooting took the lives of 17. The students who organized on March 24, 2018 against the gun lobby probably know that their community was built on a cemented over parcel of the Everglades, and that the Marjory Stoneman Douglas High School was named to honor an advocate who could not save it all, but had to try.

Leadership and power

Though leadership often brings power, power is not always a given. This is often the case with many individuals who take up the gauntlet, who have a mission. When power is defined as the capacity through sheer influence to exclusively secure crucial impact through expertise and role designation that could not otherwise be attained by others, many women can still leave a mark. There are examples of women who have achieved a presence in areas that facilitate change – the women who did not avert their eyes[8]: social activists, research and development cogs, whistle blowers and rebels. Sometimes they operate on the margins, taking chances and living lives of unusual courage and personal loss.[9] But too often women still fail the prestige test – that is, the attainment of legitimacy, the inherent power of "unqualified devotion" and of the rule of law (Gerth and Mills, 1972, p. 172). "The sentiment of prestige is able to strengthen the ardent belief in the actual existence of one's own might" (ibid., p. 161). Too many must fight to have a place at the table. What allows an individual to pursue a goal, despite the interference, rejection, dismissal or absence of prestige – to remain fierce and full of conviction, whatever the cost? To maintain a measure of personal satisfaction and stable self-esteem in the face of sociopolitical forces and unconscious bias requires a special combination of resilience and resources that must be deeply rooted and sustainable over time.

Though women exercise power in many realms, often under the radar, they appear to encounter difficulty when they seek to have, or are given authority. To be legitimized under the rule of law, or to have the authority to control a system by popular consensus or election, has not been simple. Though many of our potential leaders (women) have established their credentials, often playing crucial roles by redesigning systems, nurturing colleagues and cultivating innovation, their numerous contributions may prove meaningless in the currency of patriarchal definitions of value. When efforts do not quickly manifest in profit margins, or there is an initial downward trend, prior history and qualifications bend toward amnesia – amnesia for previous contributions, and for overall value. Though regarded as providing backbone strength during the development process, women aspiring to leadership roles suggest that it is only in the last stages, prior to the acquisition of true leadership and power, that the ax falls – that the glass ceiling bears down, or the access disappears. A frustrating experience of "almost" there, a golden ring within reach, but never held. This is often repeated in business, academic and medical arenas, and clearly, in the political and government spheres.

It is clear that when a woman has a wish for personal gain, and wants to be in charge, she seems suspect. While some women have famously attained higher status and taken command associated with the top of the hierarchy, it is too often because powerful men who have the authority to do so have taken steps to give them entry. Madeleine Albright, Condoleezza Rice, and Hillary Clinton are given high marks for their negotiating skills and qualifications to serve as Secretaries of State. As crucial members of the team, their abilities to negotiate, to forge relationships, and to show loyalty, communicated a coherent Presidential voice, and a stable Executive Office. These women exerted an *acceptable* female presence: dependable, smart and with no wish to outdo, compete with or manipulate a boss. When authority is sanctioned, often by a legal structure, community consensus, influence or control, leadership is construed as legitimate. But sometimes power is exerted under the radar, defiant, perhaps in rejection of the rule of law. Though women are still offered unquestionable authority, within the domestic sphere, there are unquestionable limits when they try to exit, when they assert authority in the public arena – when they seek to change or raise their status (Rosaldo, 1974). If women are to be in leadership positions, do men feel they will be toppled? A recent article in the *New York Times* points out that:

> women are often seen as dependable, less often as visionary. Women tend to be less comfortable with self-promotion – and more likely to be criticized if they grab the spotlight. Men remain threatened by assertive women. Most women are not socialized to be unapologetically competitive. Some women get discouraged and drop out along the way. And many are disproportionately penalized for stumbles.
>
> *(Chira, 2017)*

The leadership identity

Another term is recommended now, to affirmatively address an egregious absence in psychoanalytic theory and process regarding women, though it may be applied to any one, of any gender or gender inclination. *Leadership identity* may be described as the ability to see oneself as capable of mobilizing internal and external resources towards a mutually valued purpose. Most importantly, it is the expression of a distinctive, competent and confident voice that is utilized to fulfill a defining personal mission. Important factors that may contribute to the acceptance of the leader's message and goals include charisma, strength, intelligence, energy and conviction. While the goal may be personal, the mission is likely far reaching, inclusive of those in the obvious territory of the leader, but capable of steering others toward additional goals of individual meaning. Leadership identity has relational force for it requires the participation of individuals who endorse, support, respect and are inspired by the woman leader, her message and her vision.

In the context of a gendered world, the postmodern female leader acquires authority by combining a personal belief in her ability, a commitment to possibility, and a willingness to assume risk. A recent conversation[10] with one of our book contributors articulates how leadership identity need not be limited to a corporate hierarchical structure or political context. Rather the leadership identity is revealed in any situation or dynamic structure in which a series of unencumbered actions may unfold: the capacity to articulate a mission fueled by passion, to seize an opportunity when it arises; to take a calculated risk, likely one that will require discomfort, even fear. But when circumstances lead to hesitation or inhibition, the individual who embodies the leadership identity will assess a potential danger through a refined capacity for self-reflection, as well as a curiosity for and perceptiveness about the external world. She will be adept in her capacity to distinguish between threats that arise from personal templates, to realistic perils that may be confronted or negotiated. She is willing to bear the unexpected, because she knows that what she fears may be not what is about to happen, but what has already occurred. She will not shy away. For the individual who embodies the leadership identity, fear cannot be an impediment because "fear is the enemy of possibility" (Brody, 2016, p. 6).

The individual who embodies the leadership identity regards "no" to be a temporary obstacle. Recognizing that there are some limits that cannot be thwarted, the individual with a fierce leadership identity acknowledges what may be impossible and finds what can be accomplished. Rejection is never final, but instead leads to the next possibility, with new information to consider, and data that will shape the next step. The individual who embodies the leadership identity is determined and fervent. The individual who embodies a leadership identity is the suffragette and birth control advocate, the poet and author of anthems. She occupies the night shift and the NICU, sterilizing lines, bathrooms and kitchens, regulating conveyor belts and product development. She is Mother Courage and the Pieta; she is #Metoo *and* Times Up and Chairman of the Board of whatever world she joins, family, classroom, medical office and factory. She has authority over her body and her self. Though she is experienced in the landscape of competition, and believes in herself as a singular force of nature, she notes the value of many who share her aims, aware that many together can bear challenges more effectively and joyfully than when alone. Henceforth, the link between power and pleasure is considered as well, as society must grapple with the meaning of influence, the experience of engaging others and the personal value that results when women aspire and inspire.

Mary Beard has written that in ancient times "a woman speaking in public was, in most circumstances, by definition not a woman" (Beard, 2017, p. 17). She notes that "the abomination of women's public speaking" (ibid., p. 13) is a metaphor, one that reflects biased concepts of agency, relationship dynamics and identity that deny women access to roles that exert crucial impact in the world. But we are no longer in ancient times, when public speaking was reserved for victims or martyrs (ibid., p. 13). Like it or not, we find ourselves in a time when women speaking, persisting, refusing, and rebelling, has become purposeful and prolific. How will psychoanalysis situate itself in this dynamic force field? What role can psychoanalysis play in the development of the leadership identity?

This question should be as relevant to us as the facilitation of self-esteem, relational competence and self-reflection: that power without authority, without the legitimization that carries weight, without the right to stimulate imagination in a sociocultural context, cannot fulfill the requirements of a "facilitating environment" (Winnicott, 1965) for any who aspire to have impact, whatever the context. As psychoanalysts, it is our responsibility to consider the history of our profession: how deeply held beliefs have contributed to attitudes regarding women and gender, to clinical treatment and to theory. The sociocultural context of the past century, the culture in which psychoanalysis was created, where psychoanalysts were trained, and where patients received analytic work is now regarded with cynicism and mistrust. The authority of psychoanalysis has been weakened, not only by the emphasis on evidence-based treatment protocols that pay little attention to gender issues or bias, but because some of our past theories regarding women are antiquated and embedded with ideas that are offensive within the modern zeitgeist. Psychoanalysts, women and men, should consider alternatives that confront the inadequacy of our theory, especially when it has become bound to a history that has little relevance for the modern woman.

Though psychoanalysts have often defined personality traits and identity formation within a developmental or pathology-oriented model, psychoanalytic theory could benefit from a revision, especially as it relates to leadership (where there is a dearth of theory) and to women (where there is an abundance of bias). Too often, psychoanalysts fail to address the preconceptions that were born in our theory, especially regarding the sexism and phallocentrism in the study of women and gender. Psychoanalysts must acknowledge that we have limited our explorations, whether by conscious decision or unconscious bias, to assumptions about women and men. These assumptions alter our curiosity, and in turn, undermine the unexpected marvels of self-exploration. We have held so closely to the "analytic" focus on psychic reality that we have failed to address the degree to which social constructions of gender have inexorably shaped the imagination. Our unimpeachable rectitude is challenged by the possibility that we analysts have entered the consulting room space with underlying prejudice that skewed the dyad, caused us to treat patients differently, and led to absences in our consideration of women's relevance in the global arena. We have brought gender disparities into the consulting room, failing to explore the sparks of leadership that our patients, women and men, describe. We have failed to explore the potential that each individual has to shape a path towards the fulfillment of personal influence and widening impact, whatever the gender. We have not considered the role of the leadership identity and how it is a viable potential that can be nurtured in the clinical space.

Psychoanalysts play a part in the way women think of themselves and engage in the world as "public speakers." Psychoanalysis can help to understand and support the bold moves and passionate fantasies of women, women who strive to be leaders and activists. It is important to consider how leadership identity surfaces in our practices with our patients as well as in our own personal activism or our hesitation to act. The artifacts of language, context and bias continue to influence and limit. What moves thought into action, fantasy into agency? When embedded unconscious fantasy, fears and wishes are addressed in the consulting room and on the broader landscape of our tumultuous international stage, it is possible that wishes and fantasy will move – from unconscious reflections, to animated extensions of purpose, evidence of an evolving leadership identity. These ideas are crucial to who we are as psychoanalysts in the consulting rooms where we are no less vulnerable than our patients to social constructs: gender bias and outdated norms that shape our conscious and unconscious communications and beliefs regarding women as leaders.

Some might argue that psychoanalysis is immune to these constructs – that our profession is not defined by issues of discrimination, sexism, or class; nor are we impacted by external changes of politics, social upheaval, or injustice. The feminist, Kate Millett, once said: "It is interesting that many women do not recognize themselves as discriminated against; no better proof could be found of the totality of their conditioning" (Millett, 2016, p. 55). So too, psychoanalysts may remain deeply unaware of the forces that shape our attitudes and practices. Though psychoanalysts champion concepts regarding unconscious processes, we may be vulnerable to failures in recognition.

I propose now a challenge to my psychoanalytic colleagues – a quasi Bechdel-Wallace test for ourselves as we launch our project on women and leadership. Let's call it the *Brody Test of Women and Leadership*. The test asks for an evaluation and deconstruction of psychoanalytic discourse on this topic. How often do we pair the words "women" and "leadership" or "women" and "power" and include these three standard threads in our discussion: penis envy, men's fantasies of women and women's compensatory needs? Can we have a conversation about this critical topic and find importance in topics related to women's imaginations, missions and competencies? Can we acknowledge that when we pair the words "men" and "leadership" our discussions are not organized around men's envy of female pregnancy, on women's ideas of women's fantasies of men as leaders, or on the need to compensate for a lost womb. It just does not, and never has happened. The Brody Test asks us to confront deeply unconscious patterns that continue to affect the way we treat individuals of *any* gender, and seeks to sensitize the psychoanalytic profession to its deeply held sexism. We must understand the process by which women can be nurtured to develop a leadership identity and fulfill their underutilized potentials, and the possibility that we colluded in thwarting this developmental promise.

Our project has been to identify themes and questions, to build perspectives from analysts who have played important roles in the theory and clinical practice of our field. They are leaders who have had a role in contemporizing psychoanalytic theory. But as they have deconstructed the old bedrock of psychoanalytic ideas, they have proved to be formidable role models, building ladders – and bridges – to offer perspectives that inspire activism and understanding in other fields: sex trafficking, environmentalism, gender equality, education, diversity and politics. In the context of a volatile and deeply divided global, sociocultural and political context it feels critical to be inclusive, to invite alternative viewpoints that will be as likely to question and diverge in our psychoanalytic doctrines, as to embrace our sensitivity to individuality and agency. Indeed, the inclusion of voices that integrate ideas from outside of the psychoanalytic orbit should be of greater focus than ever before. For this reason, the contributions of postmodern psychoanalysts may be overshadowed at times by the presence of voices – past and present – that have made their mark in worlds that psychoanalysts do not often occupy. Though they do not use the psychoanalytic language that is familiar to us, many demonstrate a strategic awareness of change agents, of the significance of identity, of the power of supportive relationships and the urgency of the moment. We encourage others in our profession to seek out those voices. We have been looking for overlaps, intersections, oxymorons and gauntlets, and we believe we can learn from those who take risks, from those who have confidence, and those who speak, despite efforts to silence.

There are those in our profession who might argue that to emphasize external perspectives risks dilution of our own uniquely analytic voice, a non-analytic concession to the impact of the external, and an undervaluing of the essence of unconscious process and fantasy. There is a worry that concepts of psychic reality will fade if the world penetrates theory and practice – that radical alterations in technique will ensue, making psychoanalysis unrecognizable. But that is hardly the case for those of us who are dedicated to the significance of self-reflection and the examination of the mind. Rather, we wonder about the fate of our profession should we *fail* to include this complex context into our thinking.

We can be psychoanalytic and continue to be curious about how people become who they are from every possible perspective, and what factors facilitate wishes and fears, as well as the impediments to change. We continue to ask whether psychoanalytic acts of exclusion and the over privileging of the internal continue to limit crucial transformations in our field, and in the individuals we treat. Indeed, we believe that if we are to remain clinically and theoretically relevant, we must evolve. How we think about women, gender, identity and leadership can become part of our clinical and theoretical development, and a necessary correction over past invisibility and dismissal. In our conversations about leadership, we have begun to develop some ideas about the conditions that facilitate the movement towards visibility, the conditions that galvanize action and create freedom. Vibrant creative momentum may be set in motion when we give attention to emerging challenges from an evolving world. Our willingness to plunge in may herald a psychoanalytic renaissance. In the unfolding of the leadership identity, we may offer the option to freely run across the great green grass, in the fullness that brings the power to make a mark.

Notes

1 We deeply appreciate the assistance of Olga Umansky who discovered the Winnicott correspondence and the article on democracy.
2 Alford (2001), Burack (1997), Kramer (2012), Little (2009), Page (2003), Piterman (2010), Richards-Wilson (2004), Samuels (2000).
3 It has not been possible to confirm which papers Grossman discovered in her exploration of Winnicott's papers. The citations listed seem to express the perspectives that Winnicott

describes in his correspondence with her and in several presentations and papers from that time period (see note 4).

4 There are other obscure papers that reflect this premise. Winnicott states that "if there is no true recognition of the mother's part, then there must remain a vague fear of dependence. This fear will some times take the form of a fear of woman in general or a fear of a particular women" (Winnicott, 1957/2017 Introduction to *The Child, the Family, and the Outside World*, p. 126). In another paper, Winnicott alludes to the role society must have in the "acknowledgment of this dependence which, which is an historical fact in the initial stage of development of every individual" (Winnicott, 1957/2017, p. 294). Somewhat hesitantly, Winnicott takes up "This Feminism" (Winnicott, 1964/2017a) through his developmental filter. His attempt to clarify his position on the anatomical gender differences and their implications, Winnicott again emphasizes a unique, unequivocal aspect of human development, and its inevitable universal impact: that "at first everyone was *absolutely* dependent on a woman, and then relatively dependent" (ibid, p. 109).

5 See Chapter 1 "Desire and Women" in this book for further discussion of Chasseguet-Smirgel's ideas about women, men and desire.

6 The Bechdel-Wallace test, created by the graphic writer, Alison Bechdel (1986) asks whether a work of fiction features at least two women or girls who talk to each other about something other than a man or boy. The test reveals how common fiction narratives seem to reduce women's lives to the frequency with which important personal activity and conversations and relationships are connected to a man or men.

7 Summers (2005), Pinker (2005), and Lawrence (2006) made controversial statements about gender disparity in the fields of math and science. They argued the under-representation of women was a result of lower aptitude and cognitive abilities of women compared to men. See Dillon and Rimer (2005).

8 This phrase references a quote from the obituary of the photographer, Diane Arbus, by James Estrin (2018) who notes how the curator John Szarkowski of the Museum of Modern Art described her: "Arbus did not avert her eyes"

9 On International Women's Day (March 8, 2018) the *New York Times* devoted an Obituary section to the lives of 15 overlooked women (Padnani and Bennett, 2018). Among them are: Ida Wells (social activist/investigative reporter), Qiu Jin (feminist poet/Chinese "Joan of Arc"), Diane Arbus (photographer), Sylvia Plath (poet), Mary Ewing Outerbridge (pioneer of women's tennis), Marsha Johnson (activist of gay liberation movement), Henrietta Lacks (cell ancestor of medical research), Emily Warren Roebling (Brooklyn Bridge overseer), Ada Lovelace (mathematician/first computer programmer). With an invitation for readers to submit other overlooked women, the *Times* apologized for a century of erasure of many accomplished women who were all but forgotten.

10 Personal conversation, Vivian Pender.

References

Alford, C.G. (2001) Leadership by Interpretation and Holding. *Organ. Social Dynamics*, 1 (2):153–173.

Barres, B. (2006) Does gender matter? *Nature*, 442(13):133–136.

Beard, M. (2017) *Women and Power*. New York: Liveright Publication Company.

Bechdel, A. (1986) *Dykes to Watch Out For*. New York: Firebrand Books.

Brody, S. (2016) *Entering Night Country*. New York: Routledge.

Bruni, F. (2017) Donald Trump's Dominatrix. *New York Times*, July 26.

Burack, C. (1997) Crossing Boundaries: Black Feminism and Group Leadership. *Gender and Psychoanalysis*, 2(3):343–367.

Chasseguet-Smirgel, J. (1976) Freud and Female Sexuality – A Consideration of Some Blind Spots in the Exploration of the "Dark Continent." *IJP* 57:275–286.

Chira, S. (2017) Why Women Aren't CEOs According to the Women who Almost Were. *NY Times,* July 21.

Dillon, S. and Rimer, S. (2005) No Break in the Storm over Harvard President's Words. *New York Times,* January 19.

Douglas, M.S. (2017) *The Everglades: River of Grass* (original publication 1947). Sarasota FL: Pineapple Press.

Douglas, M.S. (2011) *Voice of the River* (original publication, 1987). Sarasota FL: Pineapple Press.

Estrin, J. (2018) Obituary, Diane Arbus. *New York Times,* March 8.

Genzlinger, N. (2017) Ben Barres, Neuroscientist and Equal Opportunity Advocate, Dies at 63. Obituary. *New York Times.* December 29.

Gerth, H. and Mills, C. (1972) *From Max Weber: Essays in Sociology.* Oxford: Oxford University Press.

Gould, S.J. (1996, 1981) *The Mismeasure of a Man.* New York: W.W. Norton and Company.

Kollwitz, K. (1988) *The Diary and Letters of Kathe Kollwitz.* Evanston IL: Northwestern University Press.

Kramer, R. (2012) Rank on Emotional Intelligence, Unlearning and Self-Leadership. *American Journal of Psychoanalysis,* 72(4):326–341.

Lawrence, P. (2006) Men, Women and Ghosts in Science. *PLoS Biology,* 4:13–15.

Little, G. (2009) Middle Way Leaders. *International Journal of Applied Psychoanalytic Studies,* 6 (2):111–128.

Mead, R. (2015) Women's Work. *The New Yorker,* November 16.

Millett, K. (2016) *Sexual Politics* (original publication, 1969). New York: Columbia University Press.

Packer, T. (2015) *Women of Will: Following the Feminism in Shakespeare's Plays.* New York: Knopf.

Padnani, A. and Bennett, J. (2018) Overlooked. Obituaries March 8, In recognition of International Women's Day. *New York Times,* March 8.

Page, M. (2003) Leadership and Collaboration Challenges in Not for Profit Partnerships. *Organ. Social Dynamics,* 3(2):207–255.

Pinker, S. (2005) Sex Ed. *New Republic.* February 14, p. 15.

Piterman, H. (2010) The Leadership Challenge: Rediscovering the Voice of Reason. *Organ. Social Dynamics,* 10(2):180–206.

Richards-Wilson, S. (2004) Introverts as Silent Leaders: Indefensible or Indomitable. *Organ. Soc. Dynamics,* 4(2):243–246.

Riviere, J. (1926) Womanliness as Masquerade. *IJP,* 10:303–313.

Rosaldo, M.Z. (1974) Woman, Culture and Society: A theoretical overview. In M. Rosaldo and L. Lamphere (eds), *Woman, Culture and Society.* Stanford, CA: Stanford University Press.

Samuels, A. (2000) The Erotic Leader. *Psychoanalytic Dialogues,* 10(2):277–280.

Summers, L (2005) Letter to the Faculty Regarding NBER Remarks. www.president.harva rd.edu/speeches/summers/2005/facletter.html

Winnicott, D.W. (1950/2017) Some Thoughts on the Meaning of the Word Democracy. In *The Collected Works of D.W. Winnicott,* Vol. 3. Oxford: Oxford University Press.

Winnicott, D.W. (1953). Transitional Objects and Transitional Phenomena—A Study of the First Not-Me Possession. *Int. J. Psycho-Anal.,* 34:89–97.

Winnicott, D.W. (1957/2017) The Mother's Contribution to Society. In *The Collected Works of D.W. Winnicott,* Vol. 5, pp. 293–296. Oxford: Oxford University Press.

Winnicott, D.W. (1964/2017a) Introduction to The Child, the Family, and the Outside World. In *The Collected Works of D.W. Winnicott*, Vol. 7, pp. 125–127. Oxford: Oxford University Press.

Winnicott, D.W. (1964/2017b) This Feminism. In *The Collected Works of D.W. Winnicott*, Vol. 7, pp. 103–111. Oxford: Oxford University Press.

Winnicott, D.W. (1965) *The Maturational Processes and The Facilitating Environment: Studies in the Theory of Emotional Development*. The International Psycho-Analytical Library, 64:1–276. London: The Hogarth Press.

Winnicott, D.W. and Grossman, R.J. (n.d.) Assorted Correspondence, Boston Psycho-analytic Society and Institute Archives. 1872–1996, Box 3 f.44.

12

THE SOCIAL CONSTRUCTION OF FEMALE POWER AND LEADERSHIP

A psychoanalytic perspective

Frances Arnold

The making of our political leaders: intersectionality of individual imagination and social discourse

We began writing this book during the 2016 presidential election, which deeply influenced the subject of this chapter: our historical moment, gender and leadership. We believe that political leaders come into being through participation (theirs and ours) with prevailing social discourse. We also view leaders as created in our collective imaginations, and therefore, as much projections of our most hopeful wishes, and darkest frustrations, as they are singular leaders in their own right. From this perspective, new leaders are shaped by sociopolitical forces, which include our collective struggle to give new meaning to ongoing dilemmas. The latter can take many forms, and certainly did in the race between Hillary Clinton and Donald Trump.

Trump both represented a radical departure from the "mainstream," and gave voice to many who believed their common, human experience had been disavowed by a political elite. For Clinton supporters, Trump seemed a caricature of a man from a time that pre-dated decades of gender and identity enlightenment. As we move through the post-election maelstrom, our belief is that any consideration of female political leadership requires a simultaneous exploration of prevailing social discourse.

Psychoanalysis has long struggled with an historical divide between those who argue that our field should confine itself to the individual psyche, and others who suggest it is impossible to understand individual subjectivity without recognition of discourse as a power structure that influences development and determines how and what we think (Dimen, 2011a, 2011b). Our subjectivity, leadership identity, and authority all emerge through social processes that are part of a larger frame of power. From this perspective, a central psychological conundrum becomes the following: "can we see when we collude in our own domination and oppression?" (Dimen, 2011a, p. 5). Our task is to comprehend our unconscious individual and group mission, and its interrelationship with broader forces. At the moment, psychoanalysis seems on the cusp of integrating social theory in a way that was previously unthinkable. Indeed, this may be a direct response to the emergent discourse of the post-2016 American political landscape.

With this frame in mind, this chapter will explore the contribution of several, iconic female leaders, beginning with Hillary Rodham Clinton and Wonder Woman, an interesting alter ego for our real-life, powerful woman. We will then consider how psychoanalytic ideas about power, gender and misogyny can help us to understand the complex reactions powerful women can and did evoke during the 2016 election. This discussion will be followed by a consideration of three female psychiatrists and psychoanalysts, Carol Nadelson, Carola Eisenberg and Margaret Morgan Lawrence, who are pioneers in our field. While all three women share certain individual and psychological characteristics, their rise to leadership is a mosaic that includes unpredictable social forces and opportunities.

Nadelson, Eisenberg and Lawrence, whose ascent to power spanned the 1940s to the present, exhibit several important traits. Most notably, they include: tremendous energy, a capacity to make things happen, the ability to inspire and to be inspired, and an engagement with larger social issues of their times. In addition, all of them share the capacity for single-minded focus and creativity about composing their lives. Costs and compromises are also part of their stories, as some paid a great price to participate in leadership roles.

HRC

As part of a Discussion Group addressing women and leadership, and focused on Hillary Rodham Clinton and the recent 2016 election, Stephanie and I presented a video of Hillary Rodham's 1969 Wellesley College commencement speech (Arnold and Brody, 2017). Many of our participants were moved by watching young HRC's courageous address, full of activism and purpose, and a mission to make the world a better place. HRC's voice and presence conveyed her leadership potential, strikingly untouched by her later history. Indeed, her speech rivaled those given by Obama in his early days and held a promise that, "here, might be someone capable of changing the natural order of leadership, as we have known it." It is sobering, yet representative of the larger landscape, to consider that just a few years after the young HRC's 1969 speech, Nixon made a recorded statement about why he would not appoint a woman to the Supreme Court:

> I don't think a woman should be in any government job whatsoever … mainly because they are erratic … and emotional … men are erratic and emotional, too, but the point is that a woman is more likely to be.
>
> *(Eagly and Carli, 2007, p. 2)*

It was not until 1981, and Reagan's appointment of Sandra Day O'Connor, that the United States confirmed its first female Supreme Court Justice.

As a young woman, and at the time of her commencement address, HRC seemed unscathed by both the social meaning of her participation in politics, and her own unflinchingly public history. Her commencement address was a reminder of how much we long for the freshness of youthful leadership, particularly when it comes from promising young women. As our Discussion Group watched the historic speech, our participants were transported to an earlier time. Many felt their previous hopefulness for new leadership possibility, yet were sadly aware of how possibility can be (and was) hijacked by time, experience, and social determinants. Some participants were moved to tears.

Reflecting on young HRC's brave address, we were reminded of the statue, recently added on Wall Street, of a young girl facing down the famous market bull – an image of youthful promise, meant to inspire girls and young women. Artistic imagery often captures the complexities of social forces; in the instance of the young girl and the bull, we might wonder if she reflects that we are more comfortable with strength and power embodied in a girlish, rather than womanly form. The young activist is, perhaps, more appealing and acceptable, while the woman in charge, with a fully lived life, is a more complex and challenging figure.

HRC and Wonder Woman – a female superhero without baggage

Our focus on women and leadership presses for both a consideration of HRC's run for presidency and also a recognition of other emblematic female figures that entered American consciousness at this time period. During the lead up to and in the wake of the 2016 election, there was a re-appearance of the female superhero, Wonder Woman. She entered our national consciousness both through a work of scholarly history and on the big screen, in a full-length box office film (2017). Having originally appeared as a comic character in the 1940s and 1950s, and in 1972 on the cover of the first *Ms. Magazine*, Wonder Woman re-appeared in Jill Lepore's (2014) historical account of the superhero's creation. Lepore explores the legacy of Wonder Woman's unusual creators, William Moulton Marston and Elizabeth Holloway, and their unconventional, triangular relationship with Olive Byrne. (Ironically, Byrne was the niece of Margaret Sanger, the famous pioneer who launched what is now the worldwide birth control movement, and whose Brooklyn birth control clinic was the forerunner to Planned Parenthood.)

HRC and Wonder Woman played, simultaneously, on our national scene. Hillary Clinton was a deeply ambitious, but flawed candidate, who came of professional age in the limelight of the American political mainstream. By contrast, Wonder Woman grew up on the all-female, Paradise Island, far from the rest of civilization. She was free of the sociopolitical and generational history of women in a gendered society. That is, except for the ominous myth that the male God, Mars (probably a play on "Marston"), might find and wreck havoc on this feminist utopia. Wonder Woman is the daughter of the female ruler of women, and from the start, is comfortable with power and agency. In the movie, played by the Israeli actress, Gal Gadot (in real life, both a beauty queen and trained in the Israeli military's IDF), Wonder Woman never worries about how she is perceived. She is supremely self-confident, and omni-competent, keeping her eye on her ambition of protecting world peace. She never panders. Portrayed with playful tongue in cheek, Wonder Woman is spared from ever seeing a man until a World War I allies' spy washes up on her island shores, with Germans in pursuit. In one sly reversal after another, of the more well-known Superman and Lois Lane duo, Wonder Woman saves the day and ventures off with her spy, to save the world from evil male destruction.

Lepore's thesis is that Wonder Woman contains the feminist history that many of us have forgotten. Wonder Woman is often portrayed as shackled, or in bondage – both a private preoccupation of Marston's and what many assume is a symbolic reference to early suffragists, and battles fought by first wave feminism. In many ways, the hidden and secret lives of Wonder Woman's creators – Marston, Holloway and Byrne – are a story of hidden identities around gender, power, intimate gender arrangements, and unconventional, fluid, family life. As the story goes, Marston wanted to keep his triangular relationship (which included four children, two mothered by each woman, all fathered by Marston) concealed, which led to secrecy and layers of double meanings about Wonder Woman's origins and history.

Perhaps most compelling about Wonder Woman is that she carries no gender baggage. In his *New York Times* review of the movie, Frank Bruni describes Wonder Woman as follows:

> [She is like] an idealist who would never think to outsource her safety, her judgment, her anything to a man. Having grown up on an all-woman island far from the rest of the world, she carries no grudges or aspirations regarding the treatment of women. In her experience, women have always been in charge and have always been self-sufficient. That's just the natural state of things.
>
> *(Bruni, 2017)*

On our other "big screen," Hillary Rodham Clinton was an ambitious woman with extensive baggage, and none of it private. Indeed, she was a heavy lifter who carried the history of her husband, their marriage, his affair with his intern, and the projections of the public. HRC was in shackles, was severely compromised by her husband's poor judgment, as well as by persistent misogyny. She was unable to become a leader and an object of identification for white, working class men and their families. Unlike Wonder Woman, who, in the comic "myth," is created free of history's shackles with the complexities of her true "creation story" concealed and hidden from public consciousness, HRC's long and full narrative, both political and private, has always been in full, public view. None of this negates the fact the HRC is accountable for her own part in failing to reach critical factions and constituencies.

Misogyny

It is hard not to miss the wild latitude that was given to HRC's presidential competitor, Donald Trump. His story was as outrageous and inconsistent as his behavior and use of language, and yet, this did not trouble a large swathe of the American psyche. For many who were concerned about his personality, but voted for him anyway, their vote was a wish for change. Differences in what was publicly tolerated in these two divisive leaders raised heated points of identification and dis-identification. Indeed, many marriages, partnerships and family relations were sorely tested when related people voted for different candidates. Misogyny clearly played a role in the election process and outcome, if we consider the divergent standards applied to the two candidates. In fact, it is difficult to recall a presidential race which was marked by as much vitriol, contempt and breakdown in civility. "Lock her up" – and all the other sordid political slogans aimed at HRC – were an expression of primitive hatred we had not experienced in previous political races. Those of us with families who cut across political lines experienced an exaggerated, visceral reaction to one another, and to each other's candidate. Hillary pillorying was visceral and highly aggressive, igniting a primitive, sexually tinged rage. Trump hating was equally embodied.

During the 2008 election, at the American Psychoanalytic Association national meetings, Drew Westin (2008), psychoanalyst and political consultant, argued that what matters most in campaigns is not content, nor debate, nor a resume, but rather the capacity to reach voters' emotions. Many of us – Hillary's majority – were out of touch with the emotional experience of Trump's constituents. A question we are left with is: how do we understand the sexist contempt that was so charged? Can psychoanalysis help us with this understanding?

One thread of the 2016 race was misogyny, the political spectacle of attacking challengers through the strategic use of gender in the service of power. Robin Ely (2017), a business school professor who has consulted to companies regarding gender issues and women's leadership, found that organizations may present problems in gender terms, when in fact the dilemmas represent larger group dynamics. This can reflect an unconscious "genderizing" of power structure biases and conflicts through the projection of larger, common issues onto "gender," an example being, turning conflict about work demand and perfectionism into a "women's issue about life balance." This lens raises important questions about hatred and how it can be played out, in the name of gender, particularly around leadership challenges.

For many of us, the misogyny of the 2016 political race seemed a conscious and strategic "otherizing" of the competent female leader, who many agree was best qualified for the presidency. Donald Moss, a psychoanalyst, has offered an understanding of hatred and "otherizing" that might add meaning to the misogyny we witnessed. This process occurs with a close encounter with an unnerving "other," whom one cannot bear to "either identify with, or love," because of the perception of intense, urgent wanting or deprivation (Moss, 2016). Moss explores the consequences of this psychic gap, including its physicality, violent impulses and the subject's wishes to attract identification with himself, to become a "we" rather than an "I," in order to rationalize the expulsion of such feelings. We might assume that the perceived unnerving experience of the other may be a product of the onlooker's own reflection. Perhaps particularly important, Moss's formulation of hatred and "otherizing" addresses the physicality, or bodily experience, that accompanies such experiences.

Trump and his supporters succeeded in "otherizing" or dehumanizing HRC by stoking rage and violent, visceral reactions that played on misogyny and group fear of the deprived, powerful woman. HRC was cast as corrupt and crazed, or deprived and inadequate. The surprise was that so many women voters dis-identified with HRC and identified with Trump's position. But, we should not be surprised by the power of internalized misogyny for women, as well as men. This power construction goes far beyond a single power contender and reflects a system in which we are all participants.

Dialectics of power and gender

One of the most influential contributors to our psychoanalytic understanding of gender and power, Jessica Benjamin (1988, 2004a, 2004b), has written prolifically about the importance of recognizing the role all of us play in maintaining psychological and institutional structures that impact individual experience. Similar to Moss, Benjamin explores domination and submission as the result of a breakdown in equal and mutual human relationships, with failure of mutual recognition at the core. For Benjamin, this breakdown occurs in the form of rigid polarization of gender, and is held in place by social and institutional structures. Benjamin describes what she sees as the central "psychic structure" and polarity prevalent in our society, a dynamic of power domination – male as subject, female as object. For Benjamin, psychic freedom involves the capacity to recognize these potentially interchangeable and shared dialectical experiences in self and other. Benjamin's work underscores the need, for all of us, to address aspects of ourselves, and our relationships with public life, that we might consciously, or unconsciously, disavow, particularly around power dynamics.

More recently, Benjamin has explored the problem of the failure to "witness," specifically its role in public denial regarding personal and collective trauma – a sociological lynchpin with relevance for our recent explosion of sexual harassment accusations and demands for accountability. While history, as always, is quickly unfolding, we hope that institutional barriers to female power and leadership are, as we are writing this book, changing rapidly and dramatically.

Female leadership: visionaries and activists

The year following the 2016 election was marked by a resurgence of women's political activism to a degree we have not seen since the 1960s. It began with the

Women's March on Inauguration Day and continued with a series of worldwide protests on behalf of women's rights and in response to what many believed was a war on women that threatened to set back the clock with repeal of basic rights. This movement was criticized for lack of coherent mission, yet, seemed part of larger activism propelling women into political positions from the grassroots level, to higher up, at an unprecedented pace. Those who track activism have wondered about the meaning of this movement. Relevant to our topic, we are interested in the importance of social action for women's leadership development overall, as well as during the recent political climate.

Heifetz, Grashow and Linsky (2009) write about "adaptive leadership" and the importance of seeing and taking the opportunity for large scale change, and doing so with full, emotional involvement. They suggest that to connect with those they are trying to reach, successful leaders must have their heart in their mission, whether it is personal, organizational or part of a larger arena. These authors also stress the importance of a sense of larger purpose. Within our own field, many women psychoanalysts who are innovative thinkers or leaders for organizational, professional, or larger change have also been activists with these qualities. While such strengths may not be unique to women, activism may be an important factor in women's leadership development, particularly for the generation of women who broke through initial barriers. Looking back at the young Hillary Rodham's Wellesley commencement speech, we see a young woman who is already a leader in the making – one who cares passionately about larger sociopolitical issues and is willing to stake her heart on her mission.

Nadelson, Eisenberg and Lawrence: early leaders in psychiatry and psychoanalysis

Relevant for female leadership, Harvard Medical School (HMS) has conducted detailed interviews of its female physicians, including some of the first generation of women to attend the medical school only a little more than 50 years ago. These archives are part of the Renaissance Women in Medicine Oral History Project, which presents an annual award in honor of a woman physician or scientist in North America:

- who has furthered the practice and understanding of medicine in our lifetime and made significant contributions outside of medicine, for example, in the humanities, arts or social sciences;
- whose determination and spirit have carried her beyond traditional pathways in medicine and science; and
- who challenges the status quo with a passion for learning.

Within psychiatry, there were two women from this generation, and from the HMS archives, whom we chose to illuminate our topic: Carol Nadelson (1936– present), who became a full professor of psychiatry and the first woman president of the American Psychiatric Association, and Carola Eisenberg (1917–present), who came to Harvard Medical School, after receiving her medical education in Buenos Aires, and was known for her humanitarian work and her mentorship of the next generation of women physicians.

Both Nadelson and Eisenberg were activists within medicine and psychiatry, and on behalf larger discourses of their time. Their interviews are a reminder of what it took to break barriers, and challenge our collective amnesia for the efforts of a preceding generation. Most astounding about these leaders is their ingenuity, their blending of the personal and the professional, and their creativity about how they constructed their lives. There is no simple way to categorize their pathways. Certainly, they "leaned in," yet "leaning in" would simplify and trivialize their complex paths to achievement.

Both Nadelson and Eisenberg went to great lengths and encountered multiple barriers in achieving their medical educations and careers in psychiatry and psychoanalysis. Each describes early developmental and relational experiences that are markers in their success stories. Their narratives highlight the importance of supportive families and community which, despite barriers of quotas, harassment and discrimination, were protective and inspirational as these female physicians came of professional age. Nadelson emphasizes her capacity to make and keep friends over her lifetime, and to this day remains in contact with childhood friends.

Activism is another critical theme for both women – Nadelson and Eisenberg had considerable impact on the next generation of women in medicine, from overseeing major changes in admissions policies, to mentoring, to initiating radical clinical and academic programs. They were also activists in larger sociopolitical arenas. Among many achievements, Nadelson made groundbreaking contributions to the standards for psychological responses to rape and pregnancy, and also contributed significantly to perinatal psychiatry. Along with colleagues, she was one of the first to identify rape as a risk factor for PTSD and to expand understanding of that disorder. Eisenberg's humanitarian work included, among many achievements, being a founding member of Physicians for Human Rights, and the 1997 co-recipient of the Nobel Peace Prize for its International Campaign to Ban Land Mines.

While not all women leaders are social activists, it is interesting to consider the role of activism in creating leaders with a mission and a connection to the larger world – perhaps particularly during their time periods. These women physicians were thoughtful activists – noteworthy, given the tendency to view "activism" as about "action" rather than thoughtfulness or intellectual rigor.

While neither Nadelson nor Eisenberg started out viewing herself as a leader, both were confident about their independence, determination and agency. Enormously energetic, they possessed high capacity for taking risks and finding solutions. Neither was from a privileged background in terms of status and wealth and both are from Eastern European Jewish immigrant families. Nadelson grew up in Brooklyn and Eisenberg in Argentina, both from working class families with more limited educational opportunity in the previous generation. Regardless of challenges, Nadelson and Eisenberg led their lives by taking risks and seizing opportunities, many of which took them far from where they began.

Several themes emerge from their extensive interviews for HMS, which occurred over several sessions and amount to hundreds of pages of transcribed autobiographic material. Vitality – physical, psychological and/or intellectual – stands out as a common trait of these leaders and others with whom we have spoken. So does an interest and capacity to connect with a wide range of people, and to be inspired and inspiring in the process. The capacity to make something new happen, often in the form of activism and out of ingenuity, is a striking trait in both these leaders and perhaps particularly characteristic of their generation. While these are undoubtedly important leadership traits, it is likely there is a synergistic effect of positive leadership, leading to increased sense of effectiveness and enhanced vitality and connection.

Along with ingenuity is creativity regarding how they construct their lives. Such creativity matters greatly in regard to the collision of child rearing with early career demands and potential for leadership track. The latter remains a difficult, seemingly immutable challenge for American women, despite obvious efforts – astounding when comparisons are made with more progressive countries. Nadelson describes raising her young children during the rise of her career through living near her work, using a strong network of colleagues and friends, and receiving childcare help from a young woman who was raising her own child at the same time. At the end of her HMS Oral History Project interview, Nadelson laments the lack of progress in this area, highlighting the challenges and backslides she anticipates for young women of the next generation. She raises concerns about the U.S. lagging behind other first world countries regarding maternity/paternity leave and also percentage of women in power or leadership positions. This mirrors the concerns of parents of daughters currently coming of age, who worry about insufficient change and potential obstacles the next female generation may encounter, particularly at the juncture of early parenthood and the press for leadership advancement. Young women often hear the advice, "just follow what you most passionately care about and the rest will follow." This advice is well meant, but we would be wise to consider the reflections of our experienced, female leaders. Describing American culture Nadelson notes,

> We have guns. Other people don't have guns. We have no childcare. We have no maternity leaves. Everybody else thinks that's insane. We have never had a woman president. Look around the world. Even third-world countries have had that. We have Merkel and Margaret Thatcher, and other countries have had women, and that's routine. It's still a problem because it's so unusual, but it happens, and we're still fighting about that. We're going backwards in all kinds of ways into another entrenchment. And I think women now, some of the young women don't have the concept that they're losing reproductive rights because most of them can get it because they have the resources. But poor women can't, and we don't even think of that.
>
> (Nadelson, 2015, p. 62)

An African American pediatrician, psychiatrist and psychoanalyst, Margaret Morgan Lawrence (1914–present), offers us another leadership story to consider. Lawrence (a former Associate Clinical Professor of Psychiatry at Columbia University College of Physicians and Surgeons) was particularly known for her work developing, and serving as chief of, the Developmental Psychiatry Service for Infants and Young Children and their Families, at Harlem Hospital. In collaboration with Robert Coles and Steven Kurtz, she was also a founding board member of the Harlem Family Institute.

Lawrence made significant contributions in the area of child development, particularly through her work focused on the resilience of inner city children (Lawrence, 1973). Drawing from both her clinical work, and her own childhood reflections, Lawrence believed that an infant's earliest sense of "a true self" is the experience of a self as "worthy of love" (Lawrence, 2001, p. 61). She also stressed that the child's "self-image becomes internalized as the infant looks into the mirror of the not too conflicted caregiver." She suggests that "love which only can exist in relationship," is "a social experience" that is organizing and leads to, among many things, the capacity for commitments – particularly, "commitments that bind a person to course of action and connection" (Lawrence, 2001, p. 61). Indeed, it is Lawrence's unusual determination and commitment to a course of action – against odds that included the double barriers of gender and race – that might be most striking about this accomplished woman, who led in so many different ways.

Preceding Nadelson by two decades and Eisenberg by several years, Lawrence was the third African American woman to attend Columbia University's Physicians and Surgeons College, graduating in 1940. She was the first African American resident admitted to the New York Psychiatry Institute and the first African American psychoanalyst to be certified at Columbia University's Center for Psychoanalytic Training.

Some of us were introduced to Lawrence several decades ago through her biography – *Balm in Gilead: Journey of a Healer* – a moving homage written by her daughter, Sarah Lawrence-Lightfoot (1988). Born in 1914, Lawrence was the second child of a mother who was a teacher, and a father who was an Episcopalian minister. Lawrence's parents traveled to New York City in order to give birth to their daughter in a Northern medical setting, having lost their firstborn son in a Southern segregated hospital, when he was 11 months old. Their act of parental protection is uncanny in light of the current, staggering mortality rate of black infants and their delivering mothers. Recent news coverage has highlighted how the decline in the infant mortality rate has slowed in the United States, since the 1990s, with black infants now "more than twice as likely to die as white infants – a racial disparity that is actually wider than in 1850, 15 years before the end of slavery" (Villarosa, 2018). The root of this problem is thought to be "societal and systemic racism which can create a kind of toxic physiological stress, resulting in conditions … that lead directly to higher rates of infant and maternal death" (Villarosa, 2018). Consideration of leadership might seem distant and irrelevant if the odds of keeping alive one's infant child are so uncertain – then again, it might seem more pressing than ever, and perhaps it did for Lawrence who, early on, wanted to become a physician. Recent press coverage reminds us these issues are, astoundingly, as alive as ever.

Lawrence was born to parents who went to great lengths to assure care as Lawrence entered their world, and who were able to provide a close, protective community, particularly important when they settled in the segregated and brutally racist town of Vicksburg, Mississippi. Lawrence recalls feeling loved, respected and sheltered from racism, within a supportive, black, middle class community, "where white folks were irrelevant" (Lawrence-Lightfoot, 1988). Despite racial insults, and the fact that a lynching had occurred on a street nearby a few years before they moved to Vicksburg, Lawrence reportedly, felt "privileged" (Lawrence-Lightfoot, 1988). As her biographer daughter notes, to have a dream of becoming a doctor (or other, similar dream) "is a privilege" – and one that came more easily a generation later, for Lawrence's own children (Lawrence-Lightfoot, 1988).

Like Nadelson and Eisenberg, Lawrence's narrative is remarkable for her resilience, independence and activism. Lawrence attributes her interest in medicine to her unknown brother's death and its impact on her parents, particularly on her mother who suffered from frequent depression. A testament to "ghosts in the nursery," Lawrence reports a recurrent childhood dream of lying in a coffin, facing the large, centrally located, photograph of her light skinned, blonde haired, baby brother – and also underscores her belief that "someone like me could have saved him" (U.S. National Library of Medicine, 2015, p. 1).

Lawrence differs from Eisenberg and Nadelson in terms of the single-mindedness of her dream and its pursuit. The intensity of her determination, and early capacity to take action, is almost unfathomable. She also differs regarding her experience of the intersectionality of race and gender – and the number of borders crossed and barriers broken. Indeed, her movement, between so many different worlds, despite the odds, is astounding.

By the age of 14, Lawrence realized that to achieve her dream, she would need to be well educated. She informed her parents that she had decided to attend a high school in New York City, and to live with her protective aunts and a domineering maternal grandmother, all of whom she had visited regularly and credits as having an important impact on her development. The following dream is reported from when Lawrence was only nine years old and seems to presage her later, bold decision:

> She and her mother are in New York. Both are dressed in their elegant city finery. On Margaret's head is a wide straw hat with black and white stripes and a streamer down the back. Her mother is also decked out in a wide hat. They are about to take a trip on an elevated train together. There is a space between the platform and the train, and Margaret experiences a moment's trepidation as she steps cautiously from one to the other. As she leaps the short distance from the platform onto the open coach at the end of the train, she suddenly realizes that her mother is no longer behind her. Mary (her mother)

has not managed to jump onto the train. Margaret looks down, and there is her mother in the street below. She is sitting on a spike at the center of a turnstile, but she doesn't seem scared or uncomfortable. She is just sitting there, looking up at Margaret on the platform. Looking down at her mother, Margaret experiences surprise but no guilt or remorse. She says, "Oh," and that is all she uttered.

(Lawrence-Lightfoot, 1988, p. 79)

Lawrence performed well at her New York high school, winning a scholarship and acceptance at Cornell University, where she was the only black student in attendance at the College of Arts and Sciences. Because of race, she was also barred from housing in the university dorms, living instead in the chilly attic of a home where she also served as a maid, to help defray costs. Despite an excellent academic record, Cornell Medical School rejected her, presumably on discriminatory grounds, although the dean's explanation was the following: "You know … twenty-five years ago there was a Negro man admitted to Cornell Medical School and it didn't work out … He got tuberculosis" (Lawrence-Lightfoot, 1988, p. 175). Describing her mother's reaction to this news, Lawrence-Lightfoot writes,

Each of the dean's words was like a knife. There was nothing to say. "I cannot remember my response … I must have said something …" She left the office in a daze, devastated by the death of a dream she had pursued with all her energy since she was a young girl. "You go along, you make your plans … you do your work, then suddenly someone has passed a sentence on you. This had been my plan since before I was fourteen … my parents expected this … they had taken me seriously … there were my aunts and the ladies in Harlem, Charles [her husband] was already involved. We already had the plan for the health clinic and social service center in Vicksburg. All these expectations, and I couldn't fulfill them …" Margaret's pain cut right to her soul. "My experience was one of depersonalization … It was as if I was lost in a strange world … I walked around like this for days and days … I remember one brief conversation with my comparative anatomy professor … but there was nobody who could really be with me where I was." The reliving of this tale nearly fifty years later brings back the pain and tears as Margaret speaks of a "lost identity." "Who am I?" she wondered.

(Lawrence-Lightfoot, 1988, p. 176)

Fortunately, Lawrence was accepted at Columbia University College of Physicians and Surgeons, and would eventually return to Columbia's Psychoanalytic Center for psychoanalytic training. However, racial barriers continued to obstruct her. She was denied pediatric residencies at two sites, one because they did not accept married residents, and another because she would have to live at the hospital's nurses' residence, which, like the dorms at Cornell, refused to accept Negro women. Later, Lawrence was blocked from certification by her psychoanalytic institute, despite having completed her course work and passing the final oral exam. She was told by Sandor Rado, Director of the Psychoanalytic Center, that she would be required to have a consultation with Abram Kardiner, a cofounder of the institute and important training analyst, in order to see if "she needed further psychoanalysis." Lightfoot writes the following about her mother's reactions to this surprising news:

> This time the blow did not leave Margaret speechless. She was fighting angry and "by now I was free enough to say my piece." "Why?" She inquired. "I won't tell you," Rado shot back. "You'll have to go to Kardiner. That was the committee's decision." "Why can't you tell me?" said Margaret, her voice steady but her insides ravaged. Dr. Rado, unaccustomed to any questioning of his authority, rose from his chair, his body rigid with anger. Margaret looked into his red and contorted face as their confrontation escalated. "You will have to go," he finally threatened, to which she replied, "I refuse to have this consultation."
>
> (Lawrence-Lightfoot, 1988, p. 180)

Rado and Margaret reached a compromise – she would agree to talk to her supervisor and her analyst instead, although Rado insisted she would be required to have the consultation with Kardiner if the matter remained unresolved. Lawrence's fate hung in the hands of several, powerful, white men. In addition, her relationship with Kardiner was complicated. Kardiner had written *Mark of Oppression*, a controversial book about the "Negro Psyche," and Lawrence had declined Kardiner's request that she become one of his research assistants interviewing African Americans in the Deep South, for his book. At the time, she was limited by the demands of her work and raising three young children. She also had concerns about Kardiner's research and his methods. By her report, Kardiner stopped talking to her after she declined the research position, although breaking his silence after his book was published to ask her opinion of his book – perhaps seeking approval from an important African American woman colleague. Later, Lawrence found out there had been a rumor that she wished not to treat black patients, which she immediately corrected. In hindsight, we might wonder if this rumor was primarily a projection of the institution's own racism, including that Lawrence, with all her achievement and aspiration, might have been seen as "different than" other African Americans.

With support from her husband and family, Lawrence overcame these setbacks, moving on to more accomplishments. She established and led important programs at Harlem Hospital and progressed as a faculty member at Columbia University College of Physicians and Surgeons. She was a co-founder of the Rockland County Center for Mental Health in New York and continued to be an activist, winning the Episcopal Peace Fellowship's Sayre Prize in 2003 in recognition of her work to promote peace, justice and non-violence. The narrative of Lawrence's rise as a pediatrician, psychiatrist and psychoanalyst, to positions of leadership, is all the more remarkable given that much of her story predates the 1960s and the civil rights movement.

Through her biographical account, Lawrence-Lightfoot set out to discover the gaps between her complex experiences of her mother and the legendary woman seen by others. She writes, "the world's image of my mother never squared with my own" (Lawrence-Lightfoot, 1988, p. 12). Addressing the complexities and costs of her mother's enormous and often single-minded drive, Lawrence-Lightfoot notes,

> I felt the impulse to look at my mother's life, more deeply, to tell of her grace against odds, of the pain that accompanied achievement, the loss of laughter that came with the single-minded pursuits. Not only would the story focus on these triumphs, it would also show how her life was filled with very ordinary twists and turns, with moments of traumatic defeat … and slow, purposeful recovery. I wanted to explore the family silences, the breaks in family stories that emerge –biases people have simply forgotten, because memories have faded with time, because images have had to be repressed in order to move on with life, because people have chosen to hide a piece of the truth for their own peace of mind … I was particularly fascinated by the way she had trans-formed hardship into strength, and loneliness into sensitivity and introspection.
>
> *(Lawrence-Lightfoot, 1988, p. 12)*

Lawrence-Lightfoot's biography is a gift to us and to psychoanalysis – a loving chronicle of an African American pioneer in our field. It is also a narrative that tells us much about the history and legacy of our institutions and our beliefs, from the 1930s to more recent times. It is certainly a reminder that our power structures, including the beliefs that hold them in place, determine a great deal about our capacity to engage difference around the development of women leaders. Law-rence's story is a complex legacy, and legend, that is complicated for the generation that follows. The latter is palpable in Lawrence-Lightfoot's efforts to locate and apprehend her mother's "pain that accompanied achievement" and the "loss of laughter that came with single-minded pursuits." There is both a deep loneliness and resilience that emanates from Lawrence-Lightfoot's account. As Lawrence-Lightfoot acknowledges, "I mistrusted the legend that seemed in its grandeur to diminish me" (Lawrence-Lightfoot, 1988, p. 12). Or:

> What others saw as peacefulness, I saw as my mother's chief survival strategy – complete concentration. I am sure that the dissonance between the idealized perceptions of Margaret and a daughter's non heroic view must also have fueled my interest in exploring her life.
>
> *(Lawrence-Lightfoot, 1988, p. 12)*

The interviews with Nadelson and Eisenberg, along with the biography of Lawrence, offer an unusually detailed and rich window into the lives of iconic female leaders who have transformed our field and the pathways, now open, for the rest of us to consider. We are left with the sense that none of this would have happened without tremendous risk, and sometimes sacrifice, that included traveling miles from where each of these iconic pioneer leaders began their lives. It also includes a rich and complex inheritance for the generation of women to follow. Ours is a deeply important, and transformative, legacy and one that we must take great care to cherish and remember, for it is a part of us, whether we are conscious of this legacy, or not.

Bibliography

Arnold, F. and Brody, S. (2017). APSA Discussion Group: Women and Leadership. APsaA Winter Meetings, NYC.

Benjamin, J. (1988). *The Bonds of Love: Psychoanalysis, Feminism and the Problem of Domination.* New York: Random House.

Benjamin, J. (2004a). Deconstructing Femininity: Understanding "Passivity" and the Daughter Position. *Ann. Psychoanal.*, 32:45–57.

Benjamin, J. (2004b). Beyond Doer and Done to: An Intersubjective View of Thirdness. *Psychoanal Q.*, 73(1):5–46. Bruni, F. (2017). The Triumph of "Wonder Woman." *New York Times Sunday Review*, June 4, 2017.

Dimen, M. (2011a). *With Culture in Mind: Psychoanalytic Stories.* Relational Perspectives Book Series, Vol. 50. New York and London: Routledge.

Dimen, M. (2011b). With Culture in Mind: The Social Third Introduction: Writing the Clinical and the Social. *Studies in Gender and Sexuality*, 12(1):1–3.

Eagly, A.H. and Carli, L.L. (2007). *Through the Labyrinth: The Truth About How Women Become Leaders.* Cambridge, MA: Harvard Business School Review Publishing.

Eagly, A.H. and Karau, S.J. (2002). Role Congruity Theory of Prejudice Toward Female Leaders. *Psychological Review*, American Psychological Association, Inc., 109(3):573–598.

Ely, R.J., (2017). Explaining the Persistence of Gender Inequality: The Work-Family Narrative as a Social Defense against the 24/7 Work Culture, Open Members Seminar, Boston Psychoanalytic Society and Institute, Newton, MA.

Heifetz, R., Grashow, A. and Linsky, M. (2009). *The Practice of Adaptive Leadership: Tools for Changing Your Organization and the Worlds.* Boston: Harvard Business School Press.

Lawrence, M.M. (1973). *Young inner city families: development of ego strength under stress.* New York: Behavioral Publications.

Lawrence, M.M. (2001). The Roots of Love and Commitment in Childhood. *Journal of Religion and Health*, 40(1):61–70.

Lawrence-Lightfoot, S. (1988). *Balm in Gilead: Journey of a Healer.* New York: Addison-Wesley Publishing.

Lepore, J. (2014). *The Secret Life of Wonder Woman.* New York: Random House.

Moss, D. (2016). The Insane Look of the Bewildered Half-Broken Animal. *JAPA*, 64 (2):345–360.

Nadelson, C. (2015). https://collections.countway.harvard.edu/onview/exhibits/show/fhwim -oral-histories/renaissance-women-in-medicine-/carol-c-nadelson/oral-history, p. 62.

U.S. National Library of Medicine (2015). Changing the Face of Medicine: Dr. Margaret Lawrence, National Institute of Health. cfmedicine.nlm.nih.gov/physicians/biography_195.html

Villarosa, L. (2018). Why America's Black Mothers and Babies Are in a Life-or-Death Crisis. *New York Times*, April 11.

Westin, D. (2008). Clinical Work Writ Large: The 2008 Presidential Campaign.Presidential Symposium, APsaA Winter Meetings, New York City.

13

CLAIRE

A story of leadership

Frances Arnold and Stephanie Brody

Leadership: respected, renounced, restrained

The following is a composite case report that gives our four clinical contributors – Brenda Bauer, Adrienne Harris, Vivian Pender and Arlene Richards an opportunity to address the highly charged context in which leadership can be nurtured or thwarted. Claire is a young, gifted woman who struggles with a sense of belonging – anywhere. Brenda Bauer considers the power structures within which women negotiate authority and develop leadership capacity. Adrienne Harris notes that when women are poised to become leaders they face extreme criticism – even when engaged in the most worthy acts of ambition. She underscores the challenges for women who may be undermined by rejecting the implicit contracts of submission. Vivian Pender explores the interrelated themes of identity, conflict and subjective reality in the context of a world that is often hostile to the achievement of girls and women. Arlene Richards looks at women's leadership through the lens of ancient myths, where powerful women wield power in cultures that may be opposed to their authority.

Case study – Claire

A woman in her 40s, and a single mother of an adolescent girl, Claire sought treatment for her anxiety and depression as she was beginning a new position, with greater responsibility, in the legal office of a prestigious financial institution. Having made a number of changes since graduating from law school, and faced with an opportunity she never imagined she would have, she found herself feeling ashamed, inadequate and miserably haunted by a sense that she was different than everyone else. In her first session, Claire talked about her fear that, in a rare moment of letting down her guard, she had divulged too much about herself. In an effort to be more real and make deeper connections, she had shared her history of having had a bi-racial child, out of wedlock, while in law school. She believed her intentions had backfired and that her colleague might now avoid her.

What emerged was a rather complicated history. Claire was the oldest of six children born to Irish Catholic parents who had never aspired to or attended college.

> My mother was a silent woman who was bitterly tied to the laundry room. It was like washing all those clothes and cleaning our house was all that mattered and she quietly hated her life, but she made sure we knew it. I don't remember my father around that much – he worked several jobs to keep us going and I think he came home to sleep, leaving the rest to my mother.

Claire was the fairy tale character – the one who landed in the wrong family – a bright light with a lot of aspiration who somehow got mismatched with parents who just survived from day to day, without dreams.

> It was a pretty closed system. Just going out the door to my Catholic school felt like crossing the Atlantic, something no one had done in my family. My mother never helped me with my homework – she had no idea how to do the math problems and even worse, I think my brain scared her.

But Claire's brain was puzzling to her as well. "I didn't know why it came up with the answers it did. All I wanted most in the world was to fit in." During her senior year of high school, her parents suggested she look into teaching or secretarial school, something that would bring in some money and get a job locally.

> I couldn't believe it! The world as I dreamt and imagined it was imploding in front of me. So, I sat them down and explained I was likely to be class valedictorian and that I could be accepted to a really good college. I had my eye on one back East, but they would have none of it! They saw those fancy schools as a waste of money. So, I hunkered down and researched everything, more determined than ever to get out.

These working-class parents simply could not understand these ambitions and had no pride in her pioneering spirit. Dreaming was cast as a frivolous, impractical activity. Claire responded to their anxieties and narrow vision of her future by doubling down. Determined to prove them wrong, she used her intellect and perseverance to focus on her goals and overcome the possibility of failure. It is a stance that has alternately propelled and dogged her over many years.

Claire went off to a "fancy Eastern school," having found a way to take full responsibility for financing her education through a series of scholarships and loans. She thrived at college, invigorated by the academics, the intellectual conversations, and especially the relationships with her instructors. Claire flourished under their interest and attention. Her capacity to formulate arguments and take diverse positions on political and social issues set her apart from the other students. She seemed uniquely able to engage her classmates in controversial topics without alienating any of them. Soon, she was elected as president of her class, then of the student body. In this role, she had regular access to the college deans who encouraged her interest in government and law. They appreciated her competence and natural interpersonal sensitivity. Her college performance and stellar recommendations led to acceptance at a top law school, this time with expenses paid.

Law school was more of a challenge, but she learned strategies and her learning curve was steep. Seeking help with the most difficult of her classes, she met an African-American law student who was a teaching assistant. Claire was a dedicated student, and had little time, or interest, in any relationships. But Mark was unlike anyone she had ever known, and she was bowled over by his charisma and brilliance. Mark's interest in her quickly grew, and soon their long tutoring sessions became personal and then intimate. Claire had trouble integrating her school work with a relationship, but their demanding schedules allowed her to quickly develop an efficient calculation of time: she slept less. She was happier than she had ever been, but hesitated to share her excitement about her new love with her family. She was sure that they would not accept an African-American man and decided it was simply better to keep this part of her life private.

In the last semester of law school, she became pregnant. Mark had been working as a law clerk, and had accepted a position in the city, not far from her family. She had no desire to terminate the pregnancy, but she had no idea how she would care for an infant and go on with the professional life she had imagined for herself. Reluctantly, she revealed her relationship, and her pregnancy to her parents. Her hope was that she might also find a job in the same law office, and that her mother might agree to care for the infant while she was at work. With a clenched jaw, her mother assumed childcare responsibilities for the healthy baby girl, born one month before Claire began her new job. Yet within weeks, life began to sour. Mark did not seem to get along with his colleagues, and he did not respect the partners' legal positions, political leanings and social strivings. It was a bad fit for him, but Claire seemed to fare better. Her natural social skills, paired with her intellectual aptitude, made her a quick study. As in law school, she knew how to make a challenging situation manageable. After a workday, parenting responsibilities seemed to fall on Claire, who found a way to survive night feedings and still get her daughter to her parents' home before work. More conflict surfaced between Claire and Mark, and Claire became alarmed when she learned that Mark had been offered a position at another firm in another city. It had never occurred to Claire that Mark would leave her, or their child, but he passionately asserted that they would resume their relationship when he was settled, and happier, in a different location.

On reflection, Claire was never sure whether she ever should have trusted that Mark intended a future with her and their daughter. The relationship did not survive. As Claire became increasingly essential at her job, she relied more and more on her mother to provide child care. Her colleagues knew nothing of her personal life, and apart from time with her parents and her daughter, she really didn't have much life outside of her job. In painful silence and guilt, she tolerated the unspoken criticism that her mother directed towards her. Though they never discussed it, she knew that she had burdened her mother, once again, with the unhappy responsibility of childcare. As soon as she established herself as an authority in the legal area of corporate finance, and her daughter was old enough to attend school, Claire found a job that placed her in an excellent school system, geographically closer to Mark, whom she secretly hoped might reconnect with his daughter, and with her. Claire was caught off guard when she shared her imminent relocation with her parents. Her mother broke into tears, and her father accused her of ungratefully abandoning them for her career. She had no inkling that they cared. But the decision had been made, and the move took place. Claire was now on her own, a single mother, with a young daughter. Her parents were too far away to help her, and Mark showed little interest in reconnecting. She found some old college friends who were awed by her ascendance to a high visibility managerial position in such a prestigious financial institution; former law school colleagues contacted her with the hope that she might help them obtain positions, as she now had a significant professional network. She enjoyed her daughter, and tried to protect their time together, but their space was often intruded upon by the deadlines of contract negotiations and demanding clients. She missed more recitals and soccer games than she wished, and though her daughter begged to visit her grandparents, Claire could never find the time to arrange a visit; though she offered to pay for their travel, her parents refused to leave their home to visit her.

It was several years after these events, and at a time she was being rapidly promoted at work, that Claire presented for treatment. She had just accepted a new managerial position and during this time period had also, as she felt, prematurely, and for confusing reasons, disclosed to a colleague that she had a child, and the information about the father. Claire was overwhelmed, felt like she could not think straight and was now worried about being able to perform at her new position. "I've ruined it for myself! It's like everyone can see through me – I might as well go to work in my underwear! Why did I allow myself to be so revealing?" As she continued to reveal herself in her treatment, a new anxiety was emerging. Claire was struggling with the emergence of contradictory feelings as she was now tasked to mentor a younger colleague.

Sarah was a brilliant woman on the fast track: the editor of her law review, the first pick for a clerkship at a superior judicial court, Sarah had a special interest in tax law and the role of government in the oversight of the banking industry. Impressive, demanding, and sometimes regarded as difficult because of her high expectations, she was nonetheless, impossible to ignore, and worthy of respect. Claire was asked to "soften" Sarah's hard edges. "You are the only one who can do this", her colleagues told her. "And you should. She'll thank you when she becomes President." To her dismay, Claire found herself jealous of the awe that Sarah inspired in others. Though Claire longed for a family and intimacy, she envied Sarah's apparent freedom from parental and relationship responsibilities. She felt strangely awkward with Sarah at their meetings, feeling suddenly self-conscious about her own attire, her history, and her intellect. More star struck fan than older instructor, Claire now revealed in therapy that it had been with Sarah that she had first shared her pain. Sarah was the one colleague she wanted to connect with, worrying that her disclosure was too revealing, fearing judgment, though hoping for compassion.

Over many weeks, an interesting bond was evolving. Sarah argued that Claire should be more assertive at work – that Claire might be recruited by another more lucrative firm, if she only showed an interest. Sarah wondered why Claire hadn't thought of "striking out" in her own law firm, where she could call the shots in a business for women, run by a woman. Flattered that Sarah thought so highly of her, she also wondered if Sarah wanted to eliminate her as a competitor. More provocative for Claire was an intensifying interest, even preoccupation, with Sarah. Since Mark, Claire had rarely found such a compatible intellectual partner. Stimulating conversations ranged from topics regarding the political landscape, gender bias, and social inequity, to literature, music and travel. Claire looked forward to their meetings and realized that she was thinking about Sarah in her free time, dreaming about her, wondering if Sarah thought about her. She wondered if she could invite her to dinner, or on a hike. But she had no idea whether Sarah was involved with anyone. For no reason in particular, she wondered if Sarah was gay. These thoughts excited her, but also made her anxious. Flooded with feelings, Claire worried that her poise and focus had been compromised, that her interest in Sarah was visible to her colleagues, and that she "looked different" and would be unable to work at the level that was expected of her. She expected to be criticized for failing to change Sarah, and that she was herself at risk of losing her position in the firm. Thinking about the possibility of starting her own law firm, or applying for a new job, she realized that what she really wanted was to run away. She struggled with regret over her past choices, but was not sure that she could trust anyone with her worries, or trust herself to be confident about her next move.

14

FEMININE AGENCY AND IDENTITY AMID MOTHER-DAUGHTER ALIENATION

Brenda Bauer

One wonders about the atmosphere, and the culture, that breeds the expectation that one professional woman should "soften" another professional woman's "hard edges." So much to unpack in that seemingly innocuous phrase! This is merely the common practice of one female easing a younger female colleague into herself, to break her into an unfamiliar professional environment, right? What could be more reasonable than enlisting a trusted senior female to show the ropes to a younger, less polished, less amenable colleague? Many law firms, of course, recognize the usefulness of a mentorship program to orient a new hire to the culture of the firm, thus engendering loyalty and cementing a particular professional identity. It can be easily rationalized, then, that the older, wiser female colleague is "paying-it-forward" out of gratitude for her own inculcation, her own proper education. It could be reasoned that such an endeavor is a kind, sensitive, soft way of "bringing along" an outspoken, forceful, unruly ingénue, of mentoring a younger female colleague. It suggests a Pygmalion/My Fair Lady allegory that in its familiarity must certainly be good and right. After all, the set-up presumes that the "big sister" or "mother" figure, Claire, will shepherd the as-yet-unformed girl-woman, Sarah, up to and into the world that she, Claire, inhabits.

That Claire is pegged for this task, however, implies certain compromises or tendencies that have no doubt shaped and marked Claire's own trajectory at the firm, and likely key to important developmental experiences we have learned about Claire. We can imagine Claire adapting herself to the institutional environment in a way required of her to "get along and go along" in the service of presenting a cooperative, non-threatening, non-demanding persona in the service of her steady professional advancement. Sarah confirms the suspicion that Claire has played it safe, and that it has perhaps never even occurred to Claire to step out of line in this conservative institutional environment. Sarah confronts Claire's passivity, thus subverting the entire enterprise that enlisted Claire to shape and direct Sarah in a similar fashion as we can conclude that she, Claire, was molded. We soon see that Sarah is impervious to such grooming and, having recognized the ruse, instead forges a friendship, kinship even, with Claire. Instead of becoming Claire's apprentice, allowing a period of grooming that will eventuate Sarah's acceptance, if not advancement in the firm, Sarah becomes Claire's mother confessor and champion.

Claire is illuminated in body, mind and spirit by Sarah's keen interest in her, thrown into a spin as Claire is by this unexpected turn of events. It is through the prism of Sarah's investment in Claire's interior that we see the perniciousness of Claire's longstanding deprivation. We are transported across space and time to the laundry room of Claire's childhood, the chronically embittered expression that Claire witnessed on her mother's face; of femininity being linked in the most mechanized of manners to childbearing, childrearing, and domestic chores. It was plain to see that being female, and mothering in particular, was a woman's cross to bear; nothing in the female experience was presented as a joy, or an achievement in the household Claire was raised in. How was Claire introduced to the curiosities and pleasures of her own body, her own mind, amid the great disappointment and discomfort that her mother had with her own body and mind? One can imagine the scene of how Claire was cared for in the context of her mother's chronic misery; each act, a perfunctory, routinized step carried out not unlike an endless succession of clothing to fold or to press into compliance. A changed diaper, a wiped nose, applying a band aid to a scraped knee, attending to a fever, all carried out largely devoid of the language and bodily gestures that denote pleasure, that link, synchronize, bring meaning, and build healthy relationality to self and other. No doubt Claire's precocious intellect blossomed and grew increasingly refined in ways that her mother could only regard as mysterious, foreign, even intimidating; and with Claire's pubescence and adolescent development we can only assume that the alienation between mother and daughter was complete.

Then it should come as no surprise that Sarah's efforts to access Claire, to interact with Claire's interior, awakened deep, long-dormant needs that had been rejected, gone unsatisfied and were hidden away by Claire, and eventually from Claire herself. The potent, shocking resurrection of these desires illustrates the psychic efficiency with which these developmental needs were obscured by Claire's formidable intellect, her desperate wish to escape her family, and to create another reality for herself. It is with a tragic sort of irony, then, that Claire has re-created certain relational aspects of her mother's deprivation within herself, if not in her immediate environment, with her own young daughter, in the absence of a romantic life, and in reflexively caving-in to fulfill the role of professional "fixer" for her firm.

It is conceivable that when Claire became pregnant with her daughter in the final semester of law school that this was an unconscious solution to the "problem" of achieving her law degree, or at least of complicating her well-laid professional plans, of punishing herself for her many academic successes and achievements, and also represented a complex identification with her long-suffering mother. Less obvious, but perhaps as likely, the pregnancy may also have represented a flight from mature female desire, ambition and advancement, and the wish for an intra-psychic reunion with her mother, as well as the concomitant fantasy that she could engineer a "redo" with the mother of her childhood. Instead Claire is again confronted with her mother's resentment upon her mother's agreement to help raise Claire's daughter. When Claire relocates to a city far away from her parents, rupturing the intimate connection that her parents have forged with their granddaughter, Claire incurs their wrath and repudiation, unable to experience her parents' attachment to the granddaughter, and perhaps by extension, to Claire herself. When the possibility of a permanent relationship with the father of her daughter fades away, she is again bereft of the potential of intimacy she so desperately desires. It is easy to imagine Claire consoling herself with her work, coming to rely on the interest and attention of her more-senior colleagues, and reasoning with herself that, if nothing else, at least she can control her career.

Claire soldiers on, until meeting her more-junior colleague, Sarah. Sarah, nothing short of a force of nature, ignites Claire's mind and body. From the margins we can see that Sarah must represent something of an ideal for Claire. Sarah uninhibitedly speaks her mind, takes open pride in her intellect, and demands respect. It is likely that Sarah's potent, awe-inspiring demeanor maps onto the omnipotent mother of Claire's infancy and early childhood, but must also represent the culmination of what Claire had herself dreamed of becoming in adolescence and early adulthood. When Sarah takes note of Claire's conflicts and constriction around her own career, and encourages Claire to take charge of her professional life, we see Claire suddenly awaken to the possibility of self, illuminated by Sarah's concern for her. It is difficult for Claire to discern if her interest in and attachment to Sarah is sexual, platonic, or something else altogether, her mind spinning as it is.

Since it is around this time that Claire finds her way into treatment, we can only assume that Sarah is both galvanizer and interloper in ways that will no doubt become powerful resistances to the treatment and transference relationship. It is Claire's intense preoccupation with Sarah that frightens her enough to eventuate her initiating treatment; however, the analyst will likely encounter in Claire a pleasant-seeming, if not frankly pleasurable, overstimulation that may make it difficult for Claire to settle into treatment, develop a trusting, reliable attachment to her analyst and progress. Claire is at something of a crossroads, it seems, even paralyzed by the decision before her to rescue herself from the well-worn path she has trod many times before, or to stay the course with limited course-correction after the tectonic shift she has encountered through Sarah.

The budding attachment that the two women form seems to have qualities of many different kinds of relationships, and yet fails to fit neatly under any one category. One is reminded of the ancient, universal figure of the woman known as "Baubo." The figure is usually positioned with her legs splayed, gesturing to her exposed vulva, often smiling or with an expression of pleasure on her face. Baubo, the Greek Goddess of Mirth, is alternately seen as fun-loving, bawdy, jesting, and sexually liberated, and yet supremely wise. The Baubo character appears in every version of the Persephone myth, in which Demeter, on a frantic search for her missing daughter meets Baubo, an older female servant, who attends to the grief-stricken Demeter, who has refused food and drink. In an attempt to cheer or provoke Demeter, Baubo lifts her skirt to reveal her genitals, eliciting a laugh and retrieving Demeter from her depressive fog. Kulish and Holtzman (1998) emphasize that the display of genitals, sexual jesting and provocation, and the intimacy of the communication and humor between two women without negativity or restraint, is considered an important ritual of female sexuality and relationality. They situate Baubo, and the myth of Persephone, amid a larger theoretical context of the so-called female Oedipus complex in general, but also in a girl's experience of her body, and her developing sense of the interpersonal and social worlds in particular. As such, Kulish and Holtzman formulated a new name, "The Persephone Complex," for this concept, to describe the experience of girls and women as they attempt to reveal a sense of agency in their lives, and in their "evolving relationships with mothers, fathers, peers and lovers."

It is fair to say that Claire had arrived at something of an impasse, both personally and professionally, in which the developmental solutions she had come to rely on were wearing thin; that is to say that Claire's reliance on her intellect, her stellar work ethic, and on her adaptability to the environment are no longer serving her in the ways that had paved a path along which she had excelled academically. Each of these solutions, quite adaptive in pursuit of one's early achievement years, can quickly become defensive liabilities where one's social, emotional, and intra-personal needs demand a "self" that is centered not on adherence and compliance, but on personal satisfaction. One is left with the impression that the rich mental life that yields the potential for personal satisfaction, that is to say, emotional attunement to the self and other, and the capacity to lovingly build bridges to available, receptive objects, is not in evidence upon Claire's commencement of treatment.

So Sarah, the ingénue allegedly in need of softening and smoothing around the edges turns out to be something of a foil to Claire, who must come to appreciate the edges of her own perimeter and find a way into her heavily obscured interior. Sarah has given Claire a shocking, stimulating, and wholly enlivening glimpse of herself (Sarah), and has enabled Claire to glance inward, if only fleetingly, which has in the process terrified Claire about all that she has denied, disowned and that of which she continues to deprive herself. The developmental "redo" that Claire sought through becoming pregnant, and then in presenting her mother with a baby granddaughter, will instead play out with the analyst. With great patience, and good fortune, an analytic staging of this dramatic developmental rift and repair allows Claire to provide not only an enriched maternal experience for her young daughter, but also engenders an environment of interiority that permits Claire's engagement with meaningful professional and intimate pursuits.

Bibliography

Kulish, N., and Holtzman, D. (1998). Persephone, the Loss of Virginity and the Female Oedipal Complex. *Int. J. Psycho-Anal.*, 79:57–71.

15

WOMEN AND AMBITION

Our ambivalent under-indulged pleasure

Adrienne Harris

This strikes me as an extraordinary and yet appropriate time to be writing an essay on women and leadership. One year after the election of Donald Trump, there has been a sudden, hard-to-theorize turn of events in response to reports of sexual harassment and exploitation of women by men holding power and advantages over them. Men in entertainment, business, media, and politics step forward, to resign or to be fired, in various states of outrage, bewilderment, pain, and fear. Virtually no woman I know or interact with has been surprised by the litany of names. A world underground and out of sight has been revealed as utterly palpably visible. Unforgotten, and unrepresentable.

Sexual harassment and exploitation of women over whom a man or men have power is in the working minds of virtually all woman. My middle aged colleague rolls her eyes and alludes to the unpleasantness of medical school and residencies. I remind friends and tell unaware younger students of the 1970s feminist take on this: Susan Brownmiller's (1975) *Against our Will.* That text led anyone who read it to have to rethink the question of consent and sexuality, re-examining the experience you thought you had agreed to. Ruefully another colleague tells me that she had imagined sleeping with her thesis chairman would give her more power. But if that is the fantasy that underlies "consent," what do we think now in retrospect?

Consent is a complex and difficult matter, always in matters of sexuality. If we approach this as psychoanalysts, we must hold the ambiguity of our incomplete mastery of ourselves and our wishes in many enterprises, not only sexuality.

But I want to suggest that there is also the incomplete mastery of the social situations in which women exercise ambition and determination to thrive and rise in the world. Sexuality may or may not be involved but I want to suggest that using and turning a psychoanalytic lens on women's ambition still yields a complex study of ambivalence and sometimes dread, a hidden conundrum on many object relations across many figures in our psychic economies.

So I have felt it necessary to begin this essay on leadership in women's lives by framing this kind of experience in a social context in which it may have been an expectable condition of advancement that a women would have to consider a conscious (or semi-conscious) participation in act(s) of sexual exploitation. Not an easy sentence to write. Before I was an academic and then a psychoanalyst, I was in the theatre where the term "casting couch" was usually conveyed with a mix of grim irony and gallows humor. It was completely visible as a practice and officially taken as unremarkable.

There are many ways to understand this moment of heightened consciousness and consequences for such exploitation. Here I want us to attend to one ubiquitous fact in these experiences we are learning about. The woman, of whom sexual submission or acquiescence is expected, is most usually in a key developmental moment which she is entering or rising in some profession, usually public, to a situation of explicit authority and meaning and presence. In other words, she is poised to become a leader, a star, a player. It is at that moment of entry that she may learn that there is an entry fee, unexpected, lethal, unavoidable. So we can see that, at a moment of acquiring power, the women is deprived of it in a secret (or worse a semi-secret) move that undercuts forever that her ambitious acts and intentions are worthy in their own right.

While not every woman in leadership has had to endure this rite of passage, every woman knows of it, probably knows individuals in these situations and at an intuitive and even unconscious level understands that there is a message being addressed to all women. Psychoanalysts have written about this process, part masochism, part strategy, part despair. Riviere (1929) wrote of this in "Womanliness as a masquerade," noting the performative way that women reassure men that they are not "really" threatening. Does some of this uncertainty about ambition and power moves overtake a women just at the point of succeeding. The sexual "price" then reassures the man (and men and herself) that she is not really a threat. Does this unsettled ambivalence about ambition continue to haunt women even as our places in the world expand and rise.

In many ways, Joan Riviere's 1929 essay on this matter is astonishingly prescient. Womanliness as a masquerade. Many have drawn on this. Lacan, feminist and postmodern discourse have seen this text as a precursor of the notion of gender as social construction. The woman performs – as Homi Bhabha (1994) might say – as an act of minstrelsy, a goofy, airhead version of herself so as not to threaten men. Would this extend to sexual submission? Why not? Many of the reports of these subjections to unwanted but impossible to step away from demands are often filled with ambiguity. Dissociation seems a likely element here. But I am wondering how much dissociation is covered by performativity, an empty shell in which an expectable enactment of a sexual performance by a woman covers both the emptiness and the horror of such moments. Perhaps the performance disguises something for the woman herself, allowing her some very compromised psychic survival in a situation that may feel and be simultaneously dangerous and shameful. Perhaps alcohol may be a self-shield as well as an aid to dissociation. Bhabha's term "minstrelsy" was designed to get us to look at the complex spirit in which the person of color behaved in a placating manner that also contained skill and performance and reassuring messages that the person posed no threat. Goofy, funny, a clown, a performer for the master. Does sexual submission as an act of minstrelsy, and perhaps this is just one of a number of masquerades, arise in conditions of harassment (which must also have some – and often a lot of – implicit danger)?

I had a quite chilling conversation with a young woman in this context. Not in our professional field but actively pursuing a middle class field of endeavor, she voiced the question: But it's her body so couldn't she use it consciously for something she wanted? Sex work, surely we know there is a substantial feminist perspective on this matter that would see the use of your body consciously as a practice for economic gain as a right? A freedom? The arguments about prostitution as work are complex and mixed. I felt a terrible collapse in myself hearing this young person make the arguments. What if sex with the boss is in the job description, silent but understood? Again one must think hard about consent. Can one consent to this? And if you consent do you continue to own the rationale for your actions?

Placating men and other women about competence and ambition takes many forms outside of the sexual. My young patient, Jenna, moving through medical school, and internship, is upset with how hard it is for her to speak authoritatively on grand rounds. Skilled, compassionate, able to write and conceptualize with grace and insight, she cannot bear the way she speaks in public moments, at grand rounds, or ward duty where she is asked publically to think about a patient. She twirls her hair, speaks in a high rising cadence. Masquerade for sure. "I am just a girly girl," her body language and her verbal tone says, even as her words are authoritative and clear. Meanwhile she is a complex, thoughtful, empathic doctor. In disguise.

I start in this way in the essay on the case of Claire to provide context for thinking of the issues, clinical and social, that bedevil the patient and her analyst. But I also do this because, on a first reading I see two instances of hierarchically organized work relationships which Claire must negotiate. In the first, she finds herself in the all too familiar difficulties with her academic supervisor. In the second she is finding herself caught up (in fantasy and enigmatically in real interactions) with a woman worker she is supervising. Sexuality, excitement and power interweave with uncertainty and shame.

Perhaps, without the social context in which I am writing, I might have not even remarked on these phenomena. But I do so now to inquire about how these relational situations – ambiguous at best, exploitative at worse – contribute to or compromise Claire's ambitions, her self-esteem, her anxieties.

With a new and evolving interest in intergenerational transmission of trauma, we can ask how have women, across the generations, consciously and unconsciously, communicated powerful prohibitions and shames around women's power and ambition? Maksimowicz (2016) examined, through ethnographies and fiction, the complex dialogues mother to daughter where she found that subtle and not so subtle messages to compromise, to stay still, to be not to do, were pervasive. Don't get too big for your britches. This insidious and demeaning and constricting message was the abiding and deep message mother to daughter for my patient Jean. Her mother was a powerful woman – intellectual, with ambition and determination to burn. But she was a daughter of the rural South, and the messages she sent her daughter came from her own instructions from an earlier generation. I think the interesting point here is that intergenerational transmission is based more on the unconscious than on the explicit and surface truth and values. A highly functioning ambitious modern woman made the unconscious choice to transmit to a gifted and creative young woman, the demand that she lived, shamed and degraded and fearful to put a foot into the world. There are interesting matters to wonder about. Another child in the same family was liberated from this charge. What goes into the selection of which child receives the pluperfect errand (Apprey, 2015)? Who is freed and who is trapped in history? And why?

In a later essay, Torok (1998, first published 1964) turns the concept of penis envy inside out, seeing it as she says as "A woman's loyalty oath to her mother" allying powerlessness and loss and lack in a genealogy of women, united in not having. Matina Horner, in the 1960s, tracked it as a "fear of success" (Horner, 1972), a process that had women's anxiety flooding her in the wake of signs of prowess and productivity and appreciation. So anxieties about empowerment and ambition can turn a woman in either direction to placate either parent, either gender. But the task is different for each parental figure. Do not threaten or castrate or shame the father. Do not abandon or separate from the mother.

It is a part of intergenerational transmission that as yet we do not know enough about. We know about transmission, enigma and translation, but we don't always have ways to explore or excavate the unique systems of transmission. Birth order, looks, circumstance, temperament, history, and as yet unknowable processes shape how intergenerational transmission works.

This case is intriguing to me for two paradoxical aspects of Claire's function. Against many odds, Claire, with abiding anxiety and self-doubt actually undertook achievements and concrete steps to success and leadership. Is she a classic example of those "wrecked by success?" Yes and no. She achieves but she pays a price, extracts a punishment. At the same time there is her paradoxical relationship to her own envy and the envious attack of others.

She seems actually not wrecked by success but more to have replicated the neglect of her childhood in the isolation and self-neglect of her pursuit of power. There is something of the ordeal of single motherhood, the isolation of her rise in educational and professional settings, her odd absence of self-awareness or self-care, that seems almost a replication of the mother in the laundry room. This may say something important about women, mothering and work, almost outside class and setting. This case may say something about the sheer impossibility of solitary parenting joined with whatever work one is set to undertake. We know that there is good evidence that even as productive work has changed in terms of the presence and space for women, reproductive work (the care of the family) has changed much less.

Claire fears the envious attack of others, surely a reproduction of family and mother-daughter dynamics from her own history. But I was also struck by her absolute dissociation from any thought of the attachment of her daughter to her grandmother, or the inability to make any arrangements for the survival of that relationship. Envy perhaps in different directions as well as being envied? Perhaps also there is the replication in her own life and in her daughter's of abandonment and indifference to the psychological state of loss and loneliness.

Although I think there is a lot about social class in this story, I think it is also deeply about the struggle of mother and daughter, the psychic danger of outdoing one's mother. When Torok says "Penis envy is a women's loyalty oath to her mother" (Torok, 1998), she meant to suggest something of the anguish of outdoing an already damaged and limited parent. Sennett and Cobb (1972) outline a similar process for men in a book on class, *The Hidden Injuries of Class*. How did Claire's conflict around her own power, including a very insidious and costly element of shame, carry some of her history of loss and longing in regard to her own mother? It may be also that for women whose relation to productive work and achievement has changed so radically over the past several generations that many mothers feel that a daughter has leapt beyond anything they might have imagined. It is as though the daughter's development is almost like a class move, or like some migratory force that has taken a daughter far from her mother's world.

In the case write-up, the author speaks of Claire as someone born into the wrong family. But I think the implication of this presentation and of so many stories of women and ambition, women and leadership is that the accomplished and intellectually talented women is always born into the wrong family. Women in leadership are subjected to extreme strictures and criticism with regard to ambition and empowerment. This has been a concern since the long ago days of 1970s feminism. It is in a perhaps neglected text of Dorothy Dinnerstein (1976), *The Mermaid and the Minotaur*, who thought that the regressive pull that a woman's body and state of being can generate was extremely powerful, in intimate and in social life.

Much of this contemporary preoccupation – long overdue – about the sexual assaults and harassments on women as they come towards power and authority needs our psychoanalytic attention. We need to re-examine the complex hatreds and envies, many of these feelings from women and from young men, that befell the campaign of Hillary Clinton. Perhaps we might say she was born into the wrong country?

References

Apprey, M. (2015) The pluperfect errand: A turbulent return to beginnings in the transgenerational transmission of destructive aggression free associations. *Psychoanalysis and Culture, Media, Groups, Politics*, 77: 15–28.

Bhabha, H. (1994) *The Bhabha Location of Culture*. New York: Routledge.

Brownmiller, S. (1975) *Against Our Will: Men, Women and Rape*. New York: Simon and Schuster.

Dinnerstein, D. (1976) *The Mermaid and the Minotaur*. New York: Beacon.

Horner, M.S. (1972) Toward an understanding of achievement-related conflicts in women. *Journal of Social Issues*, 28(2), 157–175.

Maksimowicz, C. (2016) Maternal failure and its bequest: Toxic attachment in the Neapolitan novels. In Grace Russo Bullaro and Stephanie Love (Eds), *The Works of Elena Ferrante: Reconfiguring the Margins*. New York: Palgrave Macmillan Press, pp. 207–236.

Riviere, J. (1929) Womanliness as a masquerade. *Int. J. of Psychoanal.*, 10: 303–313.

Sennett, R. and Cobb, J. (1972) *The Hidden Injuries of Class*. New York: Knopf.

Torok, M. (1998) The meaning of "penis envy" in women. In N. Abraham and M. Torok (Eds), *The Shell and the Kernel* (pp. 41–74). Chicago: University of Chicago Press.

16

DISCUSSION OF CLAIRE

Identity, conflict and subjective reality in women leaders

Vivian Pender

Three interrelated themes are elucidated in this illustrative case on leadership: identity, conflict and subjective reality. Combined, all three are psychic reflections of women's experience of leadership influenced by the context of culture. The difficulty for women is the mantle of leadership while living in an alien world. She must be positive and persistent when odds are against her; she must tolerate rejection and be generous while in isolation; her drive to lead must be ego-syntonic.

Claire is described as a highly achieving professional woman. She is ambitious and accomplished by societal standards. However it is presented that her psyche is in turmoil. Her story is not an uncommon one for such women who seek psychoanalytic consultation. For women like Claire, it is all too often the case that she finds herself in crisis with identity issues, intra-psychic conflicts and difficulty managing the reality of her world. In a profession that is largely dominated by men she must alter her female perspective to compete and fit in. She is simultaneously outside the structure and by necessity working in it. She must accommodate by taking on a male attitude that may include a more overt expression of aggression, a more stoic work ethic, and less involvement with care-taking activities. She feels she must over-compensate by being perfectionistic and overly responsible. She has strayed from her parents' patriarchal world. In a society that is largely dominated by male perspectives, Claire cannot change her larger world; she can, however, with her analyst's help, try to manage it. In this scenario her analyst would acknowledge the difficulties for Claire in her present environment rather than imply that she is responsible for achieving in such an environment and if she does not, she is implicitly to blame. Her self-esteem and confidence might improve as well. Within her own psyche, she would be stronger.

The reader may be swayed by the binary positive description of Claire. As written, the author/analyst (who I suspect is also a woman) is in a non-neutral counter-transference compromise with Claire's conscious presentation. If so, the female analyst would have her own similar difficulties with the reality of the male dominated psychoanalytic profession. This appears to contribute to the analyst's definition of Claire with such wishful terms as 'her pioneering spirit' and the one in the family with 'dreams' versus the more pejorative view of her parents as having 'anxieties and narrow vision', her mother as 'bitterly tied to the laundry room'. This is an either/or description rather than a multifaceted continuum and does not address her defenses and wishes. The analyst in collusion with Claire may be trying to offer a glimmer of hope in a desperate societal situation that applies to both.

Identity

Claire felt different from her family beginning at a very young age. One might think of her identity as the Other. If Claire were the fairy tale character the 'Ugly Duckling', who landed in the wrong family, then her defense and her wish are clear. Just as in the folklore tale of personal transformation, she is teased, abused and mocked. She is alone because of her difference, in her childhood and later, in her work. But because neurosis can fluctuate, depending on whether the environment nourishes or suppresses it, she was able to become a swan at school. Then she regresses to her daunting conflicts in the non-supporting environment of her personal life. She admires and identifies with the 'beautiful swan' Sarah, who she is told will become the swan she wanted to become herself. Perhaps her mother's wishes for herself were transmitted to her. Adding to her mother's bitterness was her own possible wish that she herself would have become a swan in a 'fancy Eastern school'.

Her sense of difference is further revealed in her implied racism. She has the idea that a bi-racial daughter is shameful or a mark against her. Her shame is based on the failure of bodily integrity (dark skin) and thus her own narcissistic vulnerability. Her feelings of inadequacy may derive from her own body-shame and attractiveness. She chooses Mark, yet another identification figure whom she is sure her family will treat with hostility and indeed he is reported to feel like the Other at his new job and perhaps in his general environment where racism plays a role.

One can observe the effect of having a depressed hostile mother in real time with her young child. It evokes in children fear, anger, insecure attachment and inconsistent mirroring; one might wonder whether Claire has identified with that image of her mother. After she chooses a potential partner with whom she has an insecure attachment, she seems to do the same with her daughter. She assumed that her mother was 'burdened with the unhappy responsibility of childcare' and was surprised to learn that the opposite was true. She apparently does not develop a 'space' in which she can have a positive relationship with her daughter. Rather she seems happier at work with her colleagues. In addition, she deprives her parents of seeing her daughter even though her daughter asks to see them. This could be evidence that Claire's daughter in fact had a good relationship with her grandparents, again contradicting Claire's conscious and deliberately hostile view of her parents. Despite her parent's distress, she takes her daughter and 'runs away' so that they cannot see her as often, if at all.

Unconsciously Claire endlessly argues with her mother/parents in her head – a relationship that one would expect to play out in the treatment. To be anticipated, Claire identifies with both sides of the coin. She is for and against herself. Of course, she repressed the encouragement, the support, the willingness to help that was evidenced by her parent's care of her daughter, and possibly even her ability to aspire to be different. Obviously Claire had enough agency to strive and accomplish what she set out to do.

Conflict

'I think my brain scared her' is the narcissistic compromise formation to defend against her guilt that she was the cause of her mother's depression. She did not refer to herself but rather a dissociated part of her integrity, her brain that was to blame. As life progressed and her accomplishments grew, her guilt demanded punishment. In her psychoanalytic treatment, this may have been clarified if she had the space to express and explore the negative aspects of her transference. Instead, on the contrary, reality intervened when her parents were upset that she was leaving. Her emphasis on her brain may also be a subtext for her strong drive and agency, although she then counters her drive with a harsh superego. One would assume that conflicts between her internal state and her analyst as interpreter of the external world would be an important part of her analysis.

Her ambivalent relationships with her mother, her daughter, and her mentee may contain similarities that would be evident in her relationship with her analyst. She mistrusts her feelings and thus her assessment of herself in these various roles.

Her mother's resentment implies that she also aspired to something more than laundry. Wanting Claire close to home after high school as well as not wanting her daughter and granddaughter to leave belied her mother's wish to be close. I suspect that her mother had an unconscious wish for Claire's ambition to aspire in order to achieve something that she had wished for herself. In her treatment, her mother's ambivalence could have been explored to reveal not only the destructive fantasies that Claire incorporated but also the positive wishes she had for her.

Inevitably, conflict arose with Mark, as a representation of her own tension between work and relationships, between her self-representation and object representation, and implicitly between herself and her daughter. She herself, the oldest of six was the witness to her mother's subsequent pregnancies and apparent suffering. Her relationship with her siblings is not part of her narrative. The reader can only surmise that as the oldest, she felt the most responsible for her family. She projected her own prejudice and hostility against her daughter and her possible homophobia onto Sarah. One wonders what she projected onto the analyst. Overwhelmed with anxiety and flooded with the aggression of her affect, she defaulted to the binary of defensive splitting. She would run away, possibly from all relationships, including the one with her analyst to avoid the pain of reliving her conflicts in the transference. To be cautionary, an overly positive countertransference can exacerbate a patient's guilt as well as suppress the negative transference only to ultimately arise and possibly disrupt the treatment.

The film Brooklyn (2015) was in part a depiction of an Irish culture of deprived and envious people. In it, the relationship between a mother and daughter was a key element. The envious and grasping mother nearly led to a derailment of her daughter's development. However, the daughter 'runs away', that is, from Ireland to Brooklyn where we are led to believe she finds true happiness.

Subjective reality

Significant conflict exists between optimistic possibilities and the real limitations for girls. The real world in which girls grow and become women is frequently hostile to their achievements and accomplishments. There is much evidence of sexism and misogyny. Many women are not supported to excel, especially in leadership positions. Girls are objectified early in life and are frequently taught to use instead seduction and manipulation as sources of power. Unfortunately, this leads to further objectification. Women are not encouraged to lead in the mostly patriarchal societal structures that have prevailed. Perhaps parents anticipate that it would be too difficult for their girl child. In many women's internal experiences they feel to be the Other. Women do feel different and outside of many sectors of society. Inhibited and suppressed by social and cultural forces, very few women become real leaders of their communities. The statistics are grim. Only about 4% of Chief Executive Officers of the top 500 businesses in the United States are women. And it applies to inequities in several areas: in their economic, religious, political, social, psychological and physical environment. Thus many women find themselves to be the object of disparities and oppression, transmitted from one generation to the next (Pender, 2016). Claire is no different. She is like so many other women who simply do not have the authority to give an order or a direction. Ultimately, whatever authority they thought they had will be either hollow or an illusion.

Despite or perhaps because of her achievements, her multi-faceted identities draw on her insecure attachment, her shame, and her excessive projected caring about what others think. This belies her identities as white, Irish Catholic, poor, depressed, smart, ambitious, academic, professional, lawyer, daughter, oldest child, mother, single mother, having a biracial daughter and lesbian. Her various intersectional identities result in a de facto disenfranchisement because each is a minority, cancelling the usual support for achievement, and therefore a net loss of power, and ultimately an inability to establish power. Some studies indicate that individual women can thrive when they are placed in groups of women and where there are no men. These groups use principles such as inclusivity and are less hierarchical. Perhaps Claire's de novo idea to found her own firm is not an escape but rather an acknowledgement of women's reality.

Claire's dilemma is similar to the one in which many women find themselves. Her worry that she divulged too much of herself may mean that she has some self-awareness. However, it also may demonstrate the need that many women have to hide themselves and their talents from those who would be envious or find them threatening. Accomplished women sometimes represent a danger of intolerable humiliation to men. Unfortunately, this puts women in an isolated state in which they are truly alone, a destructive environment for most women. It is curious that Claire was asked to place herself second to a younger female rising star, that is, Sarah. Claire in turn envies Sarah for her assertiveness and freedom from a harsh conscience. Sibling rivalry may be evident, however it seems that Sarah represented a wished for soul mate that successfully navigated professional struggles.

In Claire's experience, her mother may have vicariously hoped for Claire to have achievements and been envious of them at the same time. Just as it is for Claire, she cannot be free or happy. Perhaps this is her identification with an emotionally depriving angry mother. In treatment, her relationship with the conscious mother and the repressed mother would be clarified in the transference to her analyst and could then be interpreted. It would be important for her to grieve the loss of an idealized version of a mother. As well she must reconcile the reality for any poor woman with six children to fulfill her own potential. She may then be able to acknowledge her own identity and reality. Her wish for 'deeper connections' could reflect this idealized regressed primitive relationship with an abundantly resourceful well-connected maternal image. It could also represent a wish to be connected to a world that simply doesn't exist in reality for many women.

It would be therapeutic if Claire's analyst, using attunement and attachment, acknowledged and understood women's experience in the current world. Unless the female analyst with similar identity, conflicts, and reality acknowledges these themes for such patients as Claire, she or perhaps both will feel overwhelmed, alone and have the need 'to run away'.

References

Brooklyn (2015). Film. https://www.imdb.com/title/tt2381111/ Accessed May 2018.
Pender, V. (Ed.) (2016). *The Status of Women: Violence, Identity and Activism*. London: Karnac Ltd.

17

DIFFERENCE, CONNECTION, IDENTIFICATION

Arlene Richards

Intellect and power

The question of intellectual power in a woman, as an asset or a liability, is important in thinking about women in our clinical practices, as well as women in the larger world. It is also relevant in the case example of Claire. Girls excel in elementary school math and science, yet fall behind in the middle school years and regard themselves as uninterested in their previous, successful pursuits. This is so generally accepted as to have led a former president of Harvard to pronounce that women's brains are not structured for math and science. Belief in the inferior intelligence of women in these areas bleeds over into thinking that women are intellectually inferior in general and even to a situation in which women pride themselves on being dumb. This "dumbness" includes not speaking up in class as much as men do, not getting credit for ideas in business meetings, and even not insisting on supervising others.

The earliest myth to survive in written form, the story of Inanna (Richards and Spira, 2015, pp. 4–13), serves as a stark contrast to contemporary gender dilemmas. Inanna is a female God who learns. First she wins the prizes of a bed and a throne (symbolic of sexuality and power) from her brother. Winning in the contest of sibling rivalry empowers her. Setting out on a journey to find her adult power in the wider world, she looks at her own vulva. Inspired she names herself "The Queen of Heaven" (ibid., p. 5). Next, she visits with her father. They eat and drink together until he is intoxicated and, in his inebriated state, he gives her all his holy powers: godship; kingship; priest-ship; priestess-ship; the arts, including the art of prostitution; the sciences; the emotions; the crafts; agriculture; procreation, judge-ship; and the power of decision-making (ibid., p. 5). She allows herself to gain power in the arts and sciences including politics. She chooses a husband, has children, reigns over her country and retires. This myth of female power deals with a vision that few women in reality manage to achieve or even aspire to achieve. As a myth, it allows women to see the possibility of power, even when tempted into disavowal.

Women in psychoanalysis

Women in psychoanalysis have been seen as mothers. In Freud's day women were expected to marry, have children, run a household and be content with ruling the domestic sphere. Not all women conformed to this image – Claire is one. In the past, those who chose a career might be expected to forego marriage and were certainly expected to forego having children.

One by-product of the American Civil War was the destruction of a generation of young men. Many of the young women who could not find men to marry became factory workers. The middle class women who would have married the men who died were then educated at colleges set up especially to educate them to become schoolteachers, nurses, social workers, and in exceptional cases, to become doctors, lawyers, poets, musicians and artists. Many lived in "Boston marriages": lesbian relationships that were accepted as long as the sex was not made explicit. The social changes affected Europe as well as the United States.

Psychoanalysis was a new profession that welcomed women educated as doctors, school teachers and scientists. When universities would not hire women as professors, psychoanalysis offered them intellectual challenge, a cohort of intellectual peers, and a profession in which they could support themselves. Yet psychoanalysts themselves were part of the larger culture, and reluctant to give up the idea of the woman as homemaker. Marriage and babies were thought to be the best choice for women, with careers only a substitute. Early female analysts thought of the career choice as less desirable than the wife and mother choice.

But women, in general, wanted more. They did not want to give up either career, or marriage, or motherhood. Women began to want it all and to ask for that but also became immersed in value questions, from within and without. Were the children more important than work outside the home? How much, if anything, did a father contribute to the running of the household and nurturing of children? Should a woman have children when she is young, fertile, and physically more capable of taking care of children? Or should she establish her career first so as to be able to support her family? The women who pushed the envelope, who chose to reach for more were transgressors of the social norms valued in the past. For example, in the late nineteenth and early twentieth century, many women died in childbirth. Many children died in infancy and childhood. At that time it made sense not to educate women for professional careers, but to prepare them for motherhood and childcare in order to maximize reproduction. As medical care improved, both women and children lived longer, and it made sense to educate girls, as well as boys, so that they could spend their longer lives in more satisfying careers.

Psychoanalysis came about at the moment of this change and helped innumerable women to respect their own feelings and thoughts. Bertha Pappenheim, who was the first reported analysand, had a flawed but successful analysis. Pappenheim went from being a closeted invalid to becoming a founder of social work in Europe and inspired generations of women to work in that field. Despite Freud's early theoretical mistakes in viewing women as victims of penis envy and perpetually dissatisfied by their own anatomy, his willingness to listen to women and his eagerness to understand them resulted in enough change in the women he analyzed, and the women they influenced, to make a difference in the larger society. It seemed that the experience of being listened to by an esteemed doctor was itself empowering. When academic careers were not yet available to women, psychoanalysis welcomed them. In turn, these women changed psychoanalysis so that we understood that discrimination against women in education, the sciences, the arts and government was the problem that led to discontent, not fantasied loss of a fantasy penis.

In time, psychoanalysts understood that little girls valued the pleasure they derived from their own genitals and feared damage to what they had (Balsam, 2012; Elise, 1998; Richards, 1992; Mayer, 1986). Psychoanalysts separated the social imposition of gender from the physical experience of genital sensation. Now psychoanalysts have been involved in teasing out performative gender from the felt experience. This includes addressing the more complex layering of bodily sensation, feelings about the body, perceptions of parental and caretakers' feelings about the infant's and young child's gender, and perceptions about the family values and behaviors towards men and women.

Women who have the opportunity to choose combining a career with marriage and children are seen to have it all. But the constant choice of how much time and energy to spend on children, how much on maintaining romance and intimacy in marriage, and how much on career produces stress. That stress can reach the level of *strain trauma* when the woman regards every failure in a child as a reflection of a failure on her part. It can also reach a traumatic level when a woman believes she has to do better than her male colleagues to prove that she is not short changing work in favor of her children. Even when her partner in parenting is enlightened enough to encourage her career, it often turns out that the woman refuses to take less responsibility for any flaws in her child's life and achievements.

The myth of the powerful woman

When the glass ceiling is not imposed from the outside, the need to spend enough time and energy on one's child can produce an inner ceiling on achievement for a woman wanting to be a good mother. As women understand the imperatives of early childhood and the extent of time after childbearing and child-rearing years, career issues can be dealt with by delaying the push towards career, by delaying childbearing until a career is established, or by delegating much of child-rearing to others. One woman from my practice chose to have someone else rear her children, long before her children were even born. She prided herself on having found the perfect nanny and on treating the nanny so well that she stayed with the family until the youngest child went to high school. My patient was able to do this partly because she had been raised by a stay-at-home mother who wanted her daughter to pursue the career she herself had never had. My patient had problems with her marriage and her social relationships, but not with her pursuit of a very satisfying career.

That choice, to entrust most of the childcare to a nanny, was contrary to the social norms of her time. It created problems with her husband and with the larger extended family. Friends and feminists questioned whether she was unfair to the nanny by not allowing her to have her own children. But her nanny was a woman who did not want children of her own, did not want to marry, and said that the children she reared were her children, as well as my patient's children. She, like Hecate, the goddess of demons, witchcraft and magic, chose to remain a virgin (Richards and Spira, 2015, p. 47). And also like Hecate, whose name means "she who works from afar" (ibid., p. 47), my patient was able to tolerate the criticism. Indeed, when she recounted her pride in calling into her workplace from the labor/delivery room, she was regarded as awesome, by both her children, and by those she mentored at work.

Being contrary, not accepting social norms, and thinking independently, are attitudes that allow success, creativity and enjoyment of one's own choices. Myths allow thinking of what women can do to enable such independent thinking. Dark myths, like that of Medea who murdered her children when their father took a younger wife and threatened to take the children into his new marriage, empower women to deal with threats of loss of custody, even if they never choose Medea's solution. Bible stories of women who assert their will by tricking men into doing what the woman wants done, empower women to think of ways to get what they want through indirect and even duplicitous means when they use their minds against their oppressive male relatives.

Consider the following female, Biblical tricksters, whose ability to gain power is an inspiration: Sarah who insisted that her son be separated from her husband's older son on the pretext that the older boy was abusing the younger so her son could inherit the family estate; Rachel, who hid her family's religious statues under her saddle and claimed she could not dismount because she was menstruating; Rebecca, who showed her younger son how to inherit his father's estate when primogeniture was the law; Judith, who ensnared the king of an army that was threatening her people.

Stories of Joan of Arc and Queen Elizabeth I of England describe when power and leadership coincide. One can only lead if one has a conviction of one's own power. Both of those women had that conviction. Both were virgins. Neither allowed herself to be second best to anyone, man or woman. For much of her reign Queen Victoria was a widow who dared to create an empire.

The current political situation in the United States leads us to see the dilemma of female leadership in stark terms. I think we saw a strong falling off of support for Hillary Clinton when she accepted her husband's affair with a White House intern. His claim that he "did not have sex with that woman," his failure to apologize to "that woman" publicly, and his choice of someone his daughter's age seemed to call for a feminist response from his wife.

Claire: Self-esteem and shame

Moving from the world view, to the particular, this case seems to revolve around the affect of shame, particularly as it is experienced in the mother-daughter relationship and the exploration of Claire's *present* experience of shame, difference and inadequacy. Like Inanna, Claire, the object of this discussion, surpassed her siblings. Also like Inanna, Claire learned many of her culture's valued skills. By using relationships with teachers and mentors she has attained the power of a mentor. In addition, as a single mother, she has achieved the parental power of both a mother and a father. By cutting off face-to-face contact with her own parents she has made herself the only caretaker for her daughter. She provides, she protects, she shelters, she nurtures.

Claire describes herself as "feeling different," as if different means worse. The view of the world is a view of the "other," a parallel of the self-image. The image of the "other" in the infant-caregiver experience leads to an image of the "other" that gets refined and re-edited throughout development. The self-image in interaction with the image of the "other" influences the reaction of later "others" to the self. In a series of interactions, the self-image becomes fuller, more integrated and coherent, or, in unfavorable circumstances, can become fragmented, devalued and demeaned.

Claire also describes feeling different because she did not have the same goals and aspirations as her family, and felt so unlike her mother. She describes her mother as unable to help her with homework because her mother lacked academic confidence and competence. This raises the question of why Claire still did not feel pride regarding her academic performance: to "out do," or be more competent than one's mother is a complicated issue, often fraught with conflict. We might wonder if Claire felt she had to soothe her mother's shame about her inadequacies, or otherwise felt conflicted and responsible for her mother's limitations. Alternatively, we might also wonder if Claire identified with her mother's shame.

We might also ask about what part Claire's father played in her childhood. Women who do well at work often have had the experience of a mentoring father. We might wonder if her father involved her in his passionate interests? Did he engage with her? Were they allies, even in an ongoing dispute? And if not, how did she develop both her work ethic and interpersonal capability? Answering such questions could help Claire understand her own development and resilience.

If Claire felt different from her siblings, her need to abase herself could have some connection with sibling rivalry and fear of being loved less by her mother than her siblings, who were more like the mother and less likely to produce maternal shame. Peers could also have had a big influence. Perhaps the parents of her peers took an interest in her. A serious attachment to values of hard work, achievement and intellectual excellence could have come from extended family, neighbors, and other people in her life. Her story of being an outlier seems to coincide with a feeling of being expendable, even valueless, and yet she performed very well.

Claire's teachers may have played a large role in her development. Talking about her experiences with teachers, who encouraged her, might have enabled her to see herself as someone with a foundation in her past that could sustain her present level of responsibility. Since she had attended a Catholic school, she could have had experiences with priests or nuns who gave her the ideals and ambitions beyond those of her immediate family. Reading fiction, poetry and plays could have helped to inspire her. Understanding herself as the outcome of a complex and rich development might enable her to appreciate her place in society as someone who is valuable.

To return to Claire's self-image and image of the "other," she seems to have seen herself more like a devalued, demeaned person than a fragmented one. Initially, Mark seems to have valued her. However, something in their interaction made him leave her as if she were of no value to him. While his own self-image and image of the "other" were doubtless part of what made him treat her in that way, her view of herself and of him had to be contributing factors as well. Whatever he thought of her, he also abandoned his own daughter, a possible reflection of difficulty with his own self-esteem. To think of one's child as worthless seems an expression of self-loathing. That he left Claire and their child at a time when he was failing to get along with his colleagues at work seems to indicate that he was feeling like a failure at that time. Many divorced parents abandon their families when they are unable to see themselves as capable of caring for them. Many parents who do not marry feel the same way, and break up their relationships when they do not see themselves as able to be good enough parents.

Interestingly, Claire's sex life is not mentioned. It is interesting that Claire experienced sexual desire, for the first time, for her mentor, Mark. We do not hear about the presence of Claire's desire, repudiation of desire, conflict and compromise: the events of her life are offered more externally. She reports that she "became pregnant." Courtship, foreplay, desire are all absent. We are left to wonder about some of the following questions. Was Claire's pregnancy an "accident" that expressed an unconscious wish on her part, on Mark's part, or on the part of both of them together? Did she long for a baby who was an "outsider" like herself? Did she choose Mark because he was an outsider? Did Mark want to be a father to his child? Why did they not marry? Did she want to have a baby who was an only child and could such a wish have expressed her resentment at having so many siblings?

I would talk with Claire about how her view of Mark could have influenced *his* self-image and eventuated in his remoteness. Did she think it would be better for her daughter to know her father, or not? Does this mirror her rejection of her own father, when she relocates? Would she want to eventually connect Mark to her daughter and begin to co-parent with him?

Claire's self-esteem may be related to parenting. Having raised a child is an achievement. To do this as a single mother is even more of a challenge. Being the sole financial support of her family, in addition to advancing her career, requires great strength of purpose. Having a bi-racial child in a racist society requires dealing with a huge challenge. Being the white mother of a bi-racial child means dealing with the racial challenge, without the support of a black family that has experience and tradition that enables parents to deal with this. That Claire managed all of this, without the social support of colleagues, is truly remarkable. Helping her to appreciate her own resilience and capability is directly relevant to helping to increase her self-confidence.

Desire, parental roles, and repetition

A central affect expressed in Claire's story is that of her father's reactions when she chooses to move away from her family for a better job. Her father gets angry. Claire's intellectual defense is that her daughter will be in a good school and Claire herself will get a better job. There is no acknowledgment of the daughter's feelings about being separated from the grandparents who took care of her through her early life. Claire is "too busy" to bring her daughter to visit the grandparents and therefore, separation is final for the child. Claire's cover story is that she did offer to pay the grandparents' fare for them to visit. But her resentment toward her parents is clear. She deprives them of the grandchild they had come to love as they fed, clothed, bathed and played with her from birth, through her toddler years, and up to school age. Though Claire's father is described as a warm and caring parent, Claire's experience of him as absent gets replayed when she turns passive into active by not allowing him to be with his grandchild. This would be difficult to interpret tactfully, but it could be done by phrasing it as a question with a clear openness to rejection by Claire. Such a question would go something like: "This may be off base, but I am wondering whether you could be resenting your father caring so much about your daughter when he did not seem to care as much for you?"

It might be helpful to talk to Claire about how we all, sometimes, protect ourselves from feeling uncared for by holding ourselves back from recognizing how much we want others to care about us. It might also be helpful to focus on how we sometimes harm or deprive ourselves when we expect others to do so to us.

This line of thinking could be continued by inquiring about what purpose might be served by Claire's insulating herself from her colleagues. Surely they must notice that she did not have pictures of her family, did not discuss her family and did not seem to get close with any of them. It would be awkward if they confided in her when she did not confide in them. If they did not confide in her, she would be the outsider in the group. She would then be replicating the condition of her childhood in which she felt as if she was an outsider in her own family.

I think it is important to see this as what was once called the "repetition compulsion." This compulsion may be better understood as a way of preserving a view of the world that was helpful to the person in the past. As such, it would not take much psychic energy for the person to continue her view while it would take a lot of examining her own feelings and thinking about them to see the world in a different way. By the time a person reached her forties, she would have been using a view of the world that had solidified into a certainty. I believe that it is the need for preserving this view that accounts for the need to work through insights acquired in the course of psychoanalysis. The frequency with which the person had confirmed her previous view of the world would then determine the length of time and number of repetitions required for working through.

Meanwhile, I would be thinking that Claire might have rejected her own parents when she was a little girl because they kept producing more babies, thus indicating that she was not enough for them. She might have resented the attention required by each infant as it left less and less time and attention for her. Being the oldest and a girl, she might have been pressed into service taking care of her younger siblings. She could have resented that as well. Anger at her parents and siblings would fuel a sense that she was an outsider and also a Cinderella fantasy in which she would escape her family of origin and become a princess, far above them in aspiration and achievement.

Role model, twin, or competitor?

Claire's current problem, her relationship with Sarah, seems problematic in several ways. First, Sarah's aspirations for Claire seem to be possible ways for Sarah to get rid of Claire and take her place in their current work environment. Could Claire be thinking correctly when she suspects this of Sarah? Could she figure out a way to talk with Sarah about this? Then she feels herself drawn to Sarah sexually. We do not know if Claire's history includes lesbian fantasies or experiences. We might wonder if this was a paranoid fantasy generated by homosexual wishes and conflict over these wishes. If there were any evidence for this, one approach might be to normalize these wishes by first talking about them in the abstract and then connecting these wishes with her current situation of not having a partner.

It might be helpful to Claire if she were able to feel closer to someone before it is time for her daughter to leave her for a life of her own. Applying for a new job takes time and energy; starting a law firm takes even more energy, networking, advertising, and recruiting colleagues. Making that kind of effort could distract her from considering her new life situation as the mother of an adolescent who will soon become a separate independent person. Considering Claire's own inability to maintain a loving relationship with her family of origin, how can she provide that for her daughter?

As her daughter enters college age, Claire can expect that her daughter will have her own struggles with race. Because she lives in the United States, her daughter will be seen as a black person since she has a black father. Since Claire is white, her daughter can be expected to have more complicated separation issues once she goes off to college and tries to establish herself in relation to her black peers. How will Claire feel about that? Can she bear the struggle? Does she need to prepare her daughter for a racist world that could classify her as of lesser value because she is black? And will she cope with being socially defined as a black woman when she has lived with her white mother and presumably had no close relationship with her black father or his black family?

Just as it seemed that a woman could assert her choice of being a single mother and isolating her child from an extended family from which she felt alienated, the price of surpassing social norms and expectations has become evident. By doing so well, Claire has increased social expectations of her. This is reflected in increased expectations of herself. While she distrusts the suggestion of the woman she mentors who tells her to start her own business, she is also distrusting her own capacities to do this. Rather than assessing the possibility, she projects her distrust in a fantasy that the woman she is mentoring wants to take her job away. She cannot allow herself to believe that she could have even more success than she already has achieved – and that she could achieve this in her own right.

Analytic work with Claire seems to have a long way to go. Assessing her own goals for herself and for her daughter would mean facing delicate and potentially painful conflicts. Such conflicts will inevitably enter the therapeutic relationship in the form of transference and countertransference and require great tact and patience on the part of the therapist.

Post-election after-thoughts

Feminist thinking since the election has given us a new cause, that of stopping sexual harassment in the workplace. Such harassment is very different from flirting or romance. Asking for sexual service in exchange for job opportunities or even as a quid pro quo for not being fired is a long overdue taboo. Even the most enlightened men of an earlier era did such things without thinking of the way they were harming the women involved. The less enlightened men of the present still treat women as sexual prizes rather than people. Learning of the courage of women who have spoken up about harassment in the workplace awoke a long forgotten event in my own life. Thinking about it enabled me to see why so many women have endured this without complaining publicly.

This happened in my last year of graduate school. My children were in an elementary school run by my university for faculty and graduate students' children. In order to keep them there I would need a faculty or research position. I heard of a job at a new research project located just across the street from my children's school. The project needed someone to do statistics and research design. Since I had taken all the courses offered in those fields and had great recommendations from my professors, I applied for the job. I waited to hear until the deadline. In the late afternoon of the day before the project was to start, I got a telephone call. I was offered an interview. I went as I was, in a sweater and jeans. The head of the project was a liberal law professor. He had just written the definitive book on privacy law.

He looked at my resume. "I see you have recommendations from a really prominent professor in test construction and research design. But you have three children. How do I know you won't get pregnant on me?" Really wanting that job, I blurted out, "Use a condom." Of course he was taken aback. But I got hired. He did not actually demand sex. He acted as if he was afraid of me for the next year and a half.

And I did a great job. The project made the first page of the *New York Times*. The results were adopted by the US Office of Education, which had funded the project. I never told anyone about this story, which now, would be a clear case of gender discrimination. He would never have asked that question of a man.

Now that so many women have come forward with such stories, many other women, like me, have been reminded of how we were treated unfairly, insulted, not taken seriously, reminded of what was considered socially acceptable for a women: modesty, silence, compliance, helpfulness and kindness. We were discouraged from being assertive, strong, aggressive, stubborn, or brilliant. Those traits were masculine. They were not. But by convincing girls and young women that such traits were inimical to femininity, many were intimidated into silence, passivity, acquiescence and mediocrity. Ironically, it may have been the fear of loss of their treasured femininity that led girls and women to accept a restricted and devalued version of femininity. By speaking up about the sexual devaluation and threat of loss of femininity women have attained a level of self-respect that the misogynistic social values were used to strip away from us.

Women who stand up for themselves, women who choose our own path, women who are concerned with empowering other women and are lucky enough to have been living in a time and place that allows women to be educated, to have careers and to speak up for themselves and other women, have a responsibility to encourage women like Claire. I am honored to have been asked to contribute to this book and proud of the many women whose rebellion against patriarchy has enabled everyone writing and editing it to become who we are.

References

Balsam, R. (2012) *Women's Bodies in Psychoanalysis*. New York: Routledge.
Elise, D. (1998) The absence of the paternal penis. *J. Amer. Psychoanal. Assn.* 48(2):413–442.
Mayer, E. L. (1986) "Everybody must be just like me." *Internat. J. Psychoanal.* 66:341–347.
Richards, A.K. (1992) The influence of sphincter control and genital sensation on body image and gender identity in women. *Psychoanalytic Quarterly* 61:331–351
Richards, A.K. and Spira, L. (2015) *Myths of Mighty Women*. London. Karnac.

INDEX

References to endnotes consist of the page number followed by the letter 'n' followed by the number of the note.

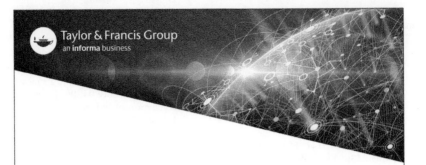